Technology, Media and Social Movements

This book offers an interdisciplinary set of contributions from leading scholars, and explores the complex relationship between media, technology and social movements. It provides a valuable resource for scholars and students working in this rapidly developing field.

Providing theoretical engagement with contemporary debates in the field of social movements and new media, the book also includes a theoretical overview of central contemporary debates, a re-evaluation of theories of social movement communication, and a critical overview of media ecology and media approaches in social movement scholarship. The theoretical contributions are also developed through empirical case studies from around the world, including the use of Facebook in student protests in the UK, the way power operates in Anonymous, the 'politics of mundanity' in China, the emotional dynamics on Twitter of India's Nirbhaya protest, and analysis of Twitter networks in the transnational feminist campaign 'Take Back The Tech!'.

This book was originally published as a special issue of *Social Movement Studies*.

Cristina Flesher Fominaya is co-Editor-in-Chief of *Social Movement Studies*, a Founding Editor of *Interface Journal*, and author of *Social Movements and Globalization* (2014). She is Reader in Social Politics and Media at Loughborough University, UK. She publishes widely on European and global social movements, hybrid parties, digital politics and media, collective identity, democracy, autonomy, and political participation.

Kevin Gillan is a Senior Lecturer in Sociology at the University of Manchester, UK, and co-Editor-in-Chief of *Social Movement Studies*. His work focuses on the generation and communication of alternative conceptions of political economy within social movements. He is currently writing a book entitled *How Capitalism Matters: Economy, Polity, Society*.

Technology, Media and Social Movements

Edited by
Cristina Flesher Fominaya and Kevin Gillan

Routledge
Taylor & Francis Group
LONDON AND NEW YORK

First published 2019
by Routledge
2 Park Square, Milton Park, Abingdon, Oxon, OX14 4RN, UK

and by Routledge
52 Vanderbilt Avenue, New York, NY 10017, USA

Routledge is an imprint of the Taylor & Francis Group, an informa business

British Library Cataloguing in Publication Data
A catalogue record for this book is available from the British Library

ISBN 13: 978-1-138-36896-5

Typeset in Minion Pro
by RefineCatch Limited, Bungay, Suffolk

Publisher's Note
The publisher accepts responsibility for any inconsistencies that may have arisen during the conversion of this book from journal articles to book chapters, namely the possible inclusion of journal terminology.

Contents

Citation Information

The chapters in this book were originally published in *Social Movement Studies*, volume 16, issue 4 (July 2017). When citing this material, please use the original page numbering for each article, as follows:

Chapter 1
Navigating the technology-media-movements complex
Cristina Flesher Fominaya and Kevin Gillan
Social Movement Studies, volume 16, issue 4 (July 2017), pp. 383–402

Chapter 2
Complex contention: analyzing power dynamics within Anonymous
Justus Uitermark
Social Movement Studies, volume 16, issue 4 (July 2017), pp. 403–417

Chapter 3
From 'moments of madness' to 'the politics of mundanity' - researching digital media and contentious collective actions in China
Jun Liu
Social Movement Studies, volume 16, issue 4 (July 2017), pp. 418–432

Chapter 4
The integrative power of online collective action networks beyond protest. Exploring social media use in the process of institutionalization
Elena Pavan
Social Movement Studies, volume 16, issue 4 (July 2017), pp. 433–446

Chapter 5
Tweeting India's Nirbhaya protest: a study of emotional dynamics in an online social movement
Saifuddin Ahmed, Kokil Jaidka and Jaeho Cho
Social Movement Studies, volume 16, issue 4 (July 2017), pp. 447–465

Chapter 6
Open networks and secret Facebook groups: exploring cycle effects on activists' social media use in the 2010/11 UK student protests
Alexander Hensby
Social Movement Studies, volume 16, issue 4 (July 2017), pp. 466–478

Chapter 7
The new information frontier: toward a more nuanced view of social movement communication
Jennifer Earl and R. Kelly Garrett
Social Movement Studies, volume 16, issue 4 (July 2017), pp. 479–493

Chapter 8
A situated understanding of digital technologies in social movements. Media ecology and media practice approaches
Alice Mattoni
Social Movement Studies, volume 16, issue 4 (July 2017), pp. 494–505

For any permission-related enquiries please visit:
http://www.tandfonline.com/page/help/permissions

Notes on Contributors

Saifuddin Ahmed is a doctoral student in the Department of Communication at the University of California, Davis, USA. His research interests lie in new and emerging media, political communication, election studies, and public opinion. He is particularly interested in the transformative role of new media in civic and political engagement in technologically emerging societies.

Jaeho Cho is an Associate Professor in the Department of Communication at the University of California, Davis, USA. His research concerns the influence of mass media and communication technologies on political decision-making and behavior.

Jennifer Earl is Professor of Sociology and (by courtesy) Government and Public Policy at the University of Arizona, USA. She is Director Emerita of the Center for Information Technology and Society and Director Emerita of the Technology and Society PhD Emphasis, both at the University of California, Santa Barbara, USA. Her research focuses on social movements, information technologies, and the sociology of law.

Cristina Flesher Fominaya is co-Editor-in-Chief of *Social Movement Studies*, a Founding Editor of *Interface Journal*, and author of *Social Movements and Globalization* (2014). She is Reader in Social Politics and Media at Loughborough University, UK. She publishes widely on European and global social movements, hybrid parties, digital politics and media, collective identity, democracy, autonomy, and political participation.

R. Kelly Garrett is an Associate Professor in the School of Communication at the Ohio State University, USA. His research interests include the study of online political communication, online news, and the ways in which citizens and activists use new technologies to shape their engagement with contentious political topics.

Kevin Gillan is a Senior Lecturer in Sociology at the University of Manchester, UK, and co-Editor-in-Chief of *Social Movement Studies*. His work focuses on the generation and communication of alternative conceptions of political economy within social movements. He is currently writing a book entitled *How Capitalism Matters: Economy, Polity, Society*.

Alexander Hensby is a Research Associate at the School of Social Policy, Sociology and Social Research at the University of Kent, UK. His current work focuses on sociological explanations for the attainment gap between white and BME students in Higher Education. He is the author of *Theorizing Global Studies* (with Darren O'Byrne, 2011), and *Participation and Non-Participation in Student Activism* (2017).

Kokil Jaidka is a Postdoctoral Research Fellow at the University of Pennsylvania, USA. Her expertise is in natural language processing, applied linguistics, and multi-document summarization. Her research interests lie in computational approaches to exploring the role of online communication for health and political outcomes.

Jun Liu is an Associate Professor in the Centre for Communication and Computing and the Department of Media, Cognition and Communication at the University of Copenhagen, Denmark. His research areas cover political communication, ICTs, and political sociology. He has published articles in *Television & New Media*, *Modern Asian Studies*, and *China Perspectives*, among other journals.

Alice Mattoni is an Assistant Professor at the Scuola Normale Superiore di Pisa, Italy. She investigates media practices, political participation, and social movements in the field of labour organization and corruption. Her work has been published in top-ranked international journals and she is the author of *Media Practices and Protest Politics. How Precarious Workers Mobilise* (2012).

Elena Pavan is an Assistant Professor at the Institute of Humanities and Social Sciences of the Scuola Normale Superiore di Pisa, Italy. Her most recent research interests pertain to the relationships between collective action and social media use. Within this area, she is conducting interdisciplinary research to study socio-technical systems, in particular through social network analysis and digital methods.

Justus Uitermark is an Associate Professor of Sociology at the University of Amsterdam, the Netherlands. He is a political sociologist interested in urban governance and social movements. His books include *Dynamics of Power in Dutch Integration Politics* (2012) and *Cities and Social Movements* (with Walter Nicholls, 2016).

Navigating the technology-media-movements complex

Cristina Flesher Fominaya and Kevin Gillan

ABSTRACT

In this article we develop the notion of the technology-media-movements complex (TMMC) as a field-definition statement for ongoing inquiry into the use of information and communication technologies (ICTs) in social and political movements. We consider the definitions and boundaries of the TMMC, arguing particularly for a historically rooted conception of technological development that allows better integration of the different intellectual traditions that are currently focused on the same set of empirical phenomena. We then delineate two recurrent debates in the literature highlighting their contributions to emerging knowledge. The first debate concerns the divide between scholars who privilege media technologies, and see them as driving forces of movement dynamics, and those who privilege media practices over affordances. The second debate broadly opposes theorists who believe in the emancipatory potential of ICTs and those who highlight the ways they are used to repress social movements and grassroots mobilization. By mapping positions in these debates to the TMMC we identify and provide direction to three broad research areas which demand further consideration: (i) questions of power and agency in social movements; (ii) the relationships between, on the one hand, social movements and technology and media *as politics* (i.e. cyberpolitics and technopolitics), and on the other, the quotidian and ubiquitous use of digital tools in a digital age; and (iii) the significance of digital divides that cut across and beyond social movements, particularly in the way such divisions may overlay existing power relations in movements. In conclusion, we delineate six challenges for profitable further research on the TMMC.

The use of information and communication technologies (ICTs) in social and political movements is an ongoing and rich area of inquiry. Research work draws from several social scientific fields including movement scholarship, information and communications studies and media research. Our purpose in this article is to set out a general framework within which to navigate this field of inquiry. We begin by developing the notion of the *technology-media-movements complex* (TMMC) as a field-definition statement, allowing for better integration of the different intellectual traditions that are currently focused on the same set of empirical phenomena. We thereby introduce the essential features required for further rigorous knowledge generation in this area. In our first section we consider the definitions and boundaries of the TMMC, arguing particularly for a historically rooted conception of technological development and an approach to 'novelty' that recognizes it as a continually reproduced feature of the TMMC, rather than as a technologically driven, momentary historical break. We describe potential routes for integration of approaches from various fields and disciplines – including political communication, media studies, technology studies, organizational studies and social psychology – whose insights can be fruitfully applied to analysis of the nexus between technology, media, and social movements. In the second section we delineate two recurrent debates. First, we examine the tension between accounts that privilege technology or social agency as drivers of social change, arguing that what has to be analysed is the interplay of collective processes, pre-existing political commitments, technological competences, and technical affordances. This approach recognizes the creative and strategic agency of social movement actors. Second, we outline debates between scholars who emphasize the emancipatory potential of digital technology and those who are much less sanguine about its liberating potential. We highlight the real insights that proponents of divergent positions have offered the field, but note the need for nuanced accounts of empirical reality to test the veracity of competing visions of digital futures.

In our third section we consider three areas of inquiry within the TMMC that merit further consideration. First, we consider differing conceptions of social movements and the implications of each position for navigating the TMMC, distinguishing between individual agglomerate, collective, and network analyses. Second, we consider the distinction between scholarship on social movements that engage with technology and media *as politics* (i.e. cyberpolitics and technopolitics) and those that focus on the quotidian and ubiquitous use of digital tools in a digital age, highlighting the need for more research on how these different understandings of the role of digital tools reciprocally influence each other in movement practice. Third, we examine the digital divide. Rather than seeing this simply as a matter of global inequalities of access to technology, we argue that complex forms of digitally mediated exclusion exist within cyberspace and social movements and call for further research on the way these divisions overlay existing power relations on and offline. In this way we call attention to the need to pay more attention to lived experience and power in our analysis of the TMMC. In conclusion, we draw from the conceptual contributions of this article to set out six challenges for further research on the TMMC.

Boundaries and definitions: technology, media, movements

The study of ICTs and social movements is not (yet) an integrated subfield. There are two important reasons for the diffuse nature of inquiry in this area. The first is that empirically led studies are often understandably interested in delineating the uptake of specific new technologies within social movements. Email, IRC channels, websites, pirate radio, mobile phones, live streaming, social media platforms; the list is potentially endless as new communicative technologies become available. From an empirical point of view one often wants to examine questions such as what ways are specific technologies put to use within particular movements, what they can contribute to mobilization or contestation, or what limitations might they place on actors. At this level, it is difficult to find broad applicability in answers to such questions. Differences in both underlying technological design and the political contexts in which they are adopted suggest that there is little hope that single cases will offer many general lessons without more concerted efforts at theoretical development. The result is that, for each technological innovation – now social media, previously, the Web, email, television and so on – there has been a tendency to cycle through a particular kind of unproductive debate: optimists see radical democratizing potential, pessimists see the reconfiguration of traditional power structures in a new arena, while others seek a middle ground.

A second barrier to integration in this area of inquiry is the fact that it necessarily draws on different fields. There is much productive potential in bringing these fields together, especially by combining insights from movement scholarship with those of (political) communication (Earl & Garett, 2017), media studies (Mattoni, 2017) and technologies studies (Pavan, 2017). At present, however, it is more a case of separate lines of inquiry with only occasional intersections. As movement scholars writing in *Social Movement Studies* we, and several contributors to the issue, tend to examine ICTs through the conceptual frameworks developed in this field and address questions concerning the utility or otherwise provided in central movement processes such as the communication of movement frames, the generation of collective identities, or the production of movement resources. Nevertheless, we acknowledge that this movement-centrism is field-specific; elsewhere, Gillan has adopted frameworks drawing more from technology studies (2008) or political communication (Gibson, Gillan, Greffet, Lee, & Ward, 2013), whereas Flesher Fominaya (2016) has drawn on insights from human–computer interaction studies and social-psychology to apply them to analysis of the TMMC. A vital first step in enabling positive cross-field developments is a more clearly defined statement of the particular complex of phenomena that has generated such a strong flow of research publications in recent years, namely: technology, media, and movements (or TMMC). We specify each in the following paragraphs.

For technology, ICTs are the core focus. It is these technologies in particular that have been the subject of so much innovation and excitement since the personal computers of the early 1960s, but especially since the creation of two major communication infrastructures: mobile phone networks beginning in the 1960s and the Internet (and various nationally specific variants) in the 1980s. A technologically vital and more recent process here is widespread digitization. Spurred by the characteristics of microchip processing and the Internet, the more that data are available in digital form the more they can be transformed and communicated. This is not a trivial technological outcome. The first mobile phone networks, drawing from their obvious predecessors on landlines, were analogue communication systems and only became digitized with the 'second generation' EU-led GSM protocol deployed from the early 1990s, which not incidentally made short message service (SMS) texting feasible (Castells, Qiu, Fernandez-Ardevol, & Sey, 2006). Without the digitization pathway, powerful and emotive imagery, audio and video would have been much harder to share online; and the visual language of contemporary information flows potentially changes the nature of the public sphere in which much movement communication is located (DeLuca & Peeples, 2002). Perhaps more fundamentally, without the digitization of mobile networks the convergence between mobile phones and Internet devices – creating complex hybrid spaces that intertwine the informational and the physical – would have been practically impossible (see De Souza e Silva, 2006; Gordon, 2006). From a communications angle, without decades of SMS texts it seems unlikely that many users would have found interaction through Twitter's 144-character messaging interface appealing or even coherent; the development of cultural competencies in ICT use is just as vital as technological affordances. It is the particular combination of the Internet and mobile infrastructures that is the source of a sense of the supposed 'ubiquity' of technologically mediated communication, which we explore further below.

It is not all ICTs, then, but specifically those ICTs which enable rapid, low-cost networked communication among individuals that have been the vital technologies studied by scholars interested in the TMMC. Understanding the characteristics of the technologies involved is important; not because social outcomes are entirely technologically determined, of course, but because design characteristics create affordances that might or might not be adopted by thinking, feeling agents in specific circumstances. Here, insights from human–computer interaction studies and social psychological work on the experience of technology use are particularly helpful (e.g. Garton & Wellman, 1995; Hargittai & Shafer, 2006; Kiesler & Sproull, 1992; Spears, Lea, Corneliussen, Postmes, & Haar, 2002). Agentic processes are evident when, for instance, individuals and groups carry out interpretative work in examining the potential utility of affordances, and may even find ways of reshaping them (within limits) for purposes for which they were never intended (Gillan 2008; Himanen, 2001). Yet such actions are hardly unconstrained: skill, time, and other resources are required to bring out the 'latent functionalities' of the technologies made available through (mostly) market means for (mostly) corporate ends (Gillan, Pickerill, & Webster, 2008, pp. 172–181). Further understanding of the role of ICTs in the TMMC may depend on making more use of social theories of technology in which a nuanced approach to both social agency and the political character of technological design are central (e.g. Feenberg, 2002; Kirkpatrick, 2008; Redshaw, 2017; Pavan 2017).

Within the investigation of ICTs and movements, technologies are primarily of interest because of their role in mediating communication, hence the focus on media in the TMMC. From a pure technology studies approach, other developments may be more crucial. The invention of, for instance, the TCP/IP protocols (that manage the packaging, addressing, and transmission of digital data) enabled the construction of the Internet on top of copper cables that had previously been intended for analogue telephone signals; this must count as one of the most significant hacks in history. Such protocols, and indeed the material hardware required (and usually privately owned), are potentially relevant 'mediators' of regular communication (Lessig, 2002). For our concerns, however, such developments are mostly mere background, too far from the practicalities of mediated communication to have much obvious relevance. Thus, technology is primarily of interest in its interrelationship with 'media' in our conception of the TMMC.

There are two senses in which 'media' can be rendered here. The first refers to the insertion of the ICTs delineated above into movement-relevant communications. The specific characteristics of communication as mediated by particular technological infrastructures presents challenges and limitations for social movement groups as is found by various studies of the affordances of such mediation (Flesher Fominaya, 2016; Gillan, 2009; Milan, 2015; Tufekci, 2014a; Wall, 2007). The term 'new media' has been adopted in many studies to refer to this collection of technological innovations, defined through the following characteristics: their hybrid or recombinant formations, bringing together pre-existing technologies in a range of innovative ways; their contribution to the development of communication systems as 'reorganizing, unfolding [...] networks of networks' structured centrally on hyperlinks; and their enabling of on-demand access to information (Lievrouw, 2011, pp. 8–16). The result is a sense of 'ubiquity' of information via new media, seemingly offering users 'an unprecedented degree of selectivity and reach in their choices of information and cultural resources and their personal interactions and expressions' (ibid). So defined, the term 'new media' remains a useful referent point because it is general enough to encompass both the 'older' web technologies (e.g. email, websites, blogs) and the growing raft of new applications of new media information networks (e.g. social media, live streaming) that come along as mobile devices with expanded capabilities and near-permanent Internet access have been more widely adopted (see also Siapera, 2011).

The notion of 'newness' is worth further consideration. As Lievrouw and others have indicated, there is genuine novelty to the forms of communication network now in wide use. But there is also a tendency to fixate on the newest formations capturing the imagination of technology enthusiasts. This can lead to a form of 'myopia of the present' (Melucci, 1994) which doesn't situate media technology use within a longer term perspective, and can ignore the ways that newer media forms evolve from previous forms and practice. It also leads to a form of presentism that fails to acknowledge the dynamic nature of technological advances in which particular platforms and their affordances – however important they might be now – may soon become modified, obsolete or replaced by other forms of media; or conversely how platforms used only by specialized activists today may become widespread tomorrow. The myopia of the present, therefore, doesn't just relate to the past but to the future. Thus, we need to be able to resist the tendency to see each technological development as radically new, as this makes it difficult to spot underlying commonalities in the nature of communications, technological adoptions, agencies and power.

We do not make this point to deny the novelty of new media. Indeed, over recent decades we have seen changes in communication, self-expression, collective identity formation, personal network building, and activist communications strategies as a result of the increasingly digitally mediated nature of the everyday lives of increasing numbers of people. However, one could not define a single innovation or a single moment at which there is a distinct break from the past (see also Ganesh & Stohl, 2013); instead we see the sometimes-fast, sometimes-slow build-up of new forms of technology alongside, crucially, the cultural competencies, practices and preferences required to make sense and use of them (e.g. Costanza-Chock, 2012). The novelty of 'new media' is thus less about a moment of change (and therefore is not a clear distinction between old and new) and much more about the fact that the production of novelties is now built into a system that is defined, as noted above, by the construction of hybrid and recombinant technological formations. Much as Daniel Bell (1974) noted the importance of planned research and development in corporate infrastructures in the changing timescale of innovation in business, we can see that today we have a networked information infrastructure that results in rapid, repeated moments of innovation that can change the characteristics and uses of the network itself.

'Media' in the TMMC thus refers in one sense to the role of technological mediation in communication between individuals and groups that make movements happen. But there is also a second, more general, sense in which 'media' is vital. This refers to the institutions of traditional news media (sometimes erroneously referred to as 'old media') – whether distributed via newspapers, television or the Internet – through which all political actors gain key information. This is a significant point of intersection with the field of political communications (Earl & Garett, 2017) as well as media studies (Mattoni, 2017). The importance for social movements of finding representation in dominant news media outlets has long been studied, especially among those interested in processes of interpretative framing (Ryan, 1991; Smith, McCarthy, McPhail, & Augustyn, 2001; Gitlin, 2003; McCarthy, Smith, & Zald, 1996; Oliver & Maney, 2000).[1] The more recent entanglement between news media and the 'new media' generated by the technological developments indicated above, however, complicate simple models of movement groups as 'outsiders' trying to gain entry to a hegemonic news agenda. In addition to our analyses of the mediated nature of group communication per se, therefore, we need to maintain an analytic gaze on the ongoing influence of those institutions which generate, select, frame, and disseminate 'the news'. Those institutions are often significantly controlled by state agencies or megalithic corporations and are now very large presences in 'new media' too, both in terms of size of websites and user traffic. Nevertheless, in the contemporary 'media ecology' (Mattoni, 2017, 2012) they become increasingly integrated with other circuits of information diffusion, especially those that present themselves as neutral 'platforms' (Gillespie, 2010), potentially making for a more responsive and diverse (if rather cacophonous) information environment. The apparent influence of 'alternative' news sources such as Breitbart in the recent US Presidential Election campaign and the related fears that we now live in a world of 'post-truth politics' are clear indicators of the potential for surprise extant in this complex information environment.

We have thus far bounded the TMMC by specifying the relationship between particular ICTs and their role in mediation – both of communication within networks and in their role in constituting the wider media ecology. The final boundary-drawing task is thus to specify how these connect with social movements. While we do not wish to get fully entangled in the 'what is a social movement?' question here (for some direct answers see Johnston, 2014), in defining the TMMC it is necessary to offer some definitional clarity. For us, the definitional features of 'social movement' must minimally include a degree collectivity through voluntary coordination of activity in the pursuit of values or interests that produce conflict with other social actors (Gillan, in press). The processes by which individuals come together, recognize common experiences of social problems, develop diagnoses of those problems, and begin to form strategies to attempt to overcome them remain, in our view, inherently collective. To identify a social movement is to prioritize processes that are inherently, and largely intentionally, collective in nature. The division between more individual and more collective approaches to the TMMC highlights a significant analytical question to which we return in the next section.

We have so far defined the core elements of the TMMC, identifying the empirical phenomena of interest by considering the intersection of technology, media, and movements. In doing so, we have highlighted especially the need to draw on insights from fields beyond our immediate frames of reference as social movement scholars. This approach is likely to yield fruitful analyses of the crucial puzzles and challenges facing social movements and scholars today. By arguing against a 'myopia of the present' we present a vision of novelty that is not the result of a particular historical break, but rather a result of varying combinations of movement action, media work, and technological play which enable the dynamic complexity of the TMMC; the tendency to reification of novelty is rendered as problematic. We now move on to consider two core analytical debates and approaches to the TMMC, before considering three vital areas for further research.

Core debates on the TMMC

By defining the TMMC above, we offered some descriptive boundaries of the empirical phenomena of interest to those working under the broad heading of 'ICTs and movements'. We now outline two recurrent core debates: the first between those who privilege either technology or social agency as drivers of mobilization; and the second between those who privilege the emancipatory versus repressive potentials of ICTs.

Technologically or socially driven changes?

While most scholars are sensitive to critiques of technological determinism, there is a continuum within the field from scholars who tend to privilege technologies and see them as driving forces of movements, among other major dynamics (e.g. Benkler, 2006; Bennett & Segerberg, 2012; Rheingold, 1993; Shirky, 2009), to those that keep their focus on social actors and the ways that they deploy these technologies, through privileging media practices over affordances (see Flesher Fominaya, 2014; Mattoni, 2017, 2012). It is undeniable that the advent of cyberspace has created an arena encompassing significant new elements in the forms and consequences of political communication, political engagement, and political conflict. Simultaneously, it is impossible to see these developments as a singular causal force in the production of movement mobilization or outcomes. Castells argues that online social networks are 'tools at the disposal of any individual or self-created network of individuals who want to have their views aired ... the diffusion of Internet-based social networks is a necessary condition for the existence of these new social movements in our time. But it is not a sufficient condition' (Castells, 2015, p. 226). Castells makes this point specifically for the category of 'new networked social movements', which emerges from his analysis of the post-2010 movements; he rightly recognizes that there are other forms of movement for which particular technologies cannot be considered a necessary condition.

Given that neither technology nor any single actor can be understood as sole driving force in the TMMC, what has to be specified is the *interplay* of collective processes, pre-existing political commitments, technological competencies and technical affordances, in which it becomes possible to recognize the creative and strategic agency of social movement actors. Two examples illuminate this point. Firstly, Bitcoin is an alternative currency based on the coming together of several key advances in highly complex uses of network technologies. The 'mining' of Bitcoin is built into the technological design as an incentive structure in which early adopters were able to receive currency by running fast computers to solve complex mathematical problems that served the needs of the network. A designed-in reduction of the rate of currency growth means that eventually the energy costs of running mining software would outstrip the value of the mined coins (Redshaw, 2017, pp. 55–56). That is to say, technological adeptness combined with access to material resources allowed the production of wealth for a clique of interested parties. As Redshaw (2017) reveals, a libertarian attitude drawn from 'cypherpunks' was embedded in the purpose and design of the technology from the start. While this has been contested during technical development, there was a neatness of fit between libertarian technological design and the rising interest in Bitcoin from people whose ideological commitment was to a Hayekian 'denationalization of money'. This demonstrates: firstly, that the exercise of technological agency need not be democratic in nature; secondly, that the significance of Bitcoin can only be understood in relation to cultural preferences and practices alongside technological competence and material capability.

A second example of technological-social interplay comes from Uitermark's study of Anonymous (2017) in which access to and adeptness with particular technologies are characteristics that shape power dynamics within that group; a form of internal digital divide that we explore further below. Because Uitermark's approach is ethnographic he is able to see beyond the characteristics of communication shaped by technological design to the social forces at play in generating power structures among a nominally horizontally organized and leaderless group. We see some mirroring of the long-known 'tyranny of structurelessness' (Freeman, 1972) here, but also other characteristics – such as the problematically 'thin' degree of shared political identity – that must finally be understood as shaped by location of Anonymous within the TMMC. In other words, specific technologies shape the precise form these power plays manifest, but the dynamics they reflect echo longstanding social movement conflicts and challenges.

Both examples suggest that there is nothing inherently progressive or democratic about technologies, such qualities are only made manifest in the use to which they are put, and even the best intentions can lead to unintended consequences; this insight underlies our position on the next recurrent debate within scholarship on the TMMC.

Emancipation and repression

Scholarly debate has distinguished theorists who believe in the emancipatory potential of new ICTs from those who are much less sanguine about their possibilities and who highlight the ways that political and economic elites and the state use these technologies to control, surveil, and limit the power of social movements and grassroots mobilization. 'Techno-utopianism' was a feature of rising initial excitement as new ICTs became widespread, with Rheingold (1993, p. 14) defining the political significance of ICTs as lying in their 'capacity to challenge the existing political hierarchies' monopoly on powerful communications media, and perhaps has revitalized citizen-based democracy' (also Benkler, 2006; Shirky, 2009). The idea that the architecture of Internet communication carries *inherent* democratic potential is now widely seen as naive (and is countered by our two examples above), but opposing this with a 'techno-pessimism' or 'cyber-skepticism' would be similarly over-simplistic, and simply 'contribute further ammunition to the tiresome binary debate' (Dencik & Leistert, 2015, p. 2). In fact, it is only logically possible to come to a pure 'techno-utopian' or 'cyber-skeptic' position on the basis of a uni-causal technological determinism; otherwise social processes of interpretation, interaction, the exercise of power and identity formation will inevitably confound the theorists' predictions. The questions for analyses of the TMMC are instead, therefore, in what ways might the interplay of technological development and social action achieve democratic visions, and in what ways does it produce barriers through repression?

Morozov (2012) argues that while the Internet can serve a democratic function, not enough attention is being paid to how states have used it as a tool of repression and control; nor how much of the cutting-edge research used to develop tools such as face recognition software, sophisticated user content analysis, and social media analysis has been harnessed by governments to repress and censor dissidents, and control citizen access to online content. Margolis and Resnick (2000) argue that political players with power in 'the real world' (offline) can also gain the upper hand in cyberspace. Tufekci (2015) further alerts us to the ways that corporate owned social media poses significant risks to democracy, including electoral processes, through their ability to modify their algorithms to manipulate and bias information that users see. The extent to which these corporate 'psycho technologies' can be used to manipulate not only users' impressions but also their emotions, allied to the opacity of data mining practices and its uses by corporate platform owners, suggests a need to pay increased attention to the negative implications for social movement actors (see e.g. Leistert, 2015).

The increasing reliance on corporate-controlled spaces for activist communication raises critical questions for movements working against neoliberal global capitalism or who are committed to critiquing and contesting political and economic elites (Hintz, 2015). The dangers posed by public discussions, organizations, and networks being observed, monitored, archived and censored by corporate enterprises has serious implications for cyber activism and for social movement organizing online (Askanius & Gustafsson, 2010; Flesher Fominaya, 2014). Stoycheff and Nisbet discuss the ways in which authoritarian governments not only restrict Internet freedoms, particularly to political content, but also establish '"psychological firewalls" that paint the internet as a scary world full of political threats. This rationale increases threat perceptions among the public. This, in turn, increases the public's support for online political censorship' (2016, n.p.). The authors highlight the limitations of techno-deterministic narratives that assume technological affordances will shape use: as they argue, we need to dispense once and for all with 'the "if we build it, they will come" philosophy underlying a great deal of Internet freedom promotion [that] doesn't take into account basic human psychology in which entertainment choices are preferred over news and attitudes toward the Internet determine its use, not the technology itself' (ibid.) Remembering too that media-based tactics such as political culture jamming are not limited to progressive radical grassroots social movements but can be used by political and social movement actors on any point of the spectrum, as well as by political parties and corporate actors, acts as a corrective to overly optimistic narratives about the emancipatory potential of new media.

Whistleblowing projects like Wikileaks and Xnet have demonstrated the capacity for small organized groups to pose significant challenges to powerful elites and states. The recent examples of the role of 'fake news' and hacking exposés in the Clinton/Trump electoral race, however, show that drawing a neat distinction between elites and grassroots actors is not simple, and the debate over the legitimacy of Wikileaks, an influential and at times widely admired group, shows how complex disentangling 'sides' – top/bottom, us/them, progressive/reactionary – and motives can be (see also Gallo-Cruz, 2017). What is clear is that any analysis of ICTs and social movements needs to be aware that the political cultures tied to Internet use matter, and that the state can and does play an important role in structuring a context which can foster or prevent movements' ability to use ICTs effectively. Rather than situate themselves on one side or the other of this debate, most scholars now recognize the tension between emancipatory and repressive tendencies, a tension inherent in the network architecture of digital communication itself (e.g. Castells, 2009, 2015; Dencik & Leistert, 2015; Jordan, 2015; Lievrouw, 2011).

Power, politics and agency in the digital age

We have thus far described two continua on which current debates around the TMMC can be organized. These positions are likely shaped, but not necessarily determined, by the pre-existing ontological and epistemological commitments or methodological choices which underpin them (on which more below). We have argued that in navigating the TMMC we must understand new technologies as always (and already) enmeshed within social processes. Neither technological design, nor decisions on adoption, can float freely of the actors participating in those processes. From that position it is only logical to understand the potential for either emancipatory or repressive outcomes as continuously unfolding and contested, a matter for empirical evaluation rather than theoretical fiat or rhetorical pronouncement. From this position, we now detail three areas in which further scholarly work is required for a better understanding of the interplay of technological and social processes in the TMMC: (1) attempts to embed both individual action and collectives within a socio-political context alive to power relations; (2) differentiation of 'cyberpolitics' and its influence (or otherwise) from quotidian ICT use; and (3) understanding the ongoing relevance of digital divides and dimensions of power on social movements.

Individuals, collectives, networks

Some scholars approach social movements as an agglomeration of individual behaviours. To some extent this follows in the footsteps of Olson's (1965) seminal treatment of collective action: reducing it to the behaviours and preferences of rational individuals highlights the need for cooperation in formal institutions to overcome the free rider problem. Here, there is an ease of fit between the aggregation of individual action and the methodological possibilities enabled by access to social media data, since that data is generally interpreted at the level of the individual (albeit located in networks of interaction). Thus predictive-explanatory models, sometimes with experimental designs, analyse online individual behaviour in order to explain mobilization without recourse to direct observation of, or contact with, mobilizing groups (but see Mercea & Yilmaz, in press for an alternative social learning process based on formal modelling of individual actions).

Margetts, John, Hale, and Yasseri (2015), for example, use experimental data to analyse and predict the role of social media in mass mobilizations, like Spain's 15-M or Egypt's Revolution. A core part of the data that shapes their model comes from online petitions, although that form of action cannot be reliably used to predict or explain other forms of mobilization (e.g. high risk protest where issues of trust, solidarity, and emotion work are brought to bear on individual decisions to participate). From these formal models and experimental designs they argue that social media enables 'mobilizations without leaders, revolutions without organizations' in line with arguments put forward by Bennett and Segerberg (2012). Bennett and Segerberg furthermore link the advent of social media use to an increase in individualization in society, thereby aligning method and theory. In these approaches, contextual factors are treated as less important than individual actions (petition signing, voting, clicking, liking, sharing and so on), or else context is seen as influencing individual rather than collective behaviour (e.g. Brym, Godbout, Hoffbauer, Menard, & Zhang, 2014; Hwang, Schmierbach, Paek, de Zuniga, & Shah, 2006).

In contrast to work adopting a summative individual agglomeration model of action, scholars adopting a collective action approach see social movements as necessarily involving meaningful and extended *collective* processes of interaction and reciprocal engagement of groups of people tied together in networks or fields of action. Such approaches are more likely to understand ICT adoption in movements as shaped by specific media ecologies, cultural repertoires, collective ideational frameworks, and subject to the dynamics of collective decision-making, including political communication strategies, protocols, and ethics (e.g. Coleman, 2010a, 2012; Firer-Blaess, 2016; Flesher Fominaya, 2016; Hensby, 2017; Kavada, 2015, 2009; Mattoni, 2017; Milan, 2013). Scholars working from this point of departure often require methodologies that involve qualitative engagement with, or observation of, internal movement processes and dynamics. Whereas the former approach focuses primarily or exclusively on mobilization (often of low-cost activities), the latter see this as only one part of what social movements do and extend analysis of media use to internal organizational and communication processes as well as external ones.

The relevance of *socio-political context* becomes particularly salient when analysing collective processes, whether enacted online or off. In work on the TMMC, that context – whether theorized as a relatively static opportunity structure or something more dynamic – is heavily shaped by the shifting landscape of technology and media described above, potentially reflecting back on the nature of collectives created (Dolata & Schrape, 2016). As Mattoni (2017) highlights, a media ecology approach recognizes not only the complexity of media use by movements (i.e. the full range of media practices and the cultural and political rationales that drive them) but also the wider media context within which they operate. This wider media context is itself open to modification by social movement actors themselves, especially those engaged in critical media practices: for example, as Flesher Fominaya's research shows,[2] Spain's 15-M movement not only effectively mobilized multiple digital media tools, but provided a support base and impetus for the development of various critical media initiatives that attempted to put into practice alternative media business models (based on collective ownership, subscriptions and crowd funding). While some such initiatives existed prior to 15-M (e.g. critical collectively produced newspaper Diagonal), the supply of and demand for independent critical media increased in a virtuous circle, with mobilization enabling the emergence of independent critical 'mass' media, thus altering the media ecology of political communication in Spain in significant ways (see also Casero-Ripollés & Feenstra, 2012). The new independent, largely worker-owned, critical media consortium 'El Salto', for example, has significant implications for social movement communication (in that the consortium is committed to covering issues related to progressive social movements), but also represents a radical media movement process in and of itself. Improving understanding of the dynamic interplay between different but overlapping movement groups and their 'contexts' is vital, then, and more likely to emerge from analytical perspectives that begin with a critical approach to the construction of movements as collectives.

The division we have set out between more individualist and more collective units of analysis is often reflective of background ontological positions and methodological choices, but this is not necessarily an insuperable dualism. Two directions for further thought emerge from the contributions to this volume. Firstly, Ahmed et al. (2017) take an interesting step in analysing the emotional valence of tweets surrounding the Nirbhaya movement reacting to a gang-rape incident in Delhi. Here, they code tweets for the sense of 'individualism' or 'collectivism' portrayed in the text. Thus, the degree of collectivism experienced in the movement becomes an empirical question for analysis rather than a matter of theoretical standpoint. Secondly, Uitermark utilizes complexity theory in his investigation of Anonymous, allowing a nuanced account of the development of power structures in an especially individualized and supposedly horizontal forum. While Uitermark argues that movements are agglomerates beyond the control of any individual or group, he also argues that they are defined by their capacity to self-organize and are essentially 'generative, creative and transgressive'. Complexity theory potentially offers a way of understanding collective activity as emergent from relational processes among individuals (c.f. Chesters & Welsh, 2006). Again, one might start from the need to empirically examine degrees of collectivity to understand the ways in which emergence might operate in the TMMC. Anonymous is perhaps at the boundaries of what one might consider a 'movement' in any traditional sense and that makes questions about the relationship between the individual and collective especially sharp. Similarly, studies that begin with social media activity or other communicative media may end up examining primarily activity that is connected, but not necessarily central to, the traditional 'stuff' of movements. These insights are pertinent to continue thinking through what is at stake in taking particular sets of individual practices as indicative of social movements per se.

A further way to overcome the danger of a dualism between more individualistic or more collectivist approaches lies in a focus on networks and the relationships of which they are composed. While formal network analyses have become increasingly popular in social movement scholarship more broadly (e.g. Diani & McAdam, 2003; Krinsky & Crossley, 2014), the network approach becomes most obviously relevant to the TMMC through Castells' (1996) conception of the network society. This opens up questions of power and culture that are especially significant. Castells has argued that power is exercised through networks in a number of ways: controlling access to, or exclusion from, particular networks; programming the purpose of networks; or controlling the connections between multiple networks (Castells, 2009, pp. 42–47). Resistance takes the form of generating counter-power through networks by the same means, but it is precisely in the interconnection of the ICT and media trends that we described as central to the TMMC that movement actors gain the possibility for new forms of contestation (Castells, 2009, pp. 47–53). It is, for Castells (2015), the capacity for 'mass self-communication' – enabled by and intersecting with new media ecologies and digitization processes – that allows the generation of counter-power by global social movements.

Two elements are missing from this conception of power, however. First, we need a stronger recognition of the ways in which communication power is shaped by other relations of power. Below, we briefly outline the ways in which the continuation of digital divides on the lines of gender, age, ethnicity, and class overlay 'traditional' power structures. Second, within Castells' account of communication power, the degree to which engaging (or refusing to engage) in mass self-communication ought to be understood as a cultural preference rooted in the cognitive and emotional characteristics of actors is curiously absent. Castells has occasionally been accused of technological determinism, although as we have already noted we do not think that charge is pertinent here. Nevertheless, if we wish to understand the operation of power in the TMMC we need to delineate the sources of preferences for engaging power in these ways, which are likely to be rooted in cultural formations, whether these are understood as ideologies, interpretative frames, collective identities, or discourses. This approach is usefully highlighted in work on the social forum movements in which it was clear that a 'cultural logic of networking' was a developing political and strategic preference among many participants (Juris, 2008; Pleyers, 2011). Further investigation of intertwining cultural formations and power structures is vital to a fuller understanding of the TMMC.

From cyberpolitics to quotidian technologies

The development of new media and the Internet has created new fields of contention over the governance of communication networks, the production of software, access to information and indeed the fundamentals of technological design (Jordan, 2002, 2015; Kirkpatrick, 2008). The creation of these new tools has inspired, and been inspired by, new forms of activism (Flesher Fominaya, 2014, pp. 135–137; Stalder, 2010). An important but not always explicit distinction in TMMC scholarship is that between the explicitly political use of digital tools in cyber and techno-political movements, and the increasingly ubiquitous and quotidian use of these tools in social movements in general. We use the term cyberpolitical movements to refer to movements who take the virtual arena as the central focus and purpose of their mobilization.

Cyberpolitics can take many forms. At times, the focus is on technologically mediated forms of action. The 'hacktivism' of early pioneers like the Electrohippies has its echoes in more recent groups such as Anonymous. Additionally, the creation of alternative citizen media of all kinds, digital guerilla communications advances, culture jamming and whistleblowing (Baker & Blaagaard, 2016; Carty, 2002; Castells et al., 2006, pp. 202–206; Coleman, 2015) all offer forms of action dependent on digital savvy that could potentially be applied with a wide range of political motives. More often, however, these techniques are used in connection with a cyberpolitical perspective in which movements are ideologically and practically committed to harnessing the emancipatory power of ICTs, and see cyberspace as a primary site of contention and mobilization. The development of a specific politics of information that is tied to the age of the Internet has a number of important expressions in broader movements for 'free culture', free and open source software (F/OSS) and attempts to create and preserve a digital commons (Coleman, 2012; Fuster Morell, 2012; Lessig, 2002; Stalder, 2010). The development of Pirate Parties in a number of European countries, and their success in Iceland (in which the Pirate Party is currently the third largest party) is instructive here (Leruth, 2016). Standing on platforms centred on civic rights, information freedom, privacy, transparency, and a radically critical stance on copyright and patent laws, their main concerns mirror the cyberpolitics found in the kinds of movements noted above. They tend to carry too a (broadly libertarian) critique of representative democracy, arguing for the development of new technologically mediated forms of deliberation (Cammaerts, 2015). This might help explain the particular popularity of the Icelandic Pirate Party, after an experimental, post-crisis 'crowd-sourced' constitutional process gained widespread participation (Oddsdóttir, 2014).

The development of both new tactical or strategic possibilities and a new discourse of information politics is clearly a significant aspect of the developing TMMC. There is some connection here with the 'hacker ethic', the influence of which has been ethnographically explored among a range of groups from F/OSS programmers (Coleman, 2012) to anti-war activists (Gillan, 2008). We do not suggest either that the hacker ethic determines the content of cyberpolitics, nor that it is everywhere the same. In Spain, for instance, the subfield of *tecnopolitica* or technopolitics exists as an activist and academic category that interrogates the nexus between digital imaginaries, digital technologies, and political action in social movements (Blanco & Duarte, 2011; Casero-Ripollés & Feenstra, 2012; Feenstra & Casero Ripollés, 2014; Monterde & Postill, 2014; Postill, 2014; Romanos & Sádaba, 2015; Subirats, Fuster, Martínez, & Berlinguer, 2014). Here, we would expect a different political tilt to that described by Coleman (2012) for (mainly) US-based programmers, although the combination of political action with digitally inscribed imaginaries is itself a common trait (Boler, 2010; Coleman, 2015; Jordan, 2013; Pickerill, 2003; Stalder, 2010).

The ideological components of cyberpolitics are enmeshed in wider ranging movement politics. Postill (2014), for example, points out the importance of various kinds of 'freedom technologists' (from programmers to lawyers and journalists) in the development of 15-M. If we only look at those groups, however, it is tempting to read 15-M as overly influenced by cyberpolitics, when of course its ideological and strategic characteristics drew from pre-existing movement cultures, the political history of Spain as well as the particular experience of economic crisis in that country (Flesher Fominaya, 2015, 2017). We think it likely that there is a multidirectional influence in terms of ideological and discursive resources as cyberpolitics bleeds into other movement spaces. Commitment to some of the values connected with the cyberpolitical realm can be evident without necessarily seeing the use of complex technologies. For example, activists might recognize the strategic benefits of corporate-owned social media but reject its use on ethical grounds (see Askanius & Gustafsson, 2010; Flesher Fominaya, 2014). Likewise, some activist groups develop technical protocols for online political communication that include prohibitions on the circulation of news from corporate-owned media sources. These ideological frameworks can lead groups sometimes to deliberately *eschew* more technologically sophisticated forms of action for ethical or strategic reasons (see Lievrouw, 2011, pp. 173–174).

Beyond cyberpolitics, the adoption of ICTs in movements may take many forms. Because digital technologies and media have also become a quotidian feature of so many people's lives, understanding how activists navigate the TMMC in movements who do *not* prioritize the digital and virtual as political is equally important. Scholars have increasingly studied the use of ICTs as a quotidian and ubiquitous aspect of social movement communication processes across a wide range of issues not directly related to digital media and the politics of cyberspace, as well as its use and importance during episodes of mobilization by actors without specialized technical skills (e.g. Fernandez-Planells, Figueras-Maz, & Pàmpols, 2014; Flesher Fominaya, 2016; Ganesh & Stohl, 2013; Kavada, 2009; Milan, 2013; Nielsen, 2013; Tufekci & Wilson, 2012). Ganesh and Stohl (2013) describe digital media ubiquity in Occupy Wellington, in which activists drew on multiple digital sources of information, and activists' personal networks were intricately embedded in digital media use. As Mattoni (2017) and Nielsen (2011) argue, we still know relatively little about the relationships between the routine use of digital tools and political agency in citizens' decisions to join or participate in movements or politics. Liu (2017) offers an analysis of the mundane digital media use in everyday resistance in China, and like Nielsen (2011) and Ganesh and Stohl (2013), highlights the deep integration of such use into recruiting and mobilizing practices. An adequate understanding of the TMMC clearly needs both kinds of research focus. Additionally, the degree to which cyberpolitics influences or is influenced by the everyday use of ICTs in social movements is another potentially fruitful area of inquiry. The role of hackers and cyber-activists in the recent wave of Occupy type movements is, for instance, understudied (but see Romanos & Sádaba, 2015), with most scholars focusing on the ubiquitous/quotidian elements of digital media use (e.g. Fernandez-Planells et al., 2014; Ganesh & Stohl, 2013).

Exclusions and divisions in the age of new media

Claims that new media use is 'ubiquitous' in some sectors of the population need to be tempered by an awareness of the continuing existence of digital divides that cut across social movements. This has implications for research methods as well as for the evaluation of the causes, dynamics, and impacts of new media use for social movements. If 'ubiquity' is understood as ICT use spreading across whole societies, it is highly misleading and needs to be interrogated. In the UK, for example, Ofcom's report on media literacy noted that 13% of adults do not use the Internet at all (Ofcom, 2016, pp. 23–25). Non-usage is clearly patterned by age, with 33% of over 65s (rising to 65% of over 75s) reporting that they never use the Internet. Volume of Internet use is also patterned: younger, wealthier people on average spend much longer online than older or poorer people and engage in a wider variety of activities (Ofcom, 2016, pp. 23–25). Around 70% of Internet users in the UK have a social media profile, which usually means Facebook. While Twitter has become an incredibly popular research tool, it is a relatively peculiar pastime. In comparing Twitter use in the UK and US, Blank (2016) finds that not only are Twitter users in both countries younger and wealthier than other Internet users (and hence even more so compared with the wider population), but they are more likely to be members of elites and have characteristically different attitudes and behaviours than the wider populations.

Moreover, while British and American Twitter users share some characteristics, there are cross-country differences too, especially pertaining to ethnicity. Not only do Twitter users not represent the wider population, but different national Twitter populations cannot be taken as representative of each other. These insights have important implications for social movement research using social media data. To take one example: the importance of 'hashtag activism' to the development of Black Lives Matter in the USA has been widely discussed in terms of its temporalities, its capacity to enable the emergence of a public counter-discourse, and its creation of solidarities (Bonilla & Rosa, 2015; Freelon, McIlwain, & Clark, 2016; Jackson & Welles, 2016). From a TMMC perspective, however, what is consequential here is that #BLM did not spring from a virtual or de-contextualized tabula rasa, but rather from a specific set of patterned relationships between black subcultures, mainstream media practices, and social media use. Blacks in the USA are disproportionately high users of Twitter, to the extent that we can talk of the emergence of a 'Black Twitter', fuelled by the technological development of hashtags and trending topics on the Twitter interface. Brock (2015) accordingly positions twitter as a cultural rather than social network, in which hashtags operate simultaneously as sign, signifier *and* signified, particularly through their performative structuring as 'call-and response' by Black Twitter users. The Twitter interface thus indirectly enables Black interventions into White public space.

Only when we grasp the interplay between these elements can we avoid the pitfalls of what Melucci (1994) calls 'the myopia of the visible', namely the tendency to focus on the most visible and easily measured aspects of mobilization, while neglecting the cultural codes and practices that generate them. The methodological point is that studying online participation exclusively cannot tell us anything about non-participation; it only captures the behaviour of those who are already participating (Flesher Fominaya, 2016; Tufekci, 2014a). This makes it harder to explore factors that *inhibit* online participation, a key issue for social movements seeking to maximize the democratic potential of ICTs (Flesher Fominaya, 2016). Studies based on online participation data need, therefore, to be carefully delimited. Online participation should not be taken as a proxy or indicator of movement organization or mobilization strength, and online forms of mobilization need to be clearly distinguished from offline forms of mobilization. One illustrative example comes from the relation between Twitter use and mobilization. Much has been made of the role of Twitter in Spain's 15-M/Indignados movement (see e.g. Peña-López, Congosto, & Aragón, 2014), yet the 2013 data for Spain shows that Twitter users represented 15% of the total Internet user population and 4% of the total population, with an average age of 22.6 for Twitter users, according to Peer Reach.[3] This does not mean Twitter is irrelevant or unimportant; quite the contrary. Activists with effective communication strategies are aware of the problems caused by social media 'echo chambers' and the need to break through the social media barrier to connect to mass media outlets which will then broadcast movement messages beyond the limited Twitter-sphere. Twitter is also a crucial communication resource during intense periods of mobilization. But recognition of the limits of the Twitter-sphere and its problematic relation to offline mobilization is necessary for activists and scholars. Calls to street protest, for example, might become a trending topic on Twitter, but not yield the necessary or anticipated bodies on the street. In a similar vein, Morozov (2012) argues that activist focus on online tools can distract them from effectively engaging in those actions needed to realize significant or lasting political change.

There is not necessarily a direct correlation, therefore, between online and offline participation, a fact that can be overlooked when all that is being measured is online participation. Selecting successful cases where intense online mobilization is accompanied by intense offline mobilization can further reinforce the idea the social media use is *driving* mobilization processes. As Castells argued in the midst of the hoopla around 'Twitter Revolutions' during the Arab Uprisings, 'obviously communication technologies did not give birth to the insurgency' (Castells, quoted in Khondker, 2011, p. 678). It is obvious, but sometimes easy to forget, that 'ICTs do not cause revolutions, deep seated structural problems, mass grievances and people willing and able to act collectively do' (Flesher Fominaya, 2014, p. 166). What is also often overlooked is how often social movement media campaigns fail to create resonance and impact in a media environment full of competing demands for attention and the continuing presence of other powerful voices with greater access to the public.

These comments highlight that while social media research is essential, one needs to be very careful in constructing research designs that rely exclusively on social media data (see also Tufekci, 2014b). Attempts to represent a wider population statistically will be problematic and claims made on the basis of these data need suitable caveats. Contentious political activity on either Twitter or Facebook is undoubtedly intrinsically interesting, but using social media as either the only source of data, or as a single starting point (e.g. providing a sampling frame of people or events) means limiting one's claims about the TMMC precisely to active users of those platforms. Fortunately, emerging scholarship in this area offers many valuable contributions to the literature, including the work of Ahmed et al. (2017), Hensby (2017) and Pavan (2017).

It is clear that social media activity in particular, or online activity in general, is not ubiquitous in the sense that it is used by all social groups: usage is uneven in spread and heterogeneous in character. It is the case, however, that ICTs can have a different kind of ubiquity in which they are becoming present everywhere in the lives of those who engage with them. That is to say, while ICTs are not *socially ubiquitous*, they may be *personally ubiquitous*: for those who almost always have Internet access, online services can become the first point of call for crucial information and communication tasks. This is why Liu (2017) proposes a research programme focused on the 'politics of mundanity', in which it is recognized that explosive contentious 'moments of madness' cannot be explained without reference to the continuous presence of political online expression that has (for some groups of the population) become a constant presence in daily life. The personally ubiquitous character of ICTs is also likely to be especially important with respect to those movement groups that are most clearly intertwined with technology and the politics of cyberspace. Ganesh and Stohl (2013:425) argue that 'digital ubiquity marks the onset of a profound hybridity rather than an abrupt change in activist organizing practices'. In other words, many activists integrate new tools into existing repertoires of action, rather than radically altering their practices as a result of new technology. This is partly because as they and others have noted (Bimber, Flanagin, & Stohl, 2012; Flesher Fominaya, 2016; Lovink, 2012) when technologies become so integrated into daily life as to no longer seem remarkable, people stop being as reflexive about their use. This can pose important problems for activism and scholarship on activism with regard to navigating the TMMC (Flesher Fominaya, 2016). We highlight a few of these issues in the next section.

Digitally enabled divides within activist communities

Rethinking digitally enabled divides requires paying attention to the ways technology and media use can be at the centre of diverse forms of divisions within social movement communities. As Flesher Fominaya (2016) argues there is a tendency to neglect the emotional and subjective aspects of ICT use in favour of their technological aspects (i.e. costs, affordances, and leveraging). In addition, with some exceptions (e.g. Horton, 2004; Pickerill, 2004; Kavada, 2009) little attention has been paid to the impact of ICTs on the internal communication and cohesion of face-to-face social movement groups. This deficit means we have insufficient knowledge of the way technology and media use is experienced *subjectively* by activists and how this affects social movement processes such as communication, cohesion, collective identity formation, frustration, and burnout. A key emerging area of research studies the role of digital technologies and digitally mediated communication in fostering or hindering social movement groups' ability to meet their ideological commitments to such values as democratic or horizontal participation, openness, transparency, and collaboration, goals that are often tied into the emancipatory digital imaginaries of the groups themselves (see e.g. Flesher Fominaya, 2016; Hensby, 2017; Romanos & Sádaba, 2015; Nielsen, 2013; Uitermark, 2017).

A related issue is the role of status inequalities and power as it flows through movement spaces and is mediated by technology. Two of the key areas in this regard are the role of technological expertise, and gender. Attention to the former reveals how technological expertise can and does influence access to and control of technology and media, which can and does create important hierarchies within social movement communities, as well as affecting the closed or open nature of internal movement organizational dynamics (Costanza-Chock, 2012; Flesher Fominaya, 2016; Juris, Caruso, Couture, & Mosca, 2013; Pickerill, 2003). This digital divide can also intersect with other divides such as age (e.g. where older activists who may be less digitally connected or savvy feel left out when groups rely exclusively or unreflexively on technologically mediated forms of communication), gender (e.g. in hacker or radical geek spaces in which women are still minorities and face significant sexism), or economic inequality (e.g. where some members do not have constant access to the Internet or mobile phones). Attention to gender reveals how it shapes patterns of mediated interaction which can marginalize, silence, delegitimize or exclude women's voices (and privilege male authority), as well as how digitally mediated interactions in cyberspace are often extremely hostile for women (and people of colour) further decreasing participation and affecting their possibilities for leadership, representation and expression. Dahlberg (2001, p. 623), for example, highlights the problems stemming from a lack of reflexivity in cyber-deliberations, including the failure to achieve respectful listening or commitment to difference, the dominance of discussion by few individuals and groups, and exclusions because of social inequalities.

Perhaps due to a lingering hangover from early techno-optimism, there is still a widespread tendency to assume that the Internet is somehow either inherently democratic, or else that it is a neutral autonomous sphere, despite clear evidence to the contrary. The gendered digital divide is also extremely pronounced within the communities that paradoxically offer the greatest opportunity for harnessing the power of the digital for progressive social change: the civic-technology and open source community. Not only are women woefully underrepresented in technology engineering and coding, but they are also silenced within the community through the privileging of male voices and the value placed on male dominated roles (Maidaborn, 2014). The pervasive sexism that penetrates cyber-activist spaces on and offline is clearly an area of the TMMC that needs to be reflexively and critically analysed. Reflexivity about power then, within and beyond digital activist communities, is crucial. So too is research on the ways that activists are trying to overcome these divides and maximize the potential offered by the TMMC. Understanding the ways that digital divides signal the intersection of traditional power dynamics with the dynamics of the TMMC would go a long way to rectifying some of the deficiencies in Castell's treatment of power, which we described above, as well as combating narratives that tend to flatten or neutralize power differences in virtual spaces.

Conclusions

We started this article by highlighting the interconnections between research in the fields of technology, media and social movements, and have offered an overview of key ways these broad fields come together to provide new knowledge of social movement dynamics. But there is much more to do to understand the dynamics of the TMMC. Drawing on the conceptual clarifications and advances provided above, we now identify six broad challenges on which further attention may generate a research programme capable of transcending the current 'state of the art'.

First, we need to pay more attention to power. On the one hand, that means more concerted focus on the political economy of media and technology in order to better understand issues of the access to, control of, and surveillance of the means by which movements are mediated. On the other, it means examining the multiple ways power imbalances 'in real life' can be reproduced, manifested and magnified online (see e.g. Flesher Fominaya, 2016) and how these traverse activist spaces and strategies, with crucial implications for participation, marginalization, inclusion, and voice.

Second, we need to pay much more attention to the lived experience of the use of digital tools. Digital mediation affects both the internal life of social movements as they communicate, deliberate, and organize, and the 'public face' of movements as they interact with broader media ecologies. Both forms of mediation are shaped by culture, emotions, gender, technological savvy, and human-technology interaction. A balanced approach to culture and material life is required to understand decisions to adopt or adapt certain forms of media and technology and to trace the way these decisions impact social movement dynamics, including cohesion, conflict, collective identity formation, and internal and external communicational and organizational strategies.

Third, we need to recognize the specificities of the media ecologies in which social movements operate, especially in local and national settings. Activists able to draw on a rich network of autonomous media resources and count on a developed critical media sphere (despite limitations posed by corporate owned mass media), for example, are likely to fare better with well-developed communication strategies than activists who might be as technologically and politically savvy but face a harsher, less forgiving media climate. Activists' digital cultural repertoires likewise will influence the uptake or rejection of certain media technologies as much as, or more than, affordances.

Fourth, we need to recognize the importance of ideational frameworks and political priorities in influencing technology and media use in social movements. This means recognizing that technology itself is neither value-neutral nor value-laden, but can be harnessed by actors of all persuasions and intents. While some movement action might be driven by the excitement of novel technologies or because the manifest functionalities of those technologies fit their organizational form, others are much more embedded in the ideological commitments of activist groups, independently of the specific affordances of particular technologies.

In each of these areas, further empirical research would help us to get beyond pointing to the complexity of interactions within the TMMC, to specifying sets of cultural, material, and social conditions that in combination generate patterns of action. Doing so successfully may depend on a *fifth* core challenge: we need to expand and revise our methodological and ethical protocols to take into account the interpenetration of technological and social processes in so many areas of collective political action. This is in part due to the very nature of the data we are faced with analysing, which as Coleman (2010b, p. 494) highlights, presents researchers with the challenge of 'how to collect and represent forms of digital data whose social and material life are often infused with elements of anonymity, modalities of hypermobility, ephemerality, and mutability'. At the same time we need to be critical and cautious about enthusiastic claims about 'the power of' the Internet, social media and digital technologies when assessing causality and outcomes, as we have argued throughout. The allure of 'big data' in enabling large-scale quantitative analysis has caused considerable excitement in some parts of the social sciences, but we have expressed some caution above about the danger of reinforcing an excessively individual-centred approach to collective action. Given that access to 'big data' is typically through powerful corporations or agents of state, we must also be mindful of the same kinds of ethical challenge that activists face in considering the adoption of particular tools (Gillan, 2014).

Our *sixth* and final challenge is more theoretical in nature. The field of social movement studies has built up a set of conceptual tools that predate the digital era. We are confident most of these existing concepts are quite robust, but we should subject them to scrutiny and modification as necessary when transferring them to the TMMC. The concept of collective identity is a good example, having often been conceived as a process that requires face-to-face interaction. Despite this, re-interrogations of the concept have found that it continues to be relevant and useful even in social movements that mobilize almost entirely online, such as Anonymous (Firer-Blaess, 2016; Flesher Fominaya, in press). We believe rising to these challenges is necessary for the further development of TMMC research, which would in turn mark a positive development for social movement scholarship as a whole.

Notes

1. For an overview of the relation between mass media and social movements, see Flesher Fominaya, 2014, Chapter 6.
2. Marie Sklodowska-Curie Research Project 'Contentious Politics in an Age of Austerity: A comparative study of anti-austerity protests in Spain and Ireland' (2013–2015). This research involved extensive participant observation, over 70 interviews and secondary data analysis.
3. For details: https://peerreach.com/

Acknowledgements

We would particularly like to thank Graeme Hayes for insightful commentary on an earlier version of this article.

Disclosure statement

No potential conflict of interest was reported by the authors.

ORCID

Kevin Gillan http://orcid.org/0000-0003-1693-9170

References

Ahmed, S., Jaidka, K., & Cho, J. (2017). Tweeting India's Nirbhaya protest: a study of emotional dynamics in an online social movement. *Social Movement Studies, 16*(4), 447–465. doi:10.1080/14742837.2016.1192457

Askanius, T., & Gustafsson, N. (2010). Mainstreaming the alternative: The changing media practices of protest movements. *Interface, 2*, 23–41.

Baker, M., & Blaagaard, B. B. (Eds.). (2016). *Citizen media and public spaces*. London: Routledge.

Bell, D. (1974). *The coming of post-industrial society: A venture in social forecasting*. London: Heinemann Educational.

Benkler, Y. (2006). *The wealth of networks: How social production transforms markets and freedom*. New Haven, CT: Yale University Press.

Bennett, W. L., & Segerberg, A. (2012). The logic of connective action. *Information, Communication & Society, 15*, 739–768.

Bimber, B., Flanagin, A., & Stohl, C. (2012). *Collective action in organizations: Interaction and engagement in an era of technological change*. Cambridge: Cambridge University Press.

Blanco, V. F. S., & Duarte, J. M. S. (2011). Del 13-M Al 15-M [From 13-M to 15-M]. *Razón Y Fe [Reason and Faith]*. Retrieved from http://www.ciber-democracia.es/articulos/SAMPEDROSANCHEZ.pdf

Blank, G. (2016). The digital divide among twitter users and its implications for social research. *Social Science Computer Review*. Advance online publication. doi:10.1177/0894439316671698.

Boler, M. (2010). *Digital media and democracy*. Boston, MA: MIT Press.

Bonilla, Y., & Rosa, J. (2015). #Ferguson: Digital protest, hashtag ethnography, and the racial politics of social media in the United States. *American Ethnologist, 42*, 4–17.

Brock, A. (2015). From the blackhand side: Twitter as a cultural conversation. *Journal of Broadcasting & Electronic Media, 56*, 529–549.

Brym, R., Godbout, M., Hoffbauer, A., Menard, G., & Zhang, T. H. (2014). Social media in the 2011 Egyptian uprising. *The British Journal of Sociology, 65*, 266–292.

Cammaerts, B. (2015). Pirates on the liquid shores of liberal democracy: Movement frames of European pirate parties. *Javnost – The Public, 22*, 19–36.

Carty, V. (2002). Technology and counter-hegemonic movements: The case of nike corporation. *Social Movement Studies, 1*, 129–146.

Casero-Ripollés, A., & Feenstra, R. A. (2012). Nuevas Formas de Producción de Noticias En El Entorno Digital Y Cambios En El Periodismo: El Caso Del 15-M [New Forms of News Production in the Digital Environment, and Changes in Journalism: The Case of 15-M]. *Comunicación Y Hombre CyH 8 (10)* [Communication And Man]. Universidad Francisco de Vitoria. Retrieved from http://ddfv.ufv.es/handle/10641/896

Castells, M. (1996). *The rise of the network society*. Malden, MA: Blackwell Publishers Inc.

Castells, M. (2009). *Communication power*. Oxford: Oxford University Press.

Castells, M. (2015). *Networks of outrage and hope: Social movements in the internet age* (2nd ed.). Cambridge: Polity Press.

Castells, M., Qiu, J. L., Fernandez-Ardevol, M., & Sey, A. (2006). *Mobile communication and society: A global perspective*. Cambridge, MA: MIT Press.

Chesters, G., & Welsh, I. (2006). *Complexity and social movements: Multitudes at the edge of chaos*. London: Routledge.

Coleman, E. G. (2010a). The hacker conference: A ritual condensation and celebration of a lifeworld. *Anthropological Quarterly, 83*, 47–72.

Coleman, E. G. (2010b). Ethnographic approaches to digital media. *Annual Review of Anthropology, 39*, 487–505.

Coleman, E. G. (2012). *Coding freedom: The ethics and aesthetics of hacking*. Princeton, NJ: Princeton University Press.

Coleman, E. G. (2015). *Hacker, hoaxer, whistleblower, spy: The many faces of anonymous*. London: Verso Books.

Costanza-Chock, S. (2012). Mic check! media cultures and the occupy movement. *Social Movement Studies, 11*, 375–385.

Dahlberg, L. (2001). The internet and democratic discourse: Exploring the prospects of online deliberative forums extending the public sphere. *Information, Communication & Society, 4*, 615–633.

De Souza e Silva, A. (2006). Interfaces of hybrid spaces. In A. Kavoori & N. Arceneaux (Eds.), *The cell phone reader. Essays in social transformation* (pp. 19–44). Oxford: Peter Lang.

DeLuca, M. K., & Peeples, J. (2002). From public sphere to public screen: Democracy, activism, and the "violence" of Seattle. *Critical Studies in Media Communication, 19*, 125–151.
Dencik, L., & Leistert, O. (Eds.). (2015). *Critical perspectives on social media and protest: Between control and emancipation* (pp. 109–126). Lanham, MD: Rowman & Littlefield International.
Diani, M., & McAdam, D. (Eds.). (2003). *Social movements and networks: Relational approaches to collective action.* Oxford: Oxford University Press.
Dolata, U., & Schrape, J.-F. (2016). Masses, crowds, communities, movements: Collective action in the internet age. *Social Movement Studies, 15*(1), 1–18.
Earl, J. & Garrett, R. K. (2017). The new information frontier: toward a more nuanced view of social movement communication. *Social Movement Studies, 16*(4), 479–893. doi:10.1080/14742837.2016.1192028
Feenberg, A. (2002). *Transforming technology: A critical theory revisited* (2nd ed.). New York: Oxford University Press.
Feenstra, R. A., & Casero Ripollés, A. (2014). Democracy in the digital communication environment: A typology proposal of political monitoring processes. *International Journal of Communication, 8*, 2448–2468.
Fernandez-Planells, A., Figueras-Maz, M., & Pàmpols, C. F. (2014). Communication among young people in the #spanishrevolution: Uses of online–offline tools to obtain information about the #acampadabcn. *New Media & Society, 16*, 1287–1308.
Firer-Blaess, S. (2016). *The collective identity of anonymous: Web of meanings in a digitally enabled movement.* Uppsala: Acta Universitatis Upsaliensis: Uppsala Studies in Media and Communication 12. Retrieved May 12, 2017, from http://www.diva-portal.org/smash/record.jsf?pid=diva2%3A926671&dswid=5513
Flesher Fominaya, C. (2014). *Social movements and globalization: How protests, occupations and uprisings are changing the world.* Basingstoke: Palgrave Macmillan.
Flesher Fominaya, C. (2015). Debunking spontaneity: Spain's 15-M/*Indignados* as autonomous movement. *Social Movement Studies, 14*, 142–163.
Flesher Fominaya, C. (2016). Unintended consequences: The negative impact of e-mail use on participation and collective identity in two "horizontal" social movement groups. *European Political Science Review, 8*, 95–122.
Flesher Fominaya, C. (2017). European anti-austerity and pro-democracy movements in the wake of the global financial crisis. *Social Movement Studies, 16*(1), 1–20.
Flesher Fominaya, C. (in press). Collective identity in social movements: Assessing the limits of a theoretical framework. In D. A. Snow, S. A. Soule, H. Kriesi, & H. J. McCammon (Eds.), *Wiley-Blackwell companion to social movements* (2nd ed.). Oxford: Wiley-Blackwell.
Freelon, D., McIlwain, C. D., & Clark, M. D. (2016). *Beyond the hashtags. #ferguson, #blacklivesmatter and the online struggle for offline justice.* Washington, D.C.: American University Center for Media & Social Impact. Retrieved May 29, 2017, from http://cmsimpact.org/wp-content/uploads/2016/03/beyond_the_hashtags_2016.pdf
Freeman, J. (1972). The tyranny of structurelessness. *Berkeley Journal of Sociology, 17*, 151–165.
Fuster Morell, M. (2012). The free culture and 15M movements in Spain: Composition, social networks and synergies. *Social Movement Studies, 11*, 386–392.
Gallo-Cruz, S. (2017). The insufficient imagery of top-down, bottom-up in global movements analysis. *Social Movement Studies, 16*, 153–168.
Ganesh, S., & Stohl, C. (2013). From wall street to Wellington: Protests in an era of digital ubiquity. *Communication Monographs, 80*, 425–451.
Garton, L., & Wellman, B. (1995). Social impacts of electronic mail in organizations: A review of the research literature. *Annals of the International Communication Association, 18*, 434–453.
Gibson, R. K., Gillan, K., Greffet, F., Lee, B. J., & Ward, S. (2013). Party organizational change and ICTs: The growth of a virtual grassroots? *New Media & Society, 15*, 31–51.
Gillan, K. (2008). Diverging attitudes to technology and innovation in Anti-War movement organisations. In T. Häyhtiö & J. Rinne (Eds.), *Net working/Networking: Citizen initiated politics* (pp. 74–102). Tampere: Tampere University Press.
Gillan, K. (2009). The UK anti-war movement online: Uses and limitations of internet technologies for contemporary activism. *Information, Communication & Society, 12*, 25–43.
Gillan, K. (2014, July 15). Emotional contagion, big data and research ethics. *Movements@Manchester Blog.* Retrieved March 7, 2016, from http://www.movements.manchester.ac.uk/big-data-research-ethics/
Gillan, K. (in press). Social movements: Sequences vs. Fuzzy temporality. In P. Kivisto (Ed.), *The Cambridge handbook of social theory* (Vol. 2). Cambridge: Cambridge University Press.
Gillan, K., Pickerill, J., & Webster, F. (2008). *Anti-war activism: New media and protest in the information age.* Basingstoke: Palgrave Macmillan.
Gillespie, T. (2010). The politics of "platforms". *New Media & Society, 12*, 347–364.
Gitlin, T. (2003). *The whole world is watching: Mass media in the making and unmaking of the new left* (2nd ed.). Berkeley, CA: University of California Press.
Gordon, J. (2006). The cell phone: An artefact of popular culture and a tool of the public sphere. In A. Kavoori & N. Arceneaux (Eds.), *The cell phone reader. Essays in social transformation* (pp. 45–60). Oxford: Peter Lang.
Hargittai, E., & Shafer, S. (2006). Differences in actual and perceived online skills: The role of gender. *Social Science Quarterly, 87*, 432–448.

Hensby, A. (2017). Open networks and secret Facebook groups: exploring cycle effects on activists'social media use in the 2010/11 UK student protests. *Social Movement Studies, 16*(4), 466–478. doi:10.1080/14742837.2016.1201421.
Himanen, P. (2001). *The hacker ethic: A radical approach to the philosophy of business*. New York, NY: Random House.
Hintz, A. (2015). Social media censorship, privatized regulation and new restrictions to protest and dissent. In L. Dencik & O. Leistert (Eds.), *Critical perspectives on social media and protest: Between control and emancipation* (pp. 109–126). London: Rowman & Littlefield.
Horton, D. (2004). Local environmentalism and the internet. *Environmental Politics, 13*, 734–753.
Hwang, H., Schmierbach, M., Paek, H.-J., de Zuniga, H. G., & Shah, D. (2006). Media dissociation, internet use, and antiwar political participation: A case study of political dissent and action against the war in Iraq. *Mass Communication and Society, 9*, 461–483.
Jackson, S. J., & Welles, B. F. (2016). #Ferguson is everywhere: Initiators in emerging counterpublic networks. *Information, Communication & Society, 19*, 397–418.
Johnston, H. (2014). *What is a social movement?*. Cambridge: Policy Press.
Jordan, T. (2002). *Activism! direct action, hacktivism and the future of society*. London: Reaktion.
Jordan, T. (2013). Information as politics. *Culture Machine, 14*, 1–22.
Jordan, T. (2015). *Information politics: Liberation and exploitation in the digital society*. London: Pluto.
Juris, J. S. (2008). *Networking futures: The movements against corporate globalization*. Durham, NC: Duke University Press.
Juris, J. S., Caruso, G., Couture, S., & Mosca, L. (2013). The cultural politics of free software and technology within the social forum process. In J. S. Juris & A. Khasnabish (Eds.), *Insurgent encounters: Transnational activism, ethnography, and the political* (pp. 342–365). Durham, NC: Duke University Press.
Kavada, A. (2009). Email lists and the construction of an open and multifaceted identity. *Information, Communication & Society, 12*, 817–839.
Kavada, A. (2015). Creating the collective: Social media, the occupy movement and its constitution as a collective actor. *Information, Communication & Society, 18*, 872–886.
Khondker, H. H. (2011). Role of the new media in the Arab Spring. *Globalizations, 8*, 675–679.
Kiesler, S., & Sproull, L. (1992). Group decision making and communication technology. *Organizational Behavior and Human Decision Processes, 52*, 96–123.
Kirkpatrick, G. (2008). *Technology and social power*. Basingstoke: Palgrave Macmillan.
Krinsky, J., & Crossley, N. (2014). Social movements and social networks: Introduction. *Social Movement Studies, 13*(1), 1–21.
Leistert, O. (2015). The revolution will not be liked: On the systemic constraints of corporate social media platforms for protests. In L. Dencik & O. Leistert (Eds.), *Critical perspectives on social media and protest: Between control and emancipation* (pp. 35–52). New York, NY: Rowman & Littlefield International.
Leruth, B. (2016, October 31). Iceland's election: The Pirates failed to live up to expectations, but this was still a landmark result. *LSE European Politics and Policy (EUROPP) Blog*. Retrieved May 15, 2017, from http://blogs.lse.ac.uk/europpblog/
Lessig, L. (2002). *The future of ideas: The fate of the commons in a connected world*. New York, NY: Vintage.
Lievrouw, L. (2011). *Alternative and activist new media*. Cambridge: Polity Press.
Liu, J. (2017). From 'moments of madness' to 'the politics of mundanity' - researching digital media and contentious collective actions in China. *Social Movement Studies, 16*(4), 418–432. doi:10.1080/14742837.2016.1192027
Lovink, G. (2012). *Networks without a Cause: A critique of social media*. Cambridge: Polity Press.
Maidaborn, V. (2014). Open sourcing feminism: The challenge of collective intelligence in 2014. *Loomio Blog*. Retrieved from http://blog.loomio.org/2014/03/08/open-sourcing-feminism-the-challenge-of-collective-intelligence-in-2014/
Margetts, H., John, P., Hale, S., & Yasseri, T. (2015). *Political turbulence: How social media shape collective action*. Princeton, NJ: Princeton University Press.
Margolis, M., & Resnick, D. (2000). *Politics as usual: The cyberspace 'revolution'*. Thousand Oaks, CA: SAGE Publications.
Mattoni, A. (2012). *Media practices and protest politics: How precarious workers mobilise*. Farnham: Ashgate Publishing.
Mattoni, A. (2017). A situated understanding of digital technologies in social movements. Media ecology and media practice approaches. *Social Movement Studies, 16*(4), 494–505. doi:10.1080/14742837.2017.1311250.
McCarthy, J. D., Smith, J., & Zald, M. N. (1996). Accessing public, media, electoral and governmental agendas. In D. McAdam, J. D. McCarthy, & M. N. Zald (Eds.), *Comparative perspectives on social movements. Political opportunities, mobilizing structures and cultural framings* (pp. 291–311). Cambridge: Cambridge University Press.
Melucci, A. (1994). A strange kind of newness: What's 'new' in new social movements?. In E. Laraña, H. Johnston, & J. R. Gusfield (Eds.), *New social movements: From ideology to identity* (pp. 103–130). Philadelphia, PA: Temple University Press.
Mercea, D., & Yilmaz, K. E. (in press). Movement social learning on twitter: The case of the people's assembly. *The Sociological Review*. Retrieved May 29, 2017, from https://ssrn.com/abstract=2971253
Milan, S. (2013). *Social movements and their technologies: Wiring social change*. Basingstoke: Palgrave Macmillan.
Milan, S. (2015). From social movements to cloud protesting: The evolution of collective identity. *Information, Communication & Society, 18*, 887–900.

Monterde, A., & Postill, J. (2014). Mobile ensembles: The uses of mobile phones for social protest by Spain's indignados. In G. Goggin & L. Hjorth (Eds.), *Routledge companion to mobile media* (pp. 429–438). London: Routledge.
Morozov, E. (2012). *The net delusion: How not to liberate the world*. London: Penguin.
Nielsen, R. K. (2011). Mundane internet tools, mobilizing practices, and the coproduction of citizenship in political campaigns. *New Media & Society, 13*, 755–771.
Nielsen, R. K. (2013). Mundane internet tools, the risk of exclusion, and reflexive movements – occupy wall street and political uses of digital networked technologies. *The Sociological Quarterly, 54*, 173–177.
Oddsdóttir, K. (2014). Iceland: The birth of the world's first crowd-sourced constitution. *Cambridge Journal of International and Comparative Law, 3*, 1207–1220.
Ofcom. (2016). *Adults' media use and attitudes*. London: Author. Retrieved April 23, 2017, from https://www.ofcom.org.uk/__data/assets/pdf_file/0026/80828/2016-adults-media-use-and-attitudes.pdf
Oliver, P. E., & Maney, G. M. (2000). Political processes and local newspaper coverage of protest events: From selection bias to triadic interactions. *American Journal of Sociology, 106*, 463–505.
Olson, M. (1965). *The logic of collective action: Public goods and the theory of groups*. Harvard, MA.: Harvard University Press.
Pavan, E. (2017). The integrative power of online collective action networks beyond protest. Exploring social media use in the process of institutionalization. *Social Movement Studies, 16*(4), 433–446. doi:10.1080/14742837.2016.1268956.
Peña-López, I., Congosto, M., & Aragón, P. (2014). Spanish Indignados and the evolution of the 15M movement on Twitter: Towards networked para-institutions. *Journal of Spanish Cultural Studies, 15*, 189–216.
Pickerill, J. (2003). *Cyberprotest: Environmental activism online*. Manchester: Manchester UniversityPress.
Pickerill, J. (2004). Rethinking political participation: Experiments in internet activism in Australia and Britain. In R. Gibson, A. Rommele, & S. Ward (Eds.), *Electronic democracy: Mobilisation, organisation and participation via new ICTs* (pp. 170–193). London: Routledge.
Pleyers, G. (2011). *Alter-globalization: Becoming actors in the global age*. Cambridge: Polity Press.
Postill, J. (2014). Freedom technologists and the new protest movements: A theory of protest formulas. *Convergence, 20*, 402–418.
Redshaw, T. (2017). Bitcoin beyond ambivalence: Popular rationalization and Feenberg's technical politics. *Thesis Eleven, 138*, 46–64.
Rheingold, H. (1993). *The virtual community*. Boston, MA: Addison Wesley.
Romanos, E., & Sádaba, I. (2015). La Evolución de Los Marcos (Tecno) Discursivos Del Movimiento 15M Y Sus Consecuencias [The Evolution of the (Techno) Discourses of the 15M Movement and its Consequences]. *Empiria. Revista de Metodología de Ciencias Sociales, 32*, 15–36.
Ryan, C. (1991). *Prime time activism: Media strategies for grassroots organizing*. Boston, MA: South End Press.
Shirky, C. (2009). *Here comes everybody: How change happens when people come together*. London: Penguin UK.
Siapera, E. (2011). *Understanding new media*. Thousand Oaks, CA: Sage Publications Ltd.
Smith, J., McCarthy, J. D., McPhail, C., & Augustyn, B. (2001). From protest to agenda building: Description bias in media coverage of protest events in Washington, D.C. *Social Forces, 79*, 1397–1423.
Spears, R., Lea, M., Corneliussen, R. A., Postmes, T., & Haar, W. T. (2002). Computer-mediated communication as a channel for social resistance: The strategic side of SIDE. *Small Group Research, 33*, 555–574. doi:10.1177/104649602237170
Stalder, F. (2010). Digital commons. In K. Hart, J.-L. Laville, & A. D. Cattani (Eds.), *Human economy: A citizen's guide* (pp. 313–325). Cambridge: Polity Press.
Stoycheff, E., & Nisbet, E. C. (2016). Is Internet Freedom a tool for democracy or authroitarianism? *The Conversation*. Retrieved from https://theconversation.com/is-internet-freedom-a-tool-for-democracy-or-authoritarianism-61956
Subirats, J., Fuster, M., Martínez, R., & Berlinguer, M. (2014). Jóvenes, Internet Y Política [Youth, internet and politics]. Retrieved from http://ictlogy.net/bibliography/reports/projects.php?idp=2691&lang=ca
Tufekci, Z. (2014a). The medium and the movement: Digital tools, social movement politics, and the end of the free rider problem. *Policy & Internet, 6*, 202–208.
Tufekci, Z. (2014b). Big questions for social media big data: Representativeness, validity and other methodological pitfalls. In *ICWSM '14: Proceedings of the 8th International AAAI Conference on Weblogs and Social Media*, 2014. Retrieved from https://arxiv.org/abs/1403.7400
Tufekci, Z. (2015). Algorithmic harms beyond facebook and google: Emergent challenges of computational agency. *Colorado Technology Law Journal, 13*, 203–217.
Tufekci, Z., & Wilson, C. (2012). Social media and the decision to participate in political protest: Observations from Tahrir square. *Journal of Communication, 62*, 363–379.
Uitermark, J. (2017). Complex contention: analyzing power dynamics within Anonymous. *Social Movement Studies, 16*(4), 403–417. doi:10.1080/14742837.2016.1184136.
Wall, M. A. (2007). Social movements and email: Expressions of online identity in the globalization protests. *New Media & Society, 9*, 258–277.

OPEN ACCESS

Complex contention: analyzing power dynamics within Anonymous

Justus Uitermark

ABSTRACT

Anonymous is notoriously elusive as the movement takes on radically different guises, constantly mutates, and traverses national borders and ideological divides. Since Anonymous is difficult to grasp with conventional social movement theory, this paper uses insights from complexity theory to analyze the movement's evolution in general and its dynamics of power in particular. While participants in Anonymous radically reject hierarchy and leadership, dominant groups emerged at various points in the movement's evolution. This paper aims to explain how such dominant groups emerge and concentrate power and how they subsequently dissolve and lose power. Drawing on ethnographic research as well as secondary sources, it identifies mechanisms of power concentration and diffusion within nominally horizontalist movements.

The nebulous entity Anonymous has claimed responsibility for a dizzying number and variety of actions, ranging from outing child molesters and chasing cat abusers to hacking into security firms and taking down websites of global corporations. Journalists often refer to Anonymous as a 'hacker collective' or a 'group of hackers,' but the movement lacks the cohesion and continuity usually associated with groups or collectives. Anonymous lacks a central authority, has no foundational ideology, does not represent categorically defined groups, does not consistently endorse ideologies, and has no fixed objectives. Anonymous can speak out against racism or promote it; Anonymous may demand military action against dictatorial regimes or oppose it; and so on. These specific qualities—the lack of a stable ideology, identity, or organizational base—mean that Anonymous' evolution is rhizomatic. Rather than being built on a foundation or directed from the top-down, the movement results from the constantly changing confluence of distributed users and systems. While participants can push the movement in a certain direction, the movement's evolution is beyond anyone's control. How are we to make sense of such a movement? If Anonymous can take on any form, then how does it take on particular guises in different episodes of contention? If there is no central coordination or leadership, how can we understand that some participants nevertheless have more power to define what the movement stands for than others?

This article analyzes the power dynamics in a movement that is, in actual fact but especially in the rhetoric of its participants, intrinsically unruly and indeterminate. While many movements have embraced networks as an egalitarian alternative to hierarchical institutions, nominally horizontal networks tend to generate highly uneven patterns of connection and marked asymmetries of power. This is also the case for Anonymous: although many participants propagate an image of the movement as leaderless agglomerate, at various points in the movement's development, specific individuals and groups had dominant positions. What we need is a theoretical perspective that acknowledges Anonymous' intrinsic pluriformity and complexity while at the same time providing the analytical tools to grasp the movement's qualitative changes over time. Following recent theorizing in social and natural sciences as well as a few pioneers in social movement studies, I propose to use concepts derived from complexity theory to understand Anonymous' development and identify specific mechanisms of power concentration and diffusion. The literature on complexity has much to offer as it highlights how, in the absence of central coordination, highly uneven configurations can emerge. This paper's key argument is that we can understand how fundamentally polysemous, fluid, and mobile signifiers can be momentarily and partially stabilized as certain groups come to dominate by outshining and outflanking others within the movement. The empirical analysis below aims to explain how such groups emerge and concentrate power and, just as important, how they subsequently dissolve and lose power.

The next section distills from different variants of complexity theory concepts that can help understand power dynamics in movements that resist central leadership and a foundational ideology. After briefly setting out the methodology for this paper, the following section analyzes Anonymous' mutations, focusing especially on the mechanisms through which power within the movement is concentrated and diffused. The conclusion of this paper reflects on the rhizomatic qualities of social movements and asks how social movement theory should be amended to incorporate the dynamics observed in the case of Anonymous.

Complexity thinking on—and within—social movements

While social movements may exhibit certain regularities or obey certain rules, they are essentially generative, creative, and transgressive. Social movement scholars have long recognized this, and often, this attracted them to the study of social movements in the first place. But it has proven difficult to develop a framework that adequately captures these qualities (Goodwin & Jasper, 1999). Movements are defined by their capacity, however partial or precarious, to shape their own development. Movements, in order words, *self-organize*. Self-organization, a central concept within complexity theory, refers to the 'spontaneous occurrence of order' (Kauffman, 1993, p. viii). For social movements, this requires a level of autonomy from the established order that movements challenge. 'Social movements,' Castells says, 'exercise counterpower by constructing themselves in the first place through a process of autonomous communication, free from the control of those holding institutional power' (Castells, 2012, p. 9). Movements carve out online and offline spaces in which participants recursively and self-referentially enact the movement. This explains why invariant models fall short: movements are not only or primarily determined by outside causes but to at least some degree self-organize. This does not imply that movements are 'agents' or make strategic decisions. Movements are agglomerates beyond the control of any individual or groups. But they are also beyond the sole determination of environmental factors. To the degree that such self-construction succeeds and autonomy emerges, movements self-organize: they reproduce themselves with the help of their 'own logic and components' (Fuchs, 2006, p. 102). Complexity theory has provided one way to move beyond reductive analyses and emphasize the emergent, indeterminate, and iterative qualities of movements. There are two strands in the complexity literature that each have a specific contribution to make to the study of social movements.

Rhizomatic movements

One strand in the literature provides the philosophical tools to think of movements as unstable agglomerates of actors and networks traversing and defying categories and borders (cf. Chesters & Welsh, 2006; Hardt & Negri, 2004; Melucci, 1996). As recent social movements, especially the alter-globalization movement, attempt to break out of national confines and engage in the collective project of creatively rethinking the foundations of social life, authors in this strand argue for an analogous move of scholars to rethink the analytical categories and presuppositions through which they make sense of social movements (Cox & Nilsen, 2007, p. 426). The concept of rhizome is often used to highlight that social movements emerge from the contingent combination of heterogeneous impulses (Chesters & Welsh, 2006; Deleuze & Guattari, 1987). While all movements emerge from distributed interactions among heterogeneous elements, rhizomatic movements explicitly resist ideological uniformity and organizational consolidation in favor of more open-ended modes of organizing. In other words, rhizomatic movements cannot only be objectively considered as complex and emergent but are also actively conceived and modeled that way by participants (Uitermark, 2015). For instance, the Spanish *indignados* and worldwide Occupy movements categorically rejected the delegation of power and instead hoped that a set of basic rules for deliberation would enable the movement to evolve iteratively. They self-consciously declared that they had no intention of formulating a desired end state for the movement; revolution was to come about in a bottom-up evolutionary fashion, as reflected in the slogan '(r)evolution' carried on banners at various protest sites. The desire for 'ad hoc, leaderless, participatory, and horizontalist' styles of organization is not new, but 'technology has brought a new dimension to protester desires for horizontalism by allowing ad hoc organizing to address collaborative needs in an unprecedented fashion' (Tufekci, 2015, p. 13; see also Bennett, 2013; Juris, 2012; Sitrin, 2012). Anonymous thrives on and stimulates these desires; the movement is highly heterogeneous in terms of ideology (Fuchs, 2013; Goode, 2015) and has been conceptualized as 'a hybrid of swarm and network' (Wiedemann, 2014, p. 322). Anonymous participants routinely emphasize the movement's radical openness and egalitarianism. While it is practically impossible for any authority, leader, or organization to control the appropriation of Anonymous symbolism, participants in the movement have also cultivated a culture that mitigates against the concentration and imposition of power (Coleman, 2014). This finds its expression in embracing anonymity not only as a practical means of evading the persecution for illegal acts but also as a condition that allows a higher state of organization and consciousness by shedding and superseding individuality. Anonymity is expressed and dramatized by Anonymous symbols like a suit with a question mark instead of a head and the Guy Fawkes mask donned by the lead character in the movie *V for Vendetta*. The conception of Anonymous as an emergent creature that is more than the sum of its parts finds expression in slogans like 'because none of us are as cruel as all of us' and analogies of the movement to a 'swarm,' 'giant globs of digital mucus,' a 'hydra,' a 'global consciousness,' or a 'hive.' While the movement's self-representations convey important dimensions of Anonymous' evolution, Anons are obviously not like bees in a hive or birds in a flock. Far from a supercreature that is effortlessly construed out of genetically pre-programmed units, like a hive or a flock, Anonymous is the emergent *and* contested outcome of Anons who work with *and* against each other.

Self-organization, power concentration, and saltations

A second strand in the literature on complexity focuses on the network dynamics that result from cooperation and competition. This strand is especially helpful for understanding processes of power concentration and power diffusion. Processes of power concentration are endemic to complex systems as well as rhizomatic movements. One central theme in research on complex systems is that networking among nominally equal nodes tends to produce highly uneven configurations (Barabási & Albert, 1999). The irony that rhizomatic movements face is that their rejection of the delegation of power can leave self-organizing processes of power concentration unchecked. Jo Freeman argues that the rejection of formal structure gives free reign to 'informal communication networks of friends' that are 'inevitably elitist and exclusive' (1973, p. 154). These observations, derived from a study of women's consciousness-raising groups in the 1970s, take on new meaning for movements that embrace networks as their preferred vehicle for organizing. Increased possibilities for networking not only allow new modes of egalitarian organizing but also revamp mechanisms of power concentration. Analyses of complex systems have identified a range of mechanisms through which inequalities emerge in the absence of design and enforcement by a central authority. For instance, pronounced patterns of stratification and segregation may be the macro-level effect of micro-decisions to socialize with similar persons (Schelling, 1971). These effects are present at the level of societies and also within movements as participants who share certain interests and ideas pull together. Many analysts have further found that complex systems are highly uneven in terms of network connectivity: some nodes and clusters of nodes have many more connections than others. New nodes tend to connect to already well-connected nodes and thereby reinforce their centrality (Barabási & Albert, 1999) and well-connected nodes tend to preferentially connect to each other, creating what is called 'rich clubs' (Colizza, Flammini, Serrano, & Vespignani, 2006). These mechanisms of concentration are found in a great variety of complex systems, ranging from the human brain (in which cortex regions are nodes connected by white tracts) and the global airline traffic network (in which nodes are airports connected through routes) (Alstott, Panzarasa, Rubinov, Bullmore, & Vértes, 2014) and can also be expected to occur in movements as they, too, emerge from distributed local interactions (cf. Uitermark, 2012). We can therefore expect that certain groups consolidate and acquire central positions within the movement's network system (cf. Nunes, 2014).

While mechanisms of power concentration are endemic to rhizomatic movements, so are mechanisms of power diffusion. Maintaining dominance in any complex system is hard work for elites as they have to expend resources and sustain internal cohesion (cf. Richards, 1993). Within rhizomatic movements, elites face the additional problem that putative challengers can call upon an egalitarian ethos to question elite dominance; due to the general antipathy against the usurpation of power, structural inequalities among participants are unlikely to remain uncontested (Coleman, 2014). In the belly of the beast—the Internet settings where Anons congregate—we do not see the harmonious collaboration of people who instinctively know their place within the collective (like birds or bees would) but an incessant struggle. Exactly because the movement lacks generally accepted procedures for making decisions and allocating power, there is a constant struggle to define what Anonymous is and how it should operate. Any hierarchy is thus fraught with tension and subject to challenges.

Out of these processes of power concentration and diffusion emerge configurations where some participants, action repertoires, and discourses are more prominent than others. While movements are unstable due to their participants' constantly changing connections, they occasionally undergo sudden changes that complexity researchers call 'phase transitions' or 'saltations.' As Woese (2004, p. 180) argues, 'evolution, as a complex dynamic process, will encounter critical points in its course, junctures that result in phase transitions (drastic changes in the character of the system as a whole).' Such phase transitions, or 'saltations,' are sudden, qualitative changes. Saltational evolution is what we are interested in when we want to examine Anonymous as this movement took on radically different guises in its short history. These saltations are related to (but not determined by) the settings in which movement participants mobilize. These settings afford (Wellman et al., 2003) different kinds of configurations, with some settings (like chat channels) allowing users to build reputations and attain privileges and other settings (like image boards) encouraging users to shed individual distinctions and identities. As the movement emerges on the interface of systems and users, it develops not only different claims and repertoires but also different configurations of power. By configuration of power, I refer to the movement's uneven network structure and the relative prominence of participants and groups of participants within it. In sum, the perspective outlined suggests movements evolve constantly and occasionally undergo drastic qualitative ruptures. The goal is to reconstruct Anonymous' evolution and tease out processes of power concentration and diffusion at various stages of its development by examining its changing logics of collective action.

Methodology

This case study is based on an ethnography and secondary literature. In December 2010, I started visiting online settings where Anons congregated, including chat channels, image boards, and various social media. Between December 2010 and August 2011, I especially spent time on the chat channels of the IRC network of Anonymous Operators, which at the time served as an important site for the preparation and coordination of Anonymous activity. By spending hours glued to my screen, chatting with anons, and doing background research, I got a 'feel for the game' (Bourdieu, 1997) without getting a full grip on the technological details or being able to observe all of the movement's activities. In the very beginning of what became my fieldwork, I considered myself a prospective activist and curious citizen more than a researcher. Over time, my interest in the movement became more academic. Every time I had conversations I might want to use for research, I identified myself as an academic researcher and explained my purposes. I shared initial insights with some Anons with different positions within the movement, including several who had been involved in high-level hacking activities. After completing one exploratory article (Uitermark, 2011), I took steps back and digested my experiences while still keeping track of developments through social media and reading secondary literature (especially Coleman, 2014; Olson, 2012). These accounts supplemented my own primary research because they validated many of my impressions and provided fuller insight into the dynamics within groups organizing within exclusive and secretive chat channels. In addition to these secondary accounts, I drew on media interviews given by arrested Anons and leaked logs from chat channels. Although I have on occasion been present in channels where hacking activities were coordinated, I did not have the nearly same level of access as Olson, Coleman, or embedded journalists like Garrett Brown (who is currently serving prison time for his involvement in Anonymous). Whereas these authors tend to focus on the groups and campaigns that caught the public's attention, most of my observations concerned campaigns that did not make news headlines. These observations thus shed light on the parts of the movement that receive little attention in journalistic and media accounts, yet constitute the bulk of activity at any moment in time. In addition, I could observe and experience how rank and file participants view elite users and the campaigns they are involved in. By triangulating data obtained from these different sources, I developed an understanding of the dynamic of the overall movement configuration and the position of dominant groups within it. It is notoriously difficult to separate fact from fiction as Anons often withhold or manipulate information to trick or manipulate Internet users and enforcement agencies. For this reason, and to protect the privacy of the movement's participants, I do not use direct quotations or observations in this piece. My interest is in the movement's general development, not in the nitty-gritty of the countless operations carried out under the Anonymous label. By abstracting away from the particularities, I hope to shed light on the broad dynamics of power concentration and power diffusion.

Anonymous' respective configurations of power

Phase 1: the quest for lulz

On so-called image boards, users usually do not use screen names other than 'Anonymous.' 4chan is the largest of these image boards with 10 million unique visitors per month (Grigoriadis, 2011). Each day, 800,000 messages are posted on the site—more than 550 per minute (*ibid.*). On the largest sub-board (/b for 'random' messages), most messages stay on the front page for less than five seconds and on the site for less than five minutes (Bernstein et al., 2011). The image boards are a swirling stream of ephemeral messages and pictures related to everything from ponies and necrophilia to religion and porn. Reflecting the demographics of the bulk of the users—teenagers and young men from the United States and Western Europe—the boards represent an absurd combination of teenage fantasies and fears. Within this setting, selection occurs by the users—if they comment on a message, they 'bump' it and push it up on the site. Because users adopt the same screen name ('Anonymous'), people profile themselves as established users through Internet dialects while slurring insults to outsiders who do not conform to the informal rules (Bernstein et al., 2011). The ruthless slandering goes together with bonding—the insiders are considered '/b/ros' or 'fellow-anons,' the outsiders are designated as 'faggots,' 'newfags,' or 'niggers.' Message boards remained the prime settings for collective trolling, but the campaigns also spawned a network of smaller and larger chat networks like 'partyvan' or 'bantown' where devoted users plotted and coordinated raids. The raid on Habbo Hotel became a landmark event for collective action springing from this environment. On 12 July 2006, Bill Cosby's birthday, thousands of black men dressed in disco outfits and with Afro haircuts, 'nigras,' flooded Habbo Hotel, an online meeting space for teenagers. The nigras blocked the swimming pools and formed swastikas. When Habbo's moderators removed the nigras, the crowds, noting that only black characters were removed, protested against the moderators' racism. The nigras dispersed, hid in libraries and private rooms, and then regrouped to again raid the pool. A year after the first Habbo raid, the nigras came back with more inciting and bizarre rhetoric. In an absurdist parody of Martin Luther King's 'million men march,' the nigras announced they were to block Habbo's swimming pools 'to stop the AIDS!' and protest the racism of the Habbo moderators. The raids on Habbo Hotel and many other targets demonstrated to participants as well as onlookers the potential of synchronized and subversive mobilizations, even if they were at this point merely ironic and playful.

The configuration of power in this phase is characterized by ephemeral collective action and unstable hierarchies. Campaigns are impulsive, whimsical, and brief, with participants typically taking interchangeable positions as faceless anons. This is not to say that degrees and types of participation are the same. Exactly because the campaigns mobilize masses, participants who put effort and wit into directing the crowd wield disproportionate power. Already early on in Anonymous' history, users opted for chat channels to plot campaigns, in effect taking on leading and coordinating roles. However, the mass dynamics on the image boards decided which campaigns took off and which did not. Such cascades are intrinsically difficult to predict (let alone steer) even in complex configurations where more influential participants can be recognized (as on Twitter, for instance; see Bakshy, Hofman, Mason, & Watts, 2011), but the default anonymization on image boards deprives users of the possibility to see whether initiators of a campaign have the qualifications to pull it off. The image boards are a 'hetacomb of failed attempts with few survivors' (Koopmans, 2004; p. 371) because the vast majority of calls to action remain unanswered. The result is an extremely volatile dynamic where campaigns that generate a positive feedback early on (i.e. they quickly draw in many participants) succeed in generating the critical mass necessary to collectively disrupt games, manipulate polls, or cause other kinds of mayhem. At this point of Anonymous' development, it 'was strength in numbers. The more people were there, the bigger the deluge' (Olson, 2012, p. 52). Anonymous had emerged from the relatively autonomous space as a self-organized and self-referential entity. Participants developed a configuration of power characterized by ephemerality of collective action and interchangeability of participants. Participants mobilized under the same banner and used a distinct set of symbols and slogans, but did not develop a stable division of labor, fixed roles, or durable networks.

Phase 2: the battle against scientology

The moment that Anonymous engaged in a sustained battle against the Church of Scientology in 2008 is widely regarded as a qualitative change of the movement (e.g. Coleman, 2014). From the 1990s on, critics had made public revelations and released classified documents to draw attention to what they considered coercive, exploitative, and manipulative strategies on the part of Scientology. These battles intensified in 2008 when Youtube removed a leaked video of scientologist Tom Cruise, attesting to the extraordinary acumen and prowess of the Church's followers. Responses to the first call for action posted on 4chan's sub-board/b were mixed, with some openly hostile to the idea ('I think scientology is cool and the guy who had this awesome idea to create a fake religion just so he can collect money from idiots is brilliant!'), others skeptical ('mission impossible—a random image board cannot take down a pseudo-religion with the backing of wealthy people and an army of lawyers'), and others falling in line with the idea ('We are the true face of the human race. We are the anti-hero, we will do good, and fuck anyone, good or bad, who happens to be in the way. The world is a fucked up place, and apathy and weak willed liberal fucks won't change it. We will, or we'll all die trying...'). A new call to action on the next day solicited more and more positive responses as users noticed that the Scientology website was experiencing downtime. Anons wrote short instructions how recruits could participate in a so-called Distributed Denial of Service (DDoS) attack in which bogus packages are send from multiple computers to clog Scientology's servers. They also published addresses of Scientology buildings so prospective participants could call for taxis and pizza delivery.

The image boards were crucial sites for mobilizations, but the campaign sprawled to other settings. Opposition against Scientology had already proliferated in many corners of the Internet and the move to 'a better place to plan' was already hinted at in the first call to action. Veteran critics of Scientology, new Anonymous recruits, and many other Internet users responding to the battle cries increasingly gravitated to Internet Relay Chat (IRC) channels. IRC affords a very different set of roles than image boards. IRC networks have network administrators that have ultimate command over the channels, chat rooms on IRC can be closed to non-invited users, chat rooms feature a range of different positions with different privileges, and last but not least, all these features are associated with user names. These characteristics of IRC imply that there are many visible differentiations among users in terms of reputations and roles.

Gregg Housh, an avid 4chan user based in Boston, came to play a key role in this period. When Housh and four other activists congregated in one chat room to discuss press strategies, they discovered that they collectively had the skills to make a clip and put together an Anonymous video press release with a computerized voice uttering declarations of injustice against a background of dramatic visuals. The video press release became a hit in obscure places like 4chan but also in more mainstream Internet venues like Gawker and Reddit. The then little known publishing platform Wikileaks released classified Scientology documents that Anonymous volunteers helped to interpret and circulate (Domscheit-Berg, 2011). Anonymous also adopted street protests in this period. Housh had applied for a permit and was subsequently targeted by Scientologists, but instead of backing off, Housh spoke out strongly against Scientology in the courts and especially in the media. To deal with the massive inflow of recruits, Housh and his fellow activists made separate chat rooms for activists based in different cities and they also set up an exclusive and secret chat room called #marblecake for people who were deemed competent and committed enough to serve as coordinators.[1] Prompted by a video from a veteran opponent of Scientology (colloquially referred to as 'wise beard man'), they also developed elaborate protest manuals, instructing activists how to challenge Scientology while keeping within the law. Housh turned from a 4chan enthusiast with an appetite for mayhem into a strict coordinator, saying he ran meetings in a designated chat room for high-level activists 'with an iron fist' (cited in Olson, 2012, p. 88).

While whimsical mass trolling continued unabated on the image boards, Anonymous had developed an entirely different configuration as it took on Scientology and settled in IRC channels—a saltation had occurred. Movement participants organizing in this setting developed a clear organizational structure, calibrated a set of protest tactics, and had pushed forward spokespersons with clearly defined talking points. Well-structured and strongly connected groups developed synchronized and sustained campaigns with the purpose of winning over the public rather than shocking it. However, the transformation of Anonymous from a ruthless and unpredictable pack into a protest machine triggered negative feedback. There were bitter complaints about 'moralfags' and Housh and his associates saw their infrastructure come under DDoS attacks. One Anon broke every rule in the protest manual by busting into Scientology's New York offices covered in a 'thick layer of petroleum jelly' with a 'generous admixture of pubic hairs and toenail clippings'—an effort not only to shock Scientology but also to upset what had become an all too predictable movement seeking respectability rather than thrills (Dibbell, 2009).

Phase 3: the battle for wikileaks

As the battle against Scientology suffered from dwindling momentum and infighting, groups of Anonymous activists initiated other campaigns, for instance, providing Iranian insurgents with software to evade surveillance during the 2009 uprising. Coordinating from a designated IRC network hosted in a number of countries to minimize chances of persecution, Anons had struck against a range of targets with DDoS attacks and occasionally with an SQL injection attack (Olson, 2012). While

Anonymous had now become a label for online activists in pursuit of structural social change, the movement did not converge on a shared goal or gravitate to a particular setting; no campaign drew near as much attention and participants as the battle against Scientology. In 2010, Operation Payback had as its goal to strike against organizations combating media piracy. In short, in 2010, Anonymous was a fragmented movement engaging in a range of campaigns on a number of different platforms—there was no dominant logic, even if some campaigns (like Operation Payback) were more prolific than others.

A qualitative change occurred when, in December 2010, Wikileaks hit the global headlines. 'Operation Payback' morphed from a campaign about copyrights into a campaign about Wikileaks. The successful disruption of websites of large financial institutions like PayPal, Mastercard, and VISA also made global headlines, creating a positive feedback loop: the number of users in the IRC channels exploded in a matter of days from hundreds to thousands. New recruits provided their bandwidth for DDoS attacks, drew attention to the campaigns on social media, and set up new communication forums. Anonymous did not only scale up but also changed qualitatively. Movement participants wrote manifestos and press releases explaining the rationale of the attacks and identifying Anonymous as a force of reason and freedom:

> The battle standard that Anonymous follows, however, is the freedom of information. Without information, one cannot fight for any other cause. Children will remain abused if their plight remains unknown. Nations will rage wars against their own people if cloaked in secrecy. Crimes will go unpunished, victims will go uncomforted, and walls will remain undefended. As Thomas Jefferson put it, 'Information is the currency of democracy.' But we would go further and say that information is the life-blood of society. (Anonymous Press Release, December 16, 2010)

The movement not only solidified its discourse but also its methods. While DDoS attacks had often been used against copyright organizations, now DDoS became a mass tactic as recruits hooked their computers into a network controlled by an operator in one of the IRC chat rooms, in effect forming a voluntary botnet. Many participants used the Low Orbit Ion Canon, an ironically named computer program designed to make participation in DDoS attacks easy for participants without specialized computer skills. LOIC predates Wikileaks by a few years, but the program was pivotal in accommodating new recruits who were willing to participate in the attacks but lacked technical competence to operate botnets or use scripts. At the highpoints of the attacks, more than a thousand participants reportedly hooked their computers into the volitional botnet, enacting the virtual equivalent of a blockade or sit-in (Coleman, 2014). The image of masses of Internet users converging on targets provided a powerful impetus to the idea of Anonymous as an egalitarian mass movement. Movement participants in IRC channels were intensely debating targets and politics but most of all they were thrilled by the experience and the idea of Anonymous as a collective and collaborative project that transcended each and therefore belonged to all. However, there were important and largely invisible inequalities among participants. Although much of the deliberation on targets took place in public channels and through instant surveys, more privileged users—those with botnets, hacking capabilities, writing skills, or administrative privileges—coordinated in channels that were invisible to other users and by invitation only. A few users in control of (non-volitional) botnets provided the majority of digital fire power. On at least one occasion, a channel administrator also manipulated the LOIC settings to make it seem as if the attacks were carried out by masses of Anons while his botnet was in fact leading the attack (Olson, 2012). Elite users consciously and effectively created a mise-en-scene where rank and file users could participate in a simulated experience of bringing down websites of major corporations.

The configuration of power at this point was characterized by marked imbalances between different groups of participants. Already during the campaigns against copyrights, influential users made decisions in a channel called #command. This channel included botnet operators whose digital fire power basically gave them the capacity to decide which targets would go down. Other users in this channel manipulated Anons in the public channels into thinking that their crowd-sourced packets were clogging the target websites while in fact the botnet operations were pulling the strings (Olson, 2012). As campaigns in retaliation for the Wikileaks blockade took off, media coverage intensified and masses of new recruits flocked to the movement, the elite users within #command consolidated their dominance. However, the users in #command could sustain their dominance for a limited amount of time only.

Phase 4: proliferation and fragmentation

As the numbers of users grew, infighting intensified and users branched off to create exclusive channels of their own. Participants who had been drawn to DDoS operations against financial institutions stuck around on the Anonymous Operators network and created channels and operations of their own. It became increasingly impossible for individuals or groups to direct and coordinate the movement, even though this did not keep some from trying. With thousands of users active in dozens of channels at any moment, the Anonymous Operators IRC network had become a tumultuous and unruly powerhouse of online activism. While Internet users were still appropriating the Anonymous label in other settings too, the Anonymous Operators IRC network by itself had become a launching pad for many different campaigns and also featured channels for different geographical regions, interests, and campaigns. While veteran and elite users were active in a number of these campaigns, connecting and coordinating dispersed efforts, many campaigns were relatively independent: their initiators embarked on their own agenda and developed hierarchies that were internal to their channels and campaigns.

Although the overall configuration was inherently fragmented, some individual campaigns came to stand out due to self-reinforcing mechanisms: if a campaign took off for whatever reason, it drew interest, and consequently attracted more participants until interest dwindled and participants changed target or moved elsewhere. This pattern continued as the revolutions associated with the so-called Arab Spring took off and one country after another attracted Anonymous' attention. For instance, the designated channel for Operation Tunisia (#optunisia) was bustling with activity as Anons engaged in crowd journalism, developed software to evade surveillance, monitored attempts by the Tunisian Government to entrap Internet users, and engaged in DDoS attacks. Experienced hackers also used their skills to deface websites operated by the Tunisian Government. While the Tunisian Government was increasingly restricting access of citizens to all but its own websites, those websites were hacked and their front pages replaced with manifestos lambasting the government and cheering on the Tunisian insurgents. After the Tunisian revolts had subsided, Anons gravitated to mobilizations for Egypt, Algeria, Libya, and other countries. Each of these operations developed its own hierarchies and divisions of labor, with some particularly active and prominent Anons being active in the chat channels of multiple or all mobilizations. In addition to the sheer number and diversity of campaigns, fissures within the elite made it increasingly difficult for them to sustain their dominance. Squabbles among elite users spilled over into public channels and on occasion escalated into full-scale conflicts involving extensive name calling, 'doxing' and DDoS attacks. The proliferation of campaigns and elite divisions created an unstable configuration of power; there were operations and Anons with more clout than others, but the overall configuration was volatile and fragmented.

Phase 5: the elite hacker spree

Hackers had been involved in Anonymous operations from the early days. While their skills provided them with resources to do things others could not, thus far, hackers had not formed a distinct clique. This slowly changed as users built up reputations and socialized in exclusive chat rooms where they could solidify their ties and reflect on their position within the overall movement. In February 2011, users in one such chat room discussed media reports on research conducted by Aaron Barr, director of the cyber security company HBGary Federal. Barr had developed a method to identify Internet users and he claimed it was so successful that he had uncovered the names of Anonymous' leaders. While Barr's claims were discussed and laughingly dismissed in the channel for Operation Egypt, the most prolific operation at the time, a group of hackers were meeting in an exclusive chat room, called #HQ, to coordinate retaliation against Barr. After a couple of days, they gained access to the servers of Barr's company, defaced his website, took over his Twitter account (and renamed it 'Colossal Faggot'), and obtained troves of emails sent by Barr and his associates. Barr's emails contained all sorts of embarrassing information, including a slide show that proposed to undertake a slandering campaign against Wikileaks. Although the hack was done by a few individuals, many Anons participated in a crowd-sourced effort to go through the emails and to ridicule Barr with memes. News on the campaign against Barr spread through social media and was covered on programs like the *Colbert Report*.

The reorientation from revolutions in the Middle East to a security company in the United States had been entirely improvised—the hackers decided to go after Barr only after he had presented his research and left his servers vulnerable to attack—but it did provide a prototype for a new model of mobilization. The hackers would obtain information by breaching systems and then involve the Anonymous community to publicize their findings. This implied a clear division of labor: groups of hackers initiated campaigns and selected targets while rank and file users engaged in applauding, exploiting, and communicating the breaches. This new division of labor and implied stratification were further buttressed by the arrests of dozens of Anons who had been involved in DDoS campaigns as coordinators or attackers. These Anons had different statuses in the movement—some were well-known and respected figures in chat rooms while others were marginal or entirely unknown—but they shared in common that they had not used botnets. While their roles in the attacks had been marginal, their incapacity to effectively hide their identities had made them targets for law enforcement. Up to that point, it was assumed that law enforcement had either no interest in going after Anons whose individual contributions were negligible, or that this was infeasible given their high numbers. These developments reinforced inequality within the movement: the masses of Anons lost their functionality for the attacks while skilled hackers became more prominent. Not only did they deploy their technical skills, they also became celebrities within the movement, with other movement participants being increasingly reduced to a role as supporters or spectators.

Olson (2012, p. 218) sums up the successive rounds of self-selection through which this dominant group emerged: 'Their group now consisted of Topiary, Sabu, Kayla, Tflow, AVunit, and occasionally the hacktivist called Q—a concentrated group of elite Anons. AnonOps had been a gathering of the elite in Anonymous; #InternetFeds a group of even more elite; and #HQ was a distillation of that.' Although Olson captures the general dynamic, chat logs and interviews reveal that the group actually was considerably larger and more fragmented; many other users were invited to #HQ and users were always active across a range of different channels on different IRC networks, creating a mishmash of networks rather than a clear hierarchy (Coleman, 2014). It is nevertheless fair to say that these few users now formed a tight core within the much larger and more ephemeral movement.

After having gradually grown closer and forming a distinct group, the hackers involved in the HBGary hack started Lulzsec. Lulzsec's Twitter bio originally stated that the group was there to aid Anonymous, but this was later replaced with 'the world's leaders in high-quality entertainment at your expense.' The members of Lulzsec hacked dozens of companies and organizations in May and June 2011, including X-factor, Sony (a couple of times), gaming platforms, the *Sun*, and contractors for the FBI. In stark contrast to the flurry of verbose statements made during the campaigns for Tunisia and other Middle Eastern countries, Lulzsec provided minimal and nihilistic explanations for its targets, emphasizing that they did it for the lulz (for laughs). On the occasion of their thousandth tweet, the group wrote a memo conveying the group's nihilistic and hedonistic approach to hacking:

> Do you feel safe with your Facebook accounts, your Google Mail accounts, your Skype accounts? What makes you think a hacker isn't silently sitting inside all of these right now, sniping out individual people, or perhaps selling them off? You are a peon to these people. A toy. A string of characters with a value....
>
> Yes, yes, there's always the argument that releasing everything in full is just as evil, what with accounts being stolen and abused, but welcome to 2011. This is the lulz lizard era, where we do things just because we find it entertaining. Watching someone's Facebook picture turn into a penis and seeing their sister's shocked response is priceless. Receiving angry emails from the man you just sent 10 dildos to because he can't secure his Amazon password is priceless. You find it funny to watch havoc unfold, and we find it funny to cause it. We release personal data so that equally evil people can entertain us with what they do with it.[2]

In an exchange with 4chan users who were infuriated that their gaming websites had been knocked offline, Lulzsec described itself as 'the concentrated success of 2005 /b' and there is some truth to that. Several hackers in the group had been involved in the Anonymous world for years and through iterated selection, they had now formed this small elite group of approximately six individuals. Although Lulzsec said that it was not part of Anonymous, its hacking spree made it into the movement's focal point. Anons flocked to Lulzsec's IRC channels, discussed their hacks on social media, and browsed through the hacked data that Lulzsec was publishing online.

The configuration of power had changed: there was one small and consolidated focal group that stood out within the movement. This is not to say that Lulzsec's members were masterminding the movement. Chat logs as well as interviews indicate that the Lulzsec members did not only cause havoc but were also caught in the storm. They acted ad hoc on vulnerabilities that others had discovered and improvised their responses to their growing number of enemies, including rival hacking groups, disgruntled Anonymous activists, and of course various branches of law enforcement. One of the first major figures to be arrested was a young man that used the screen name 'ryan' who had been providing some of the infrastructure for the group. Lulzsec closed shop after a 50-day hacking spree, but members and supporters remaining at large did not stop. Some within the group sought a return to hacking for social justice. When Lulzsec disbanded, they established #antisec, a campaign directed against the public and private security industry:

> Top priority is to steal and leak any classified government information, including email spools and documentation. Prime targets are banks and other high-ranking establishments. If they try to censor our progress, we will obliterate the censor with cannonfire anointed with lizard blood.

Hackers breached the systems of a range of different organizations, ranging from Arizona's border police to NATO. The Stratfor hack is one of the biggest carried out as part of #antisec. Following leads from Sabu and working with others, a hacker using screen names 'sup_g' and 'anarchaos' obtained more than five million emails from the security company and a wealth of credit card data that were used to make donations to charities.

Although the political emphasis changed from Lulzsec to #antisec, the configuration of power remained the same: a few skilled and well-connected users served as the movement's prime hub. Users within this hub brokered information on vulnerabilities of potential targets, connected different groups and individuals, and played a large role in representing the movement to the media. This is in particular true for Sabu, a restless and devoted hacker who incessantly incited and provoked others to strike against establishment institutions ranging from border police and banks to governments and consultancy agencies. Sabu also served as a key broker: Anons with information on vulnerabilities or in the process of a hack would approach Sabu to get him or his many associates involved. Although there were certainly many Anons who undertook actions independently of Sabu and his crew, Lulzsec and #antisec marked a period of concentration where a group of elite hackers took a position that was similar in terms of network configuration to that of Gregg Housh and his associates during the heydays of the campaign against Scientology: attention, resources, and social contacts were in very important part channeled to and through a small group of elite hackers who functioned as the movement's prime hub.

Phase 6: accelerating global protests through weak ties

Shortly after the Stratfor hack, it became clear that Sabu had become an informant for the FBI. In court documents, the FBI describes him as an 'extremely valuable and productive cooperator' who contributed directly to arrests of other Lulzsec members and spent months assisting law enforcement in the investigation of numerous hacks and hacking groups. Sabu had first been Anonymous' connection to the underground hacking scene; now, he performed the same role for the FBI. Law enforcement also arrested Anarchaos, Topiary, Kayla, and Tflow. Many Anons were devastated by the arrests and especially by Sabu's betrayal, but this did not mean that operations were halted. In fact, various hacks were committed to demonstrate that the series of arrests neither deterred nor demotivated Anonymous. But the configuration in which these actions took place changed drastically. In line with Julian Assange's network theory of power, one might say that the crackdown increased the thresholds for conspiring (Assange, 2006). First, the arrests and Sabu's delivering of fellow activists to law enforcement underscored that it is dangerous to trust others or to claim credits for a hack. Developing direct ties to undertake collective action was therefore discouraged. Second, the hub's disappearance implies that others lost indirect ties to hackers, journalists, and a huge following on social media. The crackdown did not end Anonymous, but it did fragment the movement.

Anonymous lived on, not so much as an internally cohesive social movement, but as a set of symbols and communication channels that are appropriated by a range of different groups for a range of different purposes. The masks that activists donned at the protests against Scientology have now become ubiquitous as they show up in demonstrations from Brazil to Hong Kong and from Turkey to the United States. The infrastructure that Anonymous has built up over the last years is now used to communicate about a range of protests in different countries. Rather than pushing for change itself, Anonymous accelerates the diffusion of protests that are initiated by others. For instance, Anonymous did not originate the idea to occupy Wall Street, but through Twitter, IRC, and other channels of communication, it did play a crucial role in accelerating Occupy. The configuration of power, then, is that Anonymous provides weak ties among a range of different protests in a variety of geographical contexts, serving as a relational infrastructure that connects and accelerates activism originating both within and outside of Anonymous.

Conclusion

Analyzing Anonymous is hard not only for journalists and the public, but also for social movement theorists. Attempting to understand Anonymous requires a rethinking of what movements are and how we can understand them. New movements generally challenge old frameworks and therefore prompt the reconsideration and reformulation of established theories and vocabularies (Jasper, 2012) and this rethinking is particularly urgent now that there is a consensus that deterministic models fail to recognize the contingency, creativity, and unpredictability of movement dynamics (Goodwin & Jasper, 1999; McAdam, Tarrow, & Tilly, 2001). Deterministic models assuming unitary actors or discrete factors cannot grasp Anonymous as the movement takes on radically different guises, constantly mutates, and traverses national borders and ideological divides. While familiar analytical concepts like 'resource mobilization,' 'political opportunities,' 'framing,' 'networks,' and 'emotions' may help understand certain aspects of Anonymous, they do not (individually or together) allow a comprehensive understanding of movement dynamics. Much of what is normally considered foundational to movements is absent in Anonymous. For example, while the literature has suggested that 'shared beliefs' and 'solidarities' are an essential part of social movements (e.g. Diani, 1992, p. 9), this is emphatically not the case for Anonymous, whose participants acknowledge and embrace the fact that the movement can pursue radically different goals. Anons are keen to point out that the movement does not have a foundational ideology and does not represent any particular interest, value, or identity. Although it could be suggested that Anonymous is anomalous or perhaps not a movement at all, I would rather argue that Anons highlight what in other movements is easily overlooked or downplayed: the lack of any intrinsic foundation or coherence in terms of values, solidarities, or networks. For instance, while it may seem evident that the LGBT movement revolves around the rights of lesbians, gays, bisexuals, and transgender people, in practice, this is contested. For instance, some consider same-sex marriage as the movement's ultimate goal, others vehemently oppose marriage as an institution of heteronormative sexual morality that should be dissolved rather than demanded, and yet others focus on cultural self-expression rather than legal rights. By reflexively acknowledging that it is impossible to fix what Anonymous stands for, Anons remind scholars that movements are in essence fully performative and self-referential: they are brought into being by the expressions of their participants and the participants are defined as such through their expressions. When taking on the task of developing an analytical vocabulary that can make sense of unpredictable and contingent movement dynamics, Anonymous is therefore an ideal test bed. In this context, Beraldo (2014, p. 9) proposes to analyze Anonymous as a 'movement brand,' 'a loosely connoted, but highly denotable sign, circulating through the digital ecology and mobilizing activists around disparate objectives all over the world.' Anonymous, and arguably other 'movement brands' like Occupy, represent sets of signifiers that take on radically different meanings depending on the contexts and networks in which they are mobilized. Participants are perennially engaged in struggles to settle what is intrinsically unstable: what the movement is, what it stands for, and who its legitimate spokespersons are. One of the challenges for social movement researchers is then to explain why some meanings, groups, and repertoires dominate at the expense of others. The analysis showed that this occurs when one or more power concentration mechanisms are at play. First, Anons cluster through processes of self-selection: they seek each other out based on their status, interests, and skills, with the effect that one or a few clusters contain higher concentrations of elite movement participants than others. Second, clusters with elite participants can develop collective power. As the cluster's participants develop strong internal links, they come to perceive themselves as a collective actor and they can effectively pool their resources, develop a division of labor, and coordinate actions, increasing their collective power to plan and carry out complex and high-profile collective action. Third, this group can come to serve as a hub for other clusters and individuals. Movement participants, journalists, and opponents prefer to connect to already well-connected movement participants, reinforcing the centrality of the core group and especially its celebrity figureheads (Barabási & Albert, 1999; Colizza et al., 2006). These three mechanisms were fully and jointly at play during the campaign against Scientology and in the aftermath of the HB Gary hack. As a core group concentrates power, the movement's diversity does not necessarily disappear but recedes to the background. As the spotlight is fixed on the core group, its actions and discourse increasingly define what the movement does and stands for. The group around Housh stressed the coordination, standardization, and disciplining of protest and the group around Sabu focused the movement's energies on committing and exploiting high-profile hacks. In both cases, there were countless Anons who took an altogether different approach but they received much less attention from the movement's constituents, scholars, and especially the public at large.

However, there are also mechanisms of power diffusion. First, the concentration of power antagonizes movement participants with a marginal position and a different vision of how the movement needs to develop: power concentration generates resistance from within the movement. Marginalized groups or rival elites always have incentives to question the status quo, but this is especially the case for rhizomatic movements whose participants can call upon an egalitarian discourse to criticize power holders or, in Anonymous parlance, 'leaderfags.' Second, centralization breeds vulnerability as it provides opponents—including rivals within the movement, counter-movements, and law enforcement—with a target, increasing the probability of central figures being neutralized through assault or arrest. Gregg Housh and others who spoke out publicly against Scientology were targeted by Scientologists as well as Anons who accused the group of usurping power. Sabu and others within Anonymous' circle of prominent hacktivists were almost all arrested by law enforcement and had also come under pressure from a diverse group of opponents, including rival hacker groups and disgruntled Anons seeking to uncover their identities.

If the substance of movements—their goals and means—cannot be presumed, it must be explained. The empirical analysis in this paper thus explained Anonymous' changing repertoires and goals with reference to underlying network mechanisms. The analysis presented here captures these varied connection patterns as configurations of power, focusing in particular on the degree to which logistic, symbolic, and communicative power is concentrated in one among many clusters. It is true that Anonymous is 'a hydra,' as movement participants often say, in the sense that the movement consists of multiple and relatively autonomous clusters. However, some clusters may come to play a much more prominent role than others. Investigating the underlying mechanisms and patterns of power concentration and power diffusion is, therefore, both of crucial importance in understanding Anonymous and in the study of movement dynamics in general.

Notes

1. Since Housh has become the entry point into Anonymous for both the media and academia, it is easy to overstate his role in driving the demonstrations. However, it should be recognized that the profiling of one key person as a spokesperson is not an aberration but an outcome of the structural forces driving Anonymous' move out of the image boards: Housh became identified as a result of his involvement in a street protest and became a key figure as journalists and others were looking for a reliable source and spokesperson.
2. Retrieved May 10, 2015, from http://pastebin.com/HZtH523f.

Acknowledgments

The thoughts presented here were first explored in a paper in the Dutch journal Sociologie (2011). I would like to thank Dorien Zandbergen for comments on that piece. This paper has benefited from comments from the editor, two anonymous reviewers, Davide Beraldo, and John D. Boy.

Disclosure statement

No potential conflict of interest was reported by the author.

References

Alstott, J., Panzarasa P., Rubinov M., Bullmore E. T., & Vértes P. E. (2014). A unifying framework for measuring weighted rich clubs. *Scientific Reports, 4*, article 7258.

Assange, J. (2006). Conspiracy as governance. *Cryptome*, December 6, 2006. Retrieved May 10, 2015, from http://cryptome.org/0002/ja-conspiracies.pdf

Bakshy, E., Hofman, J. M., Mason W. A., & Watts D. J. (2011). Everyone's an influencer: Quantifying influence on twitter. *WSDM '11 Proceedings of the fourth ACM international conference on Web search and data mining*, 65–74.

Barabási, A.-L., & Albert, R. (1999). Emergence of scaling in random networks. *Science, 286*, 509–512.

Bennett, W. L. (2013). *The logic of connective action*. Cambridge: Cambridge University Press.

Beraldo, D. (2014). The branding of contention. *Proceedings of the SOCIO CRI 14 Conference - Sociology and Critical Perspectives on Social Movements*, 12-14 May 2014, Istanbul, DAKAM.

Bernstein, M. S., Monroy-Hernández, A., Harry, D., André, P., Panovich, K., & Vargas, G. (2011). 4chan and /b/: An analysis of anonymity and ephemerality in a large online community. *Proceedings of the Fifth International AAAI Conference on Weblogs and Social Media*, 50–57.

Bourdieu, P. (1997). *Pascalian meditations*. Stanford: Stanford University Press.

Castells, M. (2012). *Networks of outrage and hope: Social movements in the internet age*. Cambridge: Polity Press.

Chesters, G., & Welsh, I. (2006). *Complexity and social movements: Multitudes at the edge of chaos*. London: Routledge.

Coleman, G. (2014). *Hacker, hoaxer, whistleblower, spy: The many faces of anonymous*. London: Verso.

Colizza, V., Flammini, A., Serrano, M. A., & Vespignani, A. (2006). Detecting rich-club ordering in complex networks. *Nature Physics, 2*, 110–115.

Cox, L., & Nilsen, A. G. (2007). Social movements research and the 'movement of movements': Studying resistance to neoliberal globalisation. *Sociology Compass, 1*, 424–442.

Deleuze, G., & Guattari, F. (1987). *A thousand plateaus*. Minneapolis, MN: University of Minnesota Press.

Diani, M. (1992). The concept of social movement. *The Sociological Review, 40*, 1–25.

Dibbell, J. (2009). The assclown offensive: How to enrage the church of scientology. *Wired*, September 21. Retrieved May 10, 2015, from http://archive.wired.com/culture/culturereviews/magazine/17-10/mf_chanology?currentPage=all

Domscheit-Berg, D. (2011). *Inside wikileaks. My time with Julian Assange at the world's most dangerous website*. London: Vintage.

Freeman, J. (1973). The tyranny of structurelessness. *Berkeley Journal of Sociology, 17*, 151–165.

Fuchs, C. (2006). The self-organization of social movements. *Systemic Practice and Action Research, 19*, 101–137.

Fuchs, C. (2013). The anonymous movement in the context of liberalism and socialism. *Interface, 5*, 345–376.
Goode, L. (2015). Anonymous and the political ethos of hacktivism. *Popular Communication, 13*, 74–86.
Goodwin, J., & Jasper, J. (1999). Caught in a wining, snarling vine: The structural bias of political process theory. *Sociological Forum, 14*, 27–54.
Grigoriadis, V. (2011). 4chan's chaos theory. *Vanity Fair*, April. Retrieved May 10, 2015, from http://www.vanityfair.com/news/2011/04/4chan-201104
Hardt, M., & Negri, A. (2004). *Multitude: War and democracy in the age of empire*. New York, NY: Penguin.
Jasper, J. M. (2012). Microfoundations of protest. Presented at the Amsterdam Institute for Social Science, University of Amsterdam, March 11.
Juris, J. S. (2012). Reflections on #occupy everywhere: Social media, public space, and emerging logics of aggregation. *American Ethnologist, 39*, 259–279.
Kauffman, S. A. (1993). *The origins of order: Self organization and selection in evolution*. Oxford: Oxford University Press.
Koopmans, R. (2004). Movements and media: selection processes and evolutionary dynamics in the public sphere. *Theory & Society, 33*, 367–391.
McAdam, D., Tarrow, S. G., & Tilly, C. (2001). *Dynamics of contention*. Cambridge: Cambridge University Press.
Melucci, A. (1996). *Challenging codes. Collective action in the information age*. Cambridge: Cambridge University Press.
Nunes, R. (2014). *Organisation of the organisationless: Collective action after networks*. Lüneburg, Post-Media Lab & Mute Books.
Olson, P. (2012). *We are anonymous: Inside the hacker world of LulzSec, anonymous, and the global cyber insurgency*. New York, NY: Little, Brown.
Richards, D. (1993). A chaotic model of power concentration in the international system. *International Studies Quarterly, 37*, 55–72.
Schelling, T. C. (1971). Dynamic models of segregation. *The Journal of Mathematical Sociology, 1*, 143–186.
Sitrin, M. (2012). *Everyday revolutions: Horizontalism and autonomy in Argentina*. London: Zed Books.
Tufekci, Z. (2015). Social movements and governments in the digital age: Evaluating a complex landscape. *Journal of International Affairs, 68*, 1–18.
Uitermark, J. (2011). Revolutie "for the lulz". De opkomst en transformatie van de online sociale beweging Anonymous [The emergence and transformation of the online movement Anonymous]. *Sociologie, 7*, 156–182.
Uitermark, J. (2012). *Dynamics of power in Dutch integration politics*. Amsterdam: Amsterdam University Press.
Uitermark, J. (2015). Longing for wikitopia. The study and politics of self-organization, *Urban Studies, 52*, 2301–2312.
Wellman, B., Quan-Haase A., Boase J., Chen W., Hampton K., Díaz I., & Miyata K. (2003). The social affordances of the internet for networked individualism. *Journal of Computer-Mediated Communication 8*. Retrieved May 10, 2015, from http://onlinelibrary.wiley.com/doi/10.1111/j.1083-6101.2003.tb00216.x/full
Wiedemann, C. (2014). Between swarm, network, and multitude: Anonymous and the infrastructures of the common. *Distinktion: Scandinavian Journal of Social Theory, 15*, 309–326.
Woese, C. R. (2004). A new biology for a new century. *Microbiology and Molecular Biology Reviews, 68*, 173–186.

From 'moments of madness' to 'the politics of mundanity' - researching digital media and contentious collective actions in China

Jun Liu

ABSTRACT
Information and communication technologies (ICTs) have become an essential part of contentious politics and social movements in contemporary China. Although quite a few scholars have explored ICTs, contentious politics, and collective action in China, they largely focus on the event-based analysis of discrete contentious events, failing to capture, reflect, and assess most of the political ferment in and around the routine use of digital media in people's everyday lives. This study proposes a broader research agenda by shifting the focus from contentious events – 'moments of madness' – to 'the politics of mundanity': the political dynamics in the mundanity of digitally mediated, routine daily life. The agenda includes, first, the investigation of the dynamics underlying the mundane use of digital media, which not only places the use of ICTs in contentious moments into 'a big picture' to understand the political potential of mundane use of ICTs, but also reveals 'everyday resistance,' or less publicly conspicuous tactics, as precursors of open, confrontational forms of contentious activity. Second, the agenda proposes the examination of mundane experiences to understand the sudden outburst of contention and digital media as the 'repertoire of contention.' Third, the agenda scrutinizes the adoption of mundane expressions of contentious challenges to authoritarian regimes, as they allow for the circumvention of the heavy censorship of collective action mobilization. Mundane expressions have thereby emerged as a prominent part of the mobilization mechanism of contention in China. Addressing 'the politics of mundanity' will provide a nuanced understanding of ICTs and contentious collective action in China.

> Events are *not* natural phenomena. They are always constructions and do not exist as events apart from this fact. (Kapferer, 2010, p. 17, emphasis added)

The development and proliferation of Information and Communication Technologies (ICTs) give rise to the adoption and appropriation of digital media for social movements and contentious politics around the world.[1] Against this backdrop, scholars are increasingly debating the ways in which digital media are shaping and transforming the arena of social movements. Some explore the affordances of digital media for (alternative) information distribution for political contention (e.g. Kahn & Kellner, 2004; Tufekci & Wilson, 2012). Others underline the relevance of digital media in the process of structuring and bridging networks for collective action (e.g. Bennett & Segerberg, 2012). Some argue for digital media being a catalyst for protest organization, mobilization, and participation (e.g. Bennett, Breunig, & Givens, 2008). Others observe identity- and value-driven subpolitics as key elements in digitally mediated political activism (e.g. Bakardjieva, 2009).

Among them, the use of ICTs for contentious collective action in China – the largest authoritarian state with the largest internet and mobile phone population in the world – has attracted considerable attention over the past two decades (e.g. Esarey & Xiao, 2011; Yang, 2009b). Nevertheless, most of this scholarship employs an event-based approach to analyzing discrete digitally mediated collective action. More specifically, this scholarship focuses on the alternative or antagonistic use of ICTs in contentious events,[2] or what Zolberg (1972) described as 'moments of madness,' which restricts the understanding of digital media and its effects on political contention to open, recognizable political conflicts and contentious moments *per se,* and fails to associate these specific uses with a larger living context. As such, the use of ICTs for contentious activities seems to be in isolation from other aspects of everyday life. To advance the state of the art of scholarship on ICTs, political contention, and collective action in China, this study proposes a revised research agenda by shifting the focus that is almost exclusively on contentious events to what I call '*the politics of mundanity*.' From a broader perspective, this agenda entails a focus on the political dynamics embedded in the realm of mundane, everyday life and associated with quotidian digital media practices that have come to generate, influence, or sustain contentious collective action in politically repressive regimes like China.

In this study, I take Tarrow's definition of 'contentious collective action,' which brings 'ordinary people into confrontation with opponents, elites, or authorities' with diversified forms – 'brief or sustained, institutionalized or disruptive, humdrum or dramatic' (2011, pp. 7–8). This inclusive definition allows us to observe a wide variety of contentious activities in China. Digitally mediated contentious collective action hereby refers to contentious activities in which digital media act as necessary prerequisites to the course of collective action.

I first present a critical review of current studies of ICTs, collective action, and contentious politics in China. Second, I introduce and set forth the framework of 'the mundane and the everyday' to investigate the significant value of everyday behavior and experience and contentious collective action. Third, I explicate three aspects on the politics of mundanity that comprise a broader agenda to scrutinize ICTs, contentious activities, and (possible) social movements in China. Fourth, I conclude with thoughts on the agenda that complements current scholarship by integrating the discussion of the political implications of the mundane use of digital media, presenting a more nuanced picture of digitally mediated contentious collective action beyond specific 'moments of madness' in China.

ICTs, collective action, and contentious politics in China: a critical review

The impact of ICTs on collective action and contentious politics has emerged as an enduring and substantial focus in the studies of ICTs in China (e.g. Esarey & Xiao, 2011; Yang, 2009b). Such a focus examines the emancipatory potential, albeit not necessarily democratic, of digital media in China's repressive political context (e.g. Yang, 2009b; Zheng, 2008). A number of thorough studies have elaborated the increasingly prominent role of digital media in collective action and contentious politics in the processes of information distribution (Huang & Sun, 2014; Tai, 2006), claims-making (Tong & Zuo, 2014), network-bridging (Sullivan & Xie, 2009), resource accumulation (Yang, 2005), repertoire diversification (Yang, 2009b), and movement collaboration and mobilization (Liu, 2014b, 2015a).

Among them, some believe that ICTs will overcome social, economic, and organizational barriers to collective action mobilization and participation, bringing '... the power into the hands of the individuals and marginal social groups' (Tai, 2006, p. 259), or contributing to 'a power shift in Chinese society' (Xiao, 2011b, p. 222). Others, such as Zheng (2008, pp. 89–101), acknowledge the facilitation of collective actions via ICTs such as the internet, but consider digital media as an area for both the state and society to pursue their interests and advance mutual transformation.

Yang's landmark study of online activism in China (2009b) provides a comprehensive picture of digital media and its influence on contentious politics. With a multi-interactionism approach wherein he foregrounds internet activism in interaction with multiple and intersecting forces and a major focus on contention in cyberspace, Yang defines online activism as 'contentious activities associated with the use of the Internet and other new communication technologies' (p. 3). More importantly, he indicates that online activism includes not only (contentious) political activities but also cultural and social forms 'to express or oppose values, morality, lifestyles, and identities' (p. 3). Correspondingly, Yang (2009a) categorizes four types of online activism – cultural, social, political, and nationalistic – to illustrate the uniqueness of digitally mediated contentious activities in China. Similarly, as a result of careful interrogation, a few studies have probed into humor, jokes, parody, satire, and homophones that have been used on the Chinese internet as cultural forms of contentious activity, as well as its meaning and significance (e.g. Esarey & Qiang, 2008; Yang & Jiang, 2015).

While, undoubtedly, current scholarship yields a fruitful understanding of the role of digital media in collective action and contentious politics, it largely remains dominated by an event-based approach of discrete, independent – in some cases, isolated – cases of contentious activity, the emergence of which reflects unique internal dynamics. To be clear, most existing literature approaches the issue of ICTs and contentious collective action by looking at 'internet mass incidents' (*wangluo quntixing shijian*) (Esarey & Xiao, 2011), 'new media events' (*xinmeiti shijian*) (Qiu & Chan, 2011), 'internet incidents' (*wangluo shijian*) (Yang, 2014a, p. 111), 'internet event[s]' (*wangluo shijian*) (Jiang, 2015), or 'online mass incidents' (Bondes & Schucher, 2014). This reflects, to a certain extent, a crucial characteristic of digitally mediated contentious politics in Chinese society where the politically sensitive authorities work hard with a highly repressive policy against contentious collective challenges in order to suppress the outbreak of political contention and to prevent the dispersal of its influence to a large scale, in particular, via digital media (e.g. King, Pan, & Roberts, 2013). In this sense, as some studies maintain, '[…] activism in China fails to meet the definition of a "social movement" because it is usually localized and falls short of sustained contention' (Huang & Sun, 2014, p. 87).

Nevertheless, such a focus of spontaneous, sporadic, and 'short-lived' (Tong & Zuo, 2014, p. 69) moments of madness – or 'anecdotal evidence' (Bondes & Schucher, 2014, p. 46) – presents a far too restricted view of (contentious) politics, one that privileges open, visible, and public confrontation but leaves out a great deal of what is politically significant that sets the scene for the moment of confrontation (for a general critique, see Staggenborg & Taylor, 2005, pp. 38–41; also see what Melucci, 1989, referred as 'submerged-networks'). More specifically, such a view is subject to at least three limitations. First, it fails to provide a big picture of structural change that has been introduced by the integration of ICTs into Chinese life (Yang, 2011, p. 1044) and that, in turn, facilitates contentious collective action. Second, it fails to reveal possible interconnections across periods of digitally mediated political contention.[3] Third, it fails to recognize the long-term, or 'gradual revolution' introduced by the imprints, or cumulative effects, of digitally mediated political contention on (contentious) politics in particular and Chinese society in general (Yang, 2011, pp. 1044–1045). In short, a strong preference for the analysis of disruptive events (i.e. contentious events) comes up short in the delineation of the relationship between digital media, contentious politics, and possible social change in China (also see Katz, 2009, pp. 170–171). To advance understanding, this study proposes to broaden the scope of interrogation to the everyday and to a broader array of mundane orientations.

From contentious moments to the mundane and the everyday

The importance of the mundane and the everyday to social movements has been brought out by new social movement (NSM) scholarship. Different from traditional social movements scholarship with a focus on economic interests or political conflict, NSM scholarship, based in European post-1960s movements and with a social constructivist approach, underlines the social aspect of movements, such as movement emotion, meaning, identity, and their relationships to culture, ideology, and politics, as well as the relation of the movement to wider society (e.g. Buechler, 2000; Laraña, 1994; Touraine, 1988). Among them, the realm of mundane, everyday life as a politically significant domain of social movements has attracted considerable attention particularly for feminism, environmentalism, homosexual rights, and the peace movement (e.g. Buechler, 2000). A key contribution that connects everyday practices and movements comes from Alberto Melucci's work as described below.

Along with a Foucauldian approach to power as an everyday phenomenon, Melucci (1985, 1989) suggests that we view social movements through the prism of the mundane and the everyday to achieve a full picture of movements. More specifically, addressing a processual approach to social movements, Melucci lays greater emphasis on the role of everyday processes of networking (what he coins as 'submerged networks') (1985, p. 801), experiencing, practicing, and constructing (alternative) meaning, identity, and solidarity in social movements. He identifies and differentiates *visible* movement activity that is manifested and easily recognized (e.g. demonstrations and public meetings) and *latent*, or *invisible*, movement activity that is embedded and submerged in everyday life but underpins manifest activity (Melucci, 1985, pp. 800–801). These two parts are inseparable, mutually constitutive, and integral to the understandings of social movements:

> These two poles, visibility and latency, are reciprocally correlated. Latency allows visibility in that it feeds the former with solidarity resources and with a cultural framework for mobilization. Visibility reinforces submerged networks. It provides energies to renew solidarity, facilitate creation of new groups and recruitment of new militants attracted by public mobilization who then flow into the submerged network. (Melucci, 1985, p. 801)

Here, the locus of social movements is not only situated in spaces of open defiance such as political conflicts, but, more importantly, it resides in structures of everyday life. As the key but hidden nature of social movements, these structures of everyday life become visible when they have engaged in overt political conflict. During phases of less obvious political activity, on the contrary, they serve as a latent but essential movement infrastructure that establishes and maintains the network of solidarity and identity. This conceptualization of social movements embedded, articulated, and sustained in less visible, contested forms of activity in daily life draws special attention to the political dynamics in the mundane and the everyday beyond 'complex *aggregates* of collective actions or events' (Marwell & Oliver, 1984, p. 6; emphasis in original). Consequently, as Melucci accentuates, the 'phenomenology of everyday life becomes increasingly important as *a research tool* in connecting the macro level of collective action to the individual experience in the minute textures of day-to-day practices' (Melucci & Lyyra, 1998, p. 221, emphasis added).

Melucci's view has been adopted or resonated in many later works on social movements and political contention (e.g. Katsiaficas, 1997; Staggenborg & Taylor, 2005). In their study of environmental movement participation, for instance, Almanzar, Sullivan-Catlin, and Deane (1998) show that everyday behaviors of the general public, as non-conventional social movement activities, are considerable sites of social movements. Such an approach incorporates Hanisch's famous dictum 'the personal is political' that underlines the connection 'between social movements and the everyday behaviors and choices of individuals' (Almanzar et al., 1998, p. 186). Taking activism and everyday behaviors as '... two ends of a continuum,' Almanzar et al. further suggest '... a revised model of social movement participation that includes everyday behaviors' (1998, pp. 187–188), which helps to establish individual identity, mobilization potential, and movement motivations.

In the similar vein, Reed (2005), in his study of progressive social movements, draws attention to two distinct, but related, facets of contemporary social movements: the importance of 'dramatic public actions' and 'the rather undramatic, mundane daily acts of preparation' that produce these public displays. In line with Melucci's discussion on visibility and latency, Reed states that, '[...] dramatic actions are themselves the products of usually rather undramatic, mundane daily acts of preparation, and that the impact of dramatic moments is only as great as the follow-up forms of daily organizing that accompany them.' (2005, pp. xiv–xv).

To summarize, these accounts acknowledge the political significance of the mundane, everyday practices, behaviors, and choices that not only support the very basis for open, visible moments of contention, but also represent themselves as different manifestations of social movements. Furthermore, they stress dynamic interactions between the everyday and the moment of contention, pointing out that the contentious moment cannot be examined in isolation from the context of everyday life that has come to generate and influence it. Following the argument, this study looks at 'the politics of mundanity' as *the political dynamics in quotidian practices and experiences of mundane, everyday life.* These practices and experiences not only lay the foundation for further open defiance and contentious collective action, and they are themselves part of tactical repertoires of contentious political action.

Reorienting the focus toward the mundane, everydayness of living life (in this case, mediated by ICTs) also has a significant meaning in a highly controlled authoritarian context such as China. Most current scholars consider the practice of daily life to be associated with certain kinds of social organization in Western contexts (e.g. Almanzar et al., 1998). As studies demonstrate, however, the Chinese government is working hard to impose a tightening of state control over social organizations, including non-governmental organizations. Against this backdrop, social organizations have been missing in the process of political activism, largely due to political pressure and repression (Wu & Wen, 2015, p. 113). How, then, can the politics of mundanity develop in the absence of social organizations under stern controls in authoritarian regimes? Such a politically sensitive context makes China a uniquely relevant case to understand the dynamics of the mundane, everyday politics in contentious collective action.

The following sections specify three aspects of the politics of mundanity – mundane digital media use, mundane experience, and mundane expression – followed by a synthesis of the relationship between three aspects, as well as their contributions to research on digital media, contentious politics, and social change in China.

Mundane digital media use, mobilization potentials, and 'everyday resistance'

Mundane digital media use looks at the dynamics embedded in the mundanity of everyday use of digital media that underpins digitally mediated contentious collective action in general, and less publicly conspicuous tactics of protest, or what Scott coins as 'everyday resistance' (1985), in particular. These everyday uses not only establish and prefigure the means of contention by which people engage in contentious actions, but also form and consolidate networks of mobilization and recruitment through which contentious activities are realized.

The mundanity of digital media use in everyday life and mobilization potentials

The increasing ubiquity of ICTs and the growing pervasiveness of digital communication in Chinese people's daily lives lead to the mundanity of digital media use. Mobile telecommunication was introduced into China in 1987 (Wang, 2008). Seven years later, the year 1994 marks the start of the internet in China (Xinhuanet, 2003). The first national survey of internet use in 1997, by the China Internet Network Information Center (CNNIC), reported that China had 299,000 computers with internet access and 620,000 internet users, the majority of which (43.3%) went online between 1 and 5 hours per week (CNNIC, 1997).

After around thirty years of development, the internet and mobile phones have become much more prevalent, with emerging social media becoming increasingly popular in people's everyday lives. As of December 2014, the number of internet users has skyrocketed to over 649 million, with an internet penetration rate of 47.9%, or close to half of China's population. An average Chinese user spends 26.1 hours surfing the internet per week; reportedly, over 53% internet users rely on the internet to manage their daily lives and work (CNNIC, 2015). Meanwhile, mobile phones grow as a near-ubiquitous tool for communication and information seeking in everyday life. The number of mobile phone users is close to 1.3 billion. In other words, nearly *every* Chinese person has a mobile phone these days. Ranked No. 7 in the world, Chinese people spend 170 minutes on their mobile phones per day, mostly with instant communication (91.2%), mobile searches (77.1%), and mobile news (74.6%) (*Apple Daily*, 2014; CNNIC, 2015). China also has the world's largest and most active social media user base. Ninety-five percent of internet users from major cities are regular users of social media (Chiu, Lin, & Silverman, 2012). For instance, *weibo*, a hybrid of Twitter and Facebook, emerges as one of the most widely used social media applications in China. More than 290 million *weibo* users account for over 46% of the total Chinese internet users in 2014 (CNNIC, 2015). In short, the internet, mobile phones, and social media have woven themselves into the fabric of Chinese people's everyday lives.

As digital media have become integral to the rhythms of mundane, everyday life, they are penetrating, and further embedding into, everyday practices as part of mediated life. Against this backdrop, digital media dramatically shape the habitual practices of people's everyday lives, be they expressive or instrumental ones, no matter how unobtrusively. Consequently, this means that, unlike the situation before, when there was a limited penetration of ICTs within certain social groups (e.g. the so-called middle class), different groups now have diverse ways to access digital media and are thereby involved in a diversity of digitally mediated interactions and sociality, albeit to different degrees (for the use of digital media among migrant population, see Qiu, 2009; for mobile phone use, see Liu, 2010). In other words, digital communication has become an essential part of the living environment. Hence the necessity of exploring the (political) dynamics underlying the naturalized, everyday use of digital media, as ICTs are increasingly one of the mundanities of daily life, not developed specifically for contentious situations. To be clear, the adoption of digital media for contentious collective action is but a (small) part of ICT use that is largely developed upon everyday usage. How, then, can the quotidian use of digital media rest at the foundation of contentious collective action?

Here, I would like to take the initiative by proposing two analytical topics covering the mundanity of digital media use and its effect on contentious collective action. Of course, these topics do not represent the entire field of analytical possibilities, merely a few examples. First, following Nielsen's discussion (2011), I would suggest the examination of *mundane digital media use* for contentious activities. More specifically, as Nielsen (2011, 2013) argues, instead of emerging, or special 'hypermedia' (e.g. social networking sites), it is mundane internet tools (e.g. emails and search engines)[4] that are much more deeply integrated into recruiting and mobilizing practices of political campaigns. In digitally mediated (political) practices, people rely more heavily on quotidian digital media over unfamiliar or expensive alternatives (Nielsen, 2011; p. 769). Similarly, in the case of China, Liu's study on taxi strikes reveals the mobile call – the basic function of the mobile phone – as a key means for collective mobilization (Liu, 2014a). He further stresses the relevance of 'mundane mobilization means – quotidian, commonplace methods of communication adopted for mobilization purposes,' as it is the very mundanity of such means that 'lowers the threshold for collective action by allowing ordinary people to articulate their discontent, channel their anger, and initiate collective resistance through a simple and rapid method.' (Liu, 2014a, p. 21–22). Here, mundanity does not equate to triviality. Instead, it means that (the affordances of) digital media are at hand around us, always available and easily accessible to people for contentious activities, which entails familiarity, for the appropriation for political action. In short, the key question is not whether a particular technology itself is advanced or complicated, but instead, whether it is available, accessible, affordable, and familiar to ordinary citizens for the purpose of contentious activities. Research thereby needs to interrogate the concrete use of digital media when it comes to getting people involved in contentious collective action by analyzing how the mundanity of digital media use prefigures the use in moments of contention and by placing the specific use for contention in the big picture of mundane, everyday digital media use. A key question, then, is: are some kinds of mundane digital media use and communications more suited for certain kinds of contentious activities?

Second, I would suggest the study of how the mundane use of digital media structures networks of mobilization and recruitment in the course of establishing and maintaining sociality in everyday life. A key element in collective action includes the social networks of everyday life that act as mobilizing structures (McAdam et al., 2001, p. 14). As an essential base for mobilization and recruitment of participants, these networks play an invisible but vital role in the development and activities of the movement. For instance, norms of interpersonal trust and reciprocity from 'netness' (Tilly, 1978; also see Gouldner, 1960) act as reservoirs in engendering mutual obligations for recruitment and encouraging collective action mobilization. Meanwhile, ICTs foster a sense of pervasive, personal, perpetual communication that concerns networking in people's everyday sociality: friending, chatting, discussing, flirting, and negotiating, to mention a few. A typical example of digitally mediated sociality and networking is the popularity of the New Year text-message greeting, now being replaced by WeChat, a WhatsApp-like Chinese messaging app, during the Spring Festival, the most important traditional Chinese holiday. Distributed via mobile communication, the text-message greeting has overtaken physical visits to relatives and friends and the sending of New Year greeting cards by mail, emerging as the crucial way to form, develop, and maintain social networks and cultivate social capital by greeting friends and family and spreading good cheer (Liu, 2010).

Although none of these activities are contentious, these social networks of everyday life maintain a participatory culture that 'can be employed for civic engagement and, potentially, be borrowed for meaningful participation in social movement networks' (Lim, 2014, p. 56). For instance, digitally mediated social networks of everyday life enable people to self-organize, attain a critical mass of protest participants, and consolidate solidarity for collective action without SMOs by embodying credibility, reliability, and reciprocity on the basis of mundane sociality in everyday practices (Liu, 2014b; 2015a). Here, 'the segmented, reticular, and multi-faceted structure of "movements",' which features hidden networks and latent structure/links '[...] become explicit *only* during the transient periods of collective mobilization over issues which bring the latent network to the surface and then allow it to submerge again in the fabric of the daily life' (Melucci, 1996, p. 115, emphasis added). Research thus should recognize the everyday enactment of digitally mediated social networking practices as the basis of network mechanisms of movement recruitment and mobilization through the everyday use of digital media.

The mundanity of digital media use and 'everyday resistance'

Examining the mundanity of digital media use also sheds some light on what Scott calls 'everyday resistance' (Scott, 1985) in daily use of ICTs. In his study of day-to-day peasant resistance in Southeast Asia, Scott criticizes the view that by solely focusing on observable acts of rebellion – visible 'events,' or moments of madness, such as insurrection, riot, and petition, what he calls the 'public transcript' – people would easily miss subtle, low-profile but powerful forms of 'everyday resistance,' or the 'hidden transcript.' It is clear that the event-based approach overlooks 'the immense political terrain that lies between quiescence and revolt and that [...] is the political environment of subject class' (Scott, 1990, p. 199). Scott instead outlines a framework that aims to scrutinize the 'invisible power' of the 'hidden transcript': Underreporting or concealment practices and discourses that represent a critique of power but are employed behind the backs of the dominant in mundane, quotidian practices (1985, 1990). Following Scott's discussion, empirical studies have taken up an investigation of 'the development of the "hidden transcript" of unobtrusive dissent' in China (Perry, 2007, p. 10).

An important but largely neglected aspect is that, although often taking cryptic and opaque forms such as rumor, gossip, folktale, and metaphor, under certain political conditions, everyday resistance is able to give rise to contagion and cooperation, ultimately producing overt collective actions (e.g. Thaxton, 1997). Scott accordingly proposes the concept 'infrapolitics' as 'a different logic of political action' that establishes '... the cultural and structural underpinning of the more visible political action' (1990, p. 199, 184). Beyond simply being the offstage or veiled forms of cultural struggle and political expression, infrapolitics, or everyday resistance, enables the testing and further breaching of the boundaries of politics, thereby turning into an essential force in political breakthrough. In this sense, 'an analysis of the hidden transcript can tell us something about moments that carry the portent of political breakthroughs' (Scott, 1990, p. 203).

An example of 'everyday resistance' is the easy-to-proliferate 'rumor' (*yaoyan*), a crucial but mundane phenomenon in China's digital media platforms (Larson, 2011). Through digital platforms, rumor frequently proliferates even in the face of the government's intensifying and escalating crackdown. At the very least, digitally mediated rumor diffusion not only disseminates alternative discourses, but in some cases, also ignites protest against the government, galvanizing collective action. For instance, people exploit the terminology of 'rumor' in a tactical way to promote the proliferation of certain messages by adding notes that call for the re-sending of messages to as many people as possible (e.g. 'spread the message before it becomes a [government-labelled] "rumor".') (Liu, 2012). Receivers are thus motivated to pass on these kinds of chain messages that thwart the authorities. The use of 'rumor' thereby becomes a call to actively engage. In other words, 'rumor' here is mostly symbolic but highlights its growing presence as a sort of resistance power loaded with antagonistic sentiments and, increasingly, as a strategy to facilitate collective action (e.g. alternative communication) against the authorities. With the click of a button, people spread rumors through their digital devices, whereby they challenge the government or involve themselves in resistance against authorities. Circulating rumors via digital media thus lowers the average protest threshold and vents long pent-up resentments against the entrenched authoritarian regime. It is in this sense that digitally mediated rumor becomes a key element of 'everyday resistance.' This, again, entails an intrinsic relationship and mutual conversion between everyday practices and contentious moments that research might do well to scrutinize.

To conclude, assessing the dynamics underlying the mundane use of digital media not only reveals 'everyday resistance' as a precursor of open, confrontational forms of contentious activity while using digital media, but also situates the use of ICTs in contentious moments into the big picture to understand the political potential of mundane ICT use.

Mundane experience, mobilizing motivation, and the 'repertoire of contention'

Mobilization does not occur in a vacuum but in a specific political, cultural, and social environment, so do contentious politics and collective action. As Melucci points out, 'collective action is fed by needs that originate in the social fabric of everyday life' (1996, p. 287). People make the decision to take collective action in light of their daily experience and knowledge in a given environment. In the course of movements, the closer movement framings connect, align, or resonate with everyday experiences of the target population, the greater the probability of collective action mobilization (e.g. Benford & Snow, 2000). Moreover, prior experience of contention, be it from direct participation in movements or from various media, also exerts significant impact on the decision and action of mobilization (e.g. Tarrow, 2011, p. 233). Understanding the quotidian experience of the public in general together with the experience and knowledge of prior contentions thereby enables us to contextualize and, further, systematically comprehend the sudden burst of contentious collective action.

Mundane experience as 'structure of feeling' and mobilizing motivation

Addressing the relevance of the experience to contentious activities is of special importance for the interpretation of the outbreak of political contention in China, be it mediated by digital media or not. Studies of popular protests have emphasized the widespread emergence of 'anger-venting social incidents' (*shehui xiefen shijian*), which reflect '... generalized anger that has built up over time and then is released when an incident, sometimes a relatively minor one, occurs' (Fewsmith, 2008, p. 3). In this kind of contentious activity, large numbers of people – most of whom are not necessarily victims of injustice or deprivation, and often have no relationship to those involved in the contention – mobilize and engage in sometimes extremely violent behaviors. For instance, tens of thousands torched the public security bureau and the government buildings in Weng'an County, Guizhou Province, enraged by text messages about the cover-up of a local female student's death, as the message reminded residents of other bitter experiences under the local authority's iron rule (Yu, 2008). The feeling of grievance, frustration, resentment, and anger that stems from people's daily suffering of social inequality, injustice, government inaction, and corruption is, above all, the fuse for setting off such contentious activities. Similar phenomena have been identified in studies of digitally mediated collective action (e.g. Tong & Zuo, 2014, pp. 81–82; Zheng, 2008, p. 41). Yang particularly indicates that issues of online activism are '... more relevant to the everyday experiences of the larger population' and '... have high degrees of public resonance.' (2014a, p. 57)

Although existing studies do touch upon the role of experience in the course of digital activism, they are far from specifying the (possible) causal relationship between experience and contentious activities. This study thus suggests taking lived experience as a key structural condition (Melucci, 1996, p. 300) that provides the requisite for the eruption, facilitation, and sustainability of collective actions. The concept 'lived experience' is from Williams' discussion of 'structures of feeling,' or 'social experiences *in solution*' (1961, pp. 133–134, emphasis in original): An experience that resides primarily in mundane, ordinary moments and activities, but represents a common set of perceptions and values shared by a particular social group. According to Williams,

> [...] 'feeling' is chosen to emphasize a distinction from more formal concepts of 'world-view' or 'ideology' [...] We are concerned with meanings and values as they are actively lived and felt, and the relations between these and formal or systematic beliefs are in practice variable [...] We are talking about characteristic elements of impulse, restraint, and tone; specifically affective elements of consciousness and relationships: not feeling against thought, but thought as felt and feeling as thought: practical consciousness of a present kind, in a living and interrelating continuity. (1977, p. 132)

This kind of structure articulates the lived experience of the society and generates a possible condition for the emergence of shared emotion, cultivating the collective identity that shapes and solidifies further collective activities. The articulation of feelings and emotions involves shared experiences of empowerment and collective effervescence, which is greatly affective as it inspires the move '... from framed emotion to action and from individual to collective' (Brader, 2011; Flam & King, 2005, pp. 4–5). To explore the lived experience of the society thus reveals the concrete context of contentious collective action and embodies the politics of social change. To understand digitally mediated collective action thus necessitates 'an integration [...] of structural analysis and analysis of emotional experience [...][which] would significantly improve our theoretical approach to the processes of mobilization' (Melucci, 1996, p. 301).

Experience of contention and digital media as 'repertoire of contention'

Contentious politics and collective action are not only the product of lived experience; they also open spaces in which alternative experience, or movement cultures such as new languages, rituals, tactics, and forms of artistic expression emerge, '... which may influence and affect the emergence of future social movements' (Eyerman & Jamison, 1998, p. 160; Melucci & Lyyra, 1998). In other words, contentious activities leave legacies for later actors to learn, imitate, and duplicate, further empowering the powerless with usable knowledge that facilitates their collective action. People learn from past contentious collective actions and gain knowledge and experiences for later contention. Here, one key issue regarding the experience of contention is the 'repertoire of contention.'

As Tilly defines it, the 'repertoire of contention' is '[...] a limited set of routines that are learned, shared, and acted out through a relatively deliberate process of choice' (1995, p. 42). The repertoire of contention is an array of contentious claims-making and performance that is always situated in prior societal experience. More importantly, as Tarrow writes, '... the repertoire is not only what people *do* [...] it is what they *know how to do* and what others *expect* them to do' (2011, p. 39, emphasis in original). In other words, people learn from the history and experience of contention, directly or indirectly, and '... often find inspiration elsewhere in the ideas and tactics espoused and practiced by other activists' (McAdam & Rucht, 1993, p. 58). In this way,

> [...] the demonstration effect of collective action on the part of a group of 'earlier risers' triggers a variety of processes of diffusion, extension, imitation, and reaction among groups that are normally more quiescent and have fewer resources to engage in collective action.' (Tarrow, 2011, p. 205)

These activists then borrow or imitate these 'learned conventions of contention' (Tarrow, 2011, p. 29) in later struggles. The experience and knowledge of contention or the historicity of contention, be they from direct participation in movements or from various media, also allow the outcome of a single moment of political activism to transcend beyond itself to engender and sustain collective challenges for later comers in the long run. Again, in order to make sense of concrete digital contention, it is necessary to have an integration of knowledge and experience of contention of the past into the discussion beyond the specific contentious moments. Thus, a crucial question to be answered in future research will be: under which circumstance and with what kind of knowledge and experience of contention can the latent potential of mobilization turn into visible contentious collective action?

In short, studying mundane experience, including the structure of lived experience in society in general and the experience of (digitally mediated) political activism, not only provides us with a comprehensive picture of ICTs and contentious politics beyond concrete events, but also sheds light on the interconnections that might be found within digitally mediated political contention as well as the long-term effect of contentious events in society.

The adoption and adaption of mundane expressions for collective action

The third aspect of the politics of mundanity looks at the organization tactics of contentious collective action in authoritarian regimes such as China. Along with an increasing number of political contentions and collective actions on the ground – what the government calls 'mass incidents' (*quntixing shijian*) (Lu, Li, & Chen, 2012) – is a growing tightened and complicated mechanism of censorship over the information available to people in their everyday lives, in particular via digital media (e.g. OpenNet Initiative, 2005). Among other information that contains critiques of leaders and highly sensitive topics, the one that might trigger offline collective action has drawn particular, intensive scrutiny from the censors. King, Pan, and Roberts' study of the mechanism of censorship in social media, for instance, reveals that '[...] collective expression [...] regarding actual collective action, such as protests, as well as those about events that seem likely to generate collective action but have not yet done so, are likely to be censored.' (2013, p. 327)

Despite the remarkable characteristics of censorship in China, Chinese people are magnificently skilled in maneuvering various rhetorical techniques, such as code words, homophones, spoofing, parodies, and satires, to talk about forbidden topics in political discourse, thus circumventing and challenging the authorities' censorship practices via digital media (e.g. Xiao, 2011a; Yang, 2011). A crucial yet less-addressed tactic (de Certeau, 1984) to bypass the outright censorship is to adapt and adopt mundane expressions for digitally mediated collective action.

For instance, several studies exemplify that people adopted the terms '(collective) stroll' (*jiti sanbu*) or 'taking a walk' (*sanbu*), rather than 'parade' (*youxing*) or 'demonstration' (*shiwei*), as euphemisms, distributing them via mobile phones and the internet for street protest mobilization against government-supported petrochemical projects in several cities (Liu, 2013, p. 1004). Shanghai residents employed the term 'shopping' (*gouwu*) as they disseminated mobilizing messages via bulletin board systems, internet forums, and mobile phones, to organize and facilitate protests in one of the city's most crowded shopping streets against a proposed magnetic levitation train line (Zeng, 2015, p. 110). Taxi drivers in southeast China's Guangzhou city borrowed the phase 'drink tea' (*hecha*) to mobilize strikes in response to long-standing grievances over taxi company charges, government regulation, and competition from unlicensed taxis (Shan, 2008). After the police had detained an activist-blogger, Guo Baofeng, for the accusation of using his blog to spread rumors about local police, his supporters initiated a 'postcard movement,' in which they called on Internet users to send postcards with a popular, quotidian sentence from the computer game *World of Warcraft* as a political slogan (i.e. 'Guo Baofeng, your mother calls you home to eat.') to the police station to campaign for his release (Yang, 2014a, pp. 111–112).

Addressing the relevance of the adoption of mundane expressions for contentious collective action includes the following three points. First, deploying mundane everyday expressions enables the ordinary to easily bypass the censorship of politically sensitive keywords while disseminating collective action initiatives as quickly as possible, as widely as possible via digital media. These expressions are distinguished from other rhetorical techniques such as satire, spoofing, and parodies that have been 'invented' (e.g. the term 'Grass-mud horse' [Wines, 2009]) or appropriated with either explicit or implicit political implications to subvert or criticize authorities. Instead, they are from everyday, quotidian activities (i.e. having a meal, shopping, taking a walk, and drinking tea) and are devoted to the organization and mobilization of contentious collective challenges, both online and offline. Their quotidian nature makes it difficult for the authorities to detect, identify, and censor these expressions without causing 'substantial collateral damage' (Zuckerman, 2015), such as the interruption of mundane communication in work and life that would easily trigger larger-scale discontentment with the government (e.g. to squelch people talking about 'shopping' or 'drinking tea'). In a broad sense, attention may need to be paid to the implication of digitally mediated 'casual conversation' (Scheufele, 2000) or 'informal (political) communications' (Eveland, Morey, & Hutchens, 2011) for political and civic life.

Second, the mundanity of the expressions, however, does not reduce their capacity for collective action mobilization. On the contrary, it allows the call for collective action to be conveyed and spread in a language that is understandable to people regardless of their literacy skills. The mundane expressions come from everyday life and are immediately familiar. This enables people, even without complicated knowledge of resistance, to understand and utilize these expressions for contentious collective challenges – people may not understand 'Grass-mud horse,' but everyone knows terms such as 'go shopping' and 'take a walk.'

Third, the mundanity of the expression to an extent softens the confrontational aspect of contentious collective action, which not only avoids a direct conflict with the authorities but also encourages more participations from either online or offline. For instance, in the taxi strike case, the drivers' response to customers' request was 'we are off today, [as we would like to] take a rest and drink tea!' (Shan, 2008). Such expressions save protestors from direct confrontations with either the customer or the authorities by establishing a degree of ambiguity. Meanwhile, it also opens up spaces for more participation, as the call itself is not deemed politically sensitive, inviting censorship. In this way, the adoption of mundane expressions – a key part of the mechanism of mobilization in digitally mediated activism – is of great importance for the analysis of contentious activities.

In addition to the adoption of mundane expressions for contentious mobilization, as studies already demonstrate, the linguistic exuberance of the Chinese language facilitates diversified ways of criticizing, mocking, and jeering the authorities 'beneath the radar' of censorship using political satire, spoofing, parody, jokes, humor, images (memes), and appropriation of politically correct language (e.g. Esarey & Qiang, 2008; Yang & Jiang, 2015). Moreover, Chinese phonetics mean that many characters share the same sound with a different tone, or even the same sound and same tone, which consequently allows people to use different characters with phonetics similar to a politically sensitive or censored phrases. In short, the richness and complexity of the Chinese language entails a focus on mundane expression and daily interaction in order to expose the political dynamics of everyday elements of the contentious repertoire.

Conclusion

ICTs have become an essential part of contentious politics and social movements in contemporary China. Although quite a few scholars have explored ICTs, contention politics, and collective action in China, they largely focus on the event-based analysis of discrete moments of contention, failing to capture, reflect, and assess most of the political ferment in and around the routine use of digital media as well as people's everyday lives. To advance the state of the art of scholarship, this study proposes a broader research agenda by shifting the focus from contentious events to 'the politics of mundanity': the political dynamics in the quotidian nature of digitally mediated, routine daily life. The agenda includes, first, the investigation of the dynamics underlying the mundane use of digital media. This focus will not only place the use of ICTs in contentious moments into 'a big picture' to understand the political potential of the mundane use of ICTs, but also reveals 'everyday resistance' as precursors of open, confrontational forms of contentious activities. Second, the agenda proposes to examine mundane experiences to understand the sudden outburst of contention and digital media as part of the 'repertoire of contention.' Third, the agenda scrutinizes the adoption of mundane expressions for contentious challenges in authoritarian regimes like China, as it allows for the circumvention of heavy censorship, enabling collective action mobilization.

These three aspects are reciprocally correlated to each other. The mundane use of digital media affords experiences that can be adapted to contentious collective challenges. It also offers expressions that would be maneuvered for mobilization of contention. Mundane experience enables people to locate expressions and phases that are able to bypass censorship for the mobilization of contention. The successful adoption of mundane expressions for contentious collective challenges, in turn, provides the experience and knowledge of contention for people to learn, imitate, and duplicate in future struggles, consequently encouraging the emergence of assimilation.

Finally, to emphasize the political dynamics in the routine use of digital media beyond a simple realization of overt contentious possibility also has methodological relevance in repressive contexts. As Esarey and Xiao maintain, 'due to the tightly controlled nature of the media environment in China, computerized content analysis may miss nuances of expression that communicate the presence of a subtle divergence from the official line' (2011, p. 307). Consequently, an appreciation of the multilayered and complex dimensions of digitally mediated, contentious 'micropolitics' (Deleuze & Guattari, 1987, pp. 208–231) is urgently needed to establish a widening focus of both the scope and level of interrogation by including the more routinized, informal, and inconspicuous forms and contextualized aspects of disruption, disobedience, or resistance as significant to the processes of contention. Research, for instance, may consider a 'thick description' (Geertz, 1973) of the digitally mediated quotidian practice of everyday life and how it contributes to the cultivation and activation of contentious collective action.[5] Dissecting the politics of mundanity will not only provide a nuanced understanding of ICTs and contentious collective action in China, it will also shed light on the deeper impact of digital media on social and political changes in Chinese society, both today and in the years to come.

Notes

1. This study takes McAdam, Tarrow, and Tilly's definition of 'contentious politics' as 'collective political struggle' (2001, p. 5), which involves contention, collective action, and politics (also see Tarrow, 2011, p. 6).
2. These events include, , social injustice (e.g. the Sun Zhigang case; Zheng & Wu, 2005, pp. 529–530), political scandal (e.g. the Wenzhou train collision case; Bondes & Schucher, 2014), and environmental activism (e.g. Yang, 2005).
3. Existing scholarship, however, does observe and acknowledge that earlier digitally mediated political struggles affect, facilitate, or even legitimize subsequent contentious movements (e.g. Zeng, 2015). Analysis, nevertheless, remains limited (but, see Liu, 2015b, August).
4. The perception of what refers to 'mundane' internet use, however, depends on different social groups (Nielsen, 2013, p.175–176).
5. An example is the orientation of 'deep Internet studies' (Yang, 2014b, p. 141).

Acknowledgements

The author deeply appreciates the comments from Kevin Gillan and Cristina Flesher Fominaya, two anonymous reviewers, Klaus Bruhn Jensen, Jørgen Delman, Rasmus Kleis Nielsen, and Susanne Bregnbæk.

Disclosure statement

No potential conflict of interest was reported by the author.

Funding

This work was supported by the Carlsberg Foundation [grant number CF14-0385]; S. C. Van Fonden.

References

Almanzar, N. P., Sullivan-Catlin, H., & Deane, G. (1998). Is the political personal? *Mobilization, 3*, 185–205.

Apple Daily. (2014, August 14). 全球第一 台人手机上网 [Taiwainess use of mobile phone ranks No. 1 in the world]. Retrieved from http://www.appledaily.com.tw/appledaily/article/headline/20140814/36021579/

Bakardjieva, M. (2009). Subactivism: Lifeworld and politics in the age of the Internet. *The Information Society, 25*, 91–104.

Benford, R. D., & Snow, D. A. (2000). Framing processes and social movements: An overview and assessment. *Annual Review of Sociology, 26*, 611–639.

Bennett, W. L., & Segerberg, A. (2012). The logic of connective action. *Information, Communication & Society, 15*, 739–768.

Bondes, M., & Schucher, G. (2014). Derailed emotions. *Information, Communication & Society, 17*, 45–65.

Brader, T. (2011). The political relevance of emotions: "reassessing" revisited. *Political Psychology, 32*, 337–346.

Buechler, S. M. (2000). *Social movements in advanced capitalism*. New York, NY: Oxford University Press.

China Internet Network Information Center. (1997). The first statistical report on internet development in China. Retrieved from http://www.moa.gov.cn/fwllm/xxhjs/hlwfzyj/201302/P020130201521094801183.pdf

China Internet Network Information Center. (2015). The 35th statistics report on internet development in China. Retrieved from https://www.cnnic.cn/hlwfzyj/hlwxzbg/201502/P020150203551802054676.pdf

Chiu, C., Lin, D., & Silverman, A. (2012). China's social-media boom. Retrieved from http://www.mckinseychina.com/2012/04/25/chinas-social-media-boom

de Certeau, M. (1984). *The practice of everyday life*. Berkeley: University of California Press.

Deleuze, G., & Guattari, F. (1987). *A thousand plateaus*. Minneapolis, MN: University of Minnesota Press.

Esarey, A., & Qiang, X. (2008). Political expression in the Chinese blogosphere: Below the radar. *Asian Survey, 48*, 752–772.

Esarey, A., & Xiao, Q. (2011). Digital communication and political change in China. *International Journal of Communication, 5*, 298–319.

Eveland, W. P., Morey, A. C., & Hutchens, M. J. (2011). Beyond deliberation: New directions for the study of informal political conversation from a communication perspective. *Journal of Communication, 61*, 1082–1103.

Eyerman, R., & Jamison, A. (1998). *Music and social movements*. Cambridge: Cambridge University Press.

Fewsmith, J. (2008). An "anger-venting" mass incident catches the attention of China's leadership. *China leadership monitor* (Vol. 26). Stanford, CA: Hoover Institition. Retrieved from http://www.hoover.org/sites/default/files/uploads/documents/CLM26JF.pdf

Flam, H., & King, D. (2005). Introduction. In H. Flam & D. King (Eds.), *Emotions and social movements* (pp. 1–18). New York, NY: Routledge.

Geertz, C. (1973). *The interpretation of cultures*. New York, NY: Basic Books.

Gouldner, A. W. (1960). The norm of reciprocity: A preliminary statement. *American Sociological Review, 25*, 161–178.

Huang, R., & Sun, X. (2014). Weibo network, information diffusion and implications for collective action in China. *Information, Communication & Society, 17*, 86–104.

Jiang, M. (2015). Chinese internet events (*Wang luo shi jian*). In A. Esarey & R. Kluver (Eds.), *The internet in China* (pp. 211–218). Great Barrington, MA: Berkshire Publishing.

Kahn, R., & Kellner, D. (2004). New media and internet activism. *New Media & Society, 6*, 87–95.

Kapferer, B. (2010). Introduction. *Social Analysis, 54*, 1–28.

Katsiaficas, G. (1997). *The subversion of politics*. Atlantic Highlands, NJ: Humanities Press.

Katz, E. (2009). Why sociology abandoned communication. *The American Sociologist, 40*, 167–174.

King, G., Pan, J., & Roberts, M. E. (2013). How censorship in China allows government criticism but silences collective expression. *American Political Science Review, 107*, 1–18.

Lance Bennett, W., Breunig, C., & Givens, T. (2008). Communication and political mobilization: Digital media and the organization of anti-Iraq war demonstrations in the US. *Political Communication, 25*, 269–289.

Laraña, E. (1994). *New social movements, from ideology to identity*. Philadelphia, PA: Temple University Press.

Larson, C. (2011). The people's Republic of Rumors. *Foreign Policy*. Retrieved from http://foreignpolicy.com/2011/07/08/the-peoples-republic-of-rumors/

Lim, M. (2014). Seeing spatially: People, networks and movements in digital and urban spaces. *International Development Planning Review, 36*, 51–72.

Liu, J. (2010). Mobile social network in a cultural context. In E. Canessa & M. Zennaro (Eds.), *M-Science* (pp. 211–240). Trieste: ICTP.

Liu, J. (2012). *Mobile phone rumors as "Weapons of the weak"*. Paper presented at the ICA's pre-conference "New media and citizenship in Asia", Phoenix.

Liu, J. (2013). Mobile communication, popular protests and citizenship in China. *Modern Asian Studies, 47*, 995–1018.
Liu, J. (2014a). Calling for strikes. *Georgetown Journal of International Affairs, XV*, 15–24.
Liu, J. (2014b). Mobile communication and relational mobilization in China. *Asiascape: Digital Asia, 1*, 14–38.
Liu, J. (2015a). Communicating beyond information. *Television & New Media, 16*, 503–520.
Liu, J. (2015b, August). *Digital media, cycle of contention, and sustainability of environmental activism*. Paper presented at the ECREA Political Communication Conference, Odense.
Lu, X., Li, P., & Chen, G. (2012). 社会蓝皮书 [Blue book of China's society]. Beijing: Social Science Academic Press.
Marwell, G., & Oliver, P. (1984). Collective action theory and social movements research. *Research in Social Movements, Conflict and Change, 7*, 1–27.
McAdam, D., & Rucht, D. (1993). The cross-national diffusion of movement ideas. *The ANNALS of the American Academy of Political and Social Science, 528*, 56–74.
McAdam, D., Tarrow, S. G., & Tilly, C. (2001). *Dynamics of contention*. Cambridge: Cambridge University Press.
Melucci, A. (1985). The symbolic challenge of contemporary movements. *Social Research, 52*, 789–816.
Melucci, A. (1989). *Nomads of the present*. Philadelphia, PA: Temple University Press.
Melucci, A. (1996). *Challenging codes*. Cambridge: Cambridge University Press.
Melucci, A., & Lyyra, T. (1998). Collective action, change, and democracy. In M. G. Giugni, D. McAdam, & C. Tilly (Eds.), *From contention to democracy* (pp. 203–228). Lanham, MD: Rowman & Littlefield.
Nielsen, R. K. (2011). Mundane internet tools, mobilizing practices, and the coproduction of citizenship in political campaigns. *New Media & Society, 13*, 755–771.
Nielsen, R. K. (2013). Mundane internet tools, the risk of exclusion, and reflexive movements-occupy wall street and political uses of digital networked technologies. *The Sociological Quarterly, 54*, 173–177.
OpenNet Initiative. (2005). Internet filtering in China in 2004–2005: A country study. Retrieved from: https://opennet.net/sites/opennet.net/files/ONI_China_Country_Study.pdf
Perry, E. J. (2007). Studying Chinese politics: Farewell to revolution?. *The China Journal, 57*, 1–22.
Qiu, J. L. (2009). *Working-class network society*. Cambridge, MA: The MIT Press.
Qiu, J. L., & Chan, J. M. (Eds.). (2011). 新媒介事件研究 [New media events research]. Beijing: Renmin University Press.
Reed, T. V. (2005). *The art of protest*. Minneapolis, Minn. Bristol: University of Minnesota Press.
Scheufele, D. A. (2000). Talk or conversation? *Journalism & Mass Communication Quarterly, 77*, 727–743.
Scott, J. C. (1985). *Weapons of the weak*. New Haven, CT: Yale University Press.
Scott, J. C. (1990). *Domination and the arts of resistance*. New Haven, CT: Yale University Press.
Shan, S. (2008, December 3). 公民社会的怪异表达 [Odd expressions in civil society]. *Chongqing Times*. Retrieved from http://www.chinaelections.org/NewsInfo.asp?NewsID=138915
Staggenborg, S., & Taylor, V. (2005). Whatever happened to the women's movement? *Mobilization, 10*, 37–52.
Sullivan, J., & Xie, L. (2009). Environmental activism, social networks and the internet. *The China Quarterly, 198*, 422–432.
Tai, Z. (2006). *The internet in China*. London: Routledge.
Tarrow, S. (2011). *Power in movement* (rev. & updated 3rd ed.). New York, NY: Cambridge University Press.
Thaxton, R. A. (1997). Everyday forms of resistance. In R. S. Powers, W. B. Vogele, C. Kruegler, & R. M. McCarth (Eds.), *Protest, power, and change* (pp. 173–175). London: Taylor & Francis.
Tilly, C. (1978). *From mobilization to revolution*. Reading: Addison-Wesley.
Tilly, C. (1995). *Popular contention in Great Britain, 1758–1834*. Cambridge, MA: Harvard University Press.
Tong, J., & Zuo, L. (2014). Weibo communication and government legitimacy in China. *Information, Communication & Society, 17*, 66–85.
Touraine, A. (1988). *Return of the actor, social theory in postindustrial society*. Minneapolis, MN: University of Minnesota Press.
Tufekci, Z., & Wilson, C. (2012). Social media and the decision to participate in political protest: Observations from Tahrir Square. *Journal of Communication, 62*, 363–379.
Wang, X. (2008, April 28). Upward mobility. *China Daily*, p. 2.
Williams, R. (1961). *The long revolution*. London: Hogarth Press.
Williams, R. (1977). *Marxism and literature* (Vol. 1). Oxford: Oxford University Press.
Wines, M. (2009, March 12). A dirty pun tweaks China's online censors. *New York Times*, p. A1.
Wu, F., & Wen, B. (2015). Nongovernmental organizations and environmental protests. In P. G. Harris & G. Lang (Eds.), *Routledge handbook of environment and society in Asia* (pp. 105–119). London: Routledge.
Xiao, Q. (2011a). The battle for the Chinese internet. *Journal of Democracy, 22*, 47–61.
Xiao, Q. (2011b). The rise of online public opinion and its political impact. In S. L. Shirk (Ed.), *Changing media, changing China* (pp. 202–224). New York, NY: Oxford University Press.
Xinhuanet. (2003). Internet in China. Retrieved from http://news.xinhuanet.com/ziliao/2003-01/22/content_702667.htm
Yang, G. (2005). Environmental NGOs and institutional dynamics in China. *The China Quarterly, 181*, 46–66.
Yang, G. (2009a). Online activism. *Journal of Democracy, 20*, 33–36.
Yang, G. (2009b). *The power of the internet in China*. New York, NY: Columbia University Press.

Yang, G. (2011). Technology and its contents: Issues in the study of the Chinese internet. *The Journal of Asian Studies, 70*, 1043–1050.
Yang, G. (2014a). Internet activism & the party-state in China. *Daedalus, 143*, 110–123.
Yang, G. (2014b). Political contestation in Chinese digital spaces: Deepening the critical inquiry. *China Information, 28*, 135–144.
Yang, G., & Jiang, M. (2015). The networked practice of online political satire in China: Between ritual and resistance. *International Communication Gazette, 77*, 215–231.
Yu, J. (2008). Emerging trends in violent riots. *China Security, 4*, 75–81.
Zeng, F. (2015). 环境抗争的扩散效应 [Diffusion effects of Chinese environmental contentions]. *Journal of Northwest Normal University, 52*, 110–115.
Zheng, Y. (2008). *Technological empowerment*. Stanford, CA: Stanford University Press.
Zheng, Y., & Wu, G. (2005). Information technology, public space, and collective action in China. *Comparative Political Studies, 38*, 507–536.
Zolberg, A. R. (1972). Moments of madness. *Politics & Society, 2*, 183–207.
Zuckerman, E. (2015). Cute cats to the rescue? Participatory media and political expression. In D. Allen, & J. S. Light (Eds.), *From voice to influence: Understanding citizenship in a digital age* (pp. 131–154). Chicago: University of Chicago Press.

The integrative power of online collective action networks beyond protest. Exploring social media use in the process of institutionalization

Elena Pavan

ABSTRACT

In this article, we aim at expanding the event-based and protest-centered perspective that is typically adopted to study the nexus between social media and movements. To this aim, we propose a network-based approach to explore the changing role that these tools play during the dynamic unfolding of movement processes and, more particularly, over the course of their institutionalization. In the first part, we read the added value of social media as a function of the 'integrative power' of the networks they foster – a unique and evolving form of sociotechnical power that springs from the virtuous encounter between social media networking potential and social resources. In the second part, we investigate this form of power by focusing directly on online networks' structure as well as on the type of communication and participation environments they host. We apply our proposed approach to the longitudinal exploration of the Twitter networks deployed in the period 2012–2014 during three annual editions of the transnational feminist campaign 'Take Back The Tech!' (TBTT). Results from our case study suggest that, over time, TBTT supporters do in fact make a differentiated use of social media affordances – progressively switching their communicative strategies to better sustain the campaign's efforts inside and outside institutional venues. Thus, the exploration of the TBTT case provides evidence of the usefulness of the proposed approach to reflect on the different modes in which social media can be exploited in different mobilization stages and political terrains.

An increasing number of studies that analyze social media adoption within contentious dynamics help us reach a more genuine understanding of how the diffusion and strategic use of these tools can affect the mobilization and organization of collective participation. However, so far, the research focus has been on social media usage during pivotal protests (e.g. riots, demonstrations, and/or occupations), which, although connected to broader political processes, often constitute rather short-term instances of contention. In this sense, we possess only a partial understanding of how social media use couples with the evolving nature of movement processes and with the heterogeneity of strategies collective actors can adopt to achieve their goals (Diani, 1992).

In this article, we expand the current event-based and protest-centered perspective by proposing a network approach to explore the changing role that social media can play during the dynamic unfolding of movement processes, particularly over the course of their institutionalization. Broadly speaking, movements' institutionalization consists of dynamics through which they 'traverse the official terrain of formal politics and engage with authoritative institutions such as the legislature, the judiciary, the state, and political parties to enhance their collective ability to achieve [their] goals' (Suh, 2011, p. 443). As it entails a 'conflictual cooperation' (Giugni & Passy, 1998, pp. 84–85) between different interests and strategies, institutionalization often takes the form of a long-term and multidimensional process (Bosi, 2016). Thus, in the course of this process, collective actors are required to adopt radically different strategies in comparison to when they 'stand outside and cast blame' on institutions (Ferree & McClurg Mueller, 2004, p. 591) often adjusting their forms, claims, and action repertoires to the rules and the procedures of the institutional sphere. While observers are split over the consequences of institutionalization, there is no specific reflection on how social media networking and communicative potentials intersect with it and thus mediate movements' chances of seizing increased political opportunities and resisting the 'co-optive and assimilative force of the state' (Bosi, 2016, p. 343).

In the first part of the article, we read the added value of social media for collective action dynamics as a function of the 'integrative power' of the networks they foster – a unique form of sociotechnical power that springs from the virtuous encounter between social media networking potential and human needs, desires for social change, and perceptions of technological affordances. Because of its sociotechnical nature, the integrative power of online networks can take different forms depending on how social media materiality intersects with the dynamic unfolding of movements and their changing strategies. In the second part, we investigate this form of power by focusing directly on online network structures as well as on the type of communication and participation environments they host. We argue that these two elements provide a useful entry point to capture the sociotechnical nature of online networks' integrative power and also to reflect on the different modes in which social media can be exploited in different mobilization stages (Della Porta & Mattoni, 2015) and political terrains (Suh, 2011).

We then apply our proposed approach to the exploration of Twitter networks deployed in the period 2012–2014 during three annual editions of the transnational feminist campaign 'Take Back The Tech!' (TBTT), which occurred in the context of its progressive institutionalization within the gender policy domain. After illustrating our case study and the results we derived from its exploration, we conclude by pulling the threads together and reflecting on the potentials and the limits of the proposed approach.

The integrative power of online collective action networks within and beyond protest

It is increasingly recognized that social media matter to collective action not simply by virtue of their pervasiveness but, rather, because they enable and actively intervene in shaping online networks that are intrinsic components of any current collective action system (Pavan, 2014). Movement studies have long insisted on the fact that networks provide the baseline infrastructure for mobilizing as well as for coordinating activists and organizations (see e.g. Melucci, 1996 but also Diani, 2003; Diani & Bison, 2004). Hence, social media relevance lays precisely in their capacity of boosting the inherent relational nature of collective action through the provision of a ubiquitous technical infrastructure that sustains the rapid construction of 'personal, multiuser, multitask and multithreaded communication networks' (Rainie & Wellman, 2012, p. 7) that expand and enrich the relational milieu grounding collective efforts.

In fact, some skeptical observers argue that online collective action networks are residual or even detrimental for collective efforts (see for example Diani, 2011; Morozov, 2009). Thus, the systematic exploration of digital spaces within and beyond the domain of politics has led to the identification of some typical structural features that distinguish online networks quite neatly from the interactional structures that are typically associated with social movement processes. First, online networks are sustained by ties that are more ephemeral than those laying underneath 'offline' movement networks (Barassi, 2015). In addition, online networks tend to be very sparse and locally clustered (Mislove, Marcon, Gummadi, Druschel, & Bhattacharjee, 2007) as a consequence of their large scale and also of the tendency to connect with those already connected to neighbors (González-Bailón, Borge-Holthoefer, & Moreno, 2013). Moreover, while pre-digital movements networks were far from being extraneous to the presence of leaders and prominent actors (Diani, 2003; Melucci, 1996), online structures are often shaped by severe structural asymmetries, as they are held together by few 'disproportionally connected nodes [that] keep the network small in terms of path length or average distance between any two nodes' (González-Bailón et al., 2013, p. 954).

However, the actual investigation of online collective action networks is providing increasing evidence of the multifaceted role they can play in spite of their sparseness, looseness, and centralization. This includes: the emergence of new mechanisms for the identification of leaders and frames formation (Tremayne, 2014); the redefinition of power dynamics (Bennett & Segerberg, 2014); the modification of individual recruitment and claims diffusion mechanisms (González-Bailón, Borge-Holthoefer, Rivero, & Moreno, 2011; González-Bailón et al., 2013); the fluid evolution of roles played by single activists and organizations (Varol, Ferrara, Ogan, Menczer, & Flammini, 2014); and the organization of 'offline' protest events (Howard & Hussain, 2013).

In all their heterogeneity, these studies have clarified that the asset to collective dynamics is not the mere presence of vast and easily accessible digital networks. In fact, it is the conscious and strategic effort made by social actors to shape and use these networks as spaces for political participation, as strategic communication venues to connect and remix heterogeneous competences, experiences, and skills and, in this way, to broaden and accelerate the formation of new collective meanings, frames, and action strategies to challenge the status quo. As Bennett and Segerberg eloquently put it, 'the point of the analyses is not Twitter or any type of technology as such, but what people do with what the technology 'affords' them and the structure this can create' (2013, p. 9). Indeed, social media materiality (that is, the set of features and functions that are available to all users) is not conductive, per se, of collective action networks wherein actors 'collaborate, mutually support their respective initiatives, and blend them in broader agendas' (Diani, 2015, p. 3). Only when social actors approach social media materiality with the explicit intention of enacting 'shared interests and programs' (Tilly & Tarrow, 2007, p. 5) do online networks become loci of collective action.

Ultimately, it is the virtuous encounter between social media materiality and social actors' desire for change that masters these tools' networking potential and turns it an actual 'integrative power', i.e. the unique capacity of converting loose, sparse, clustered, and centralized online networks into digital systems of transversal alliances binding a multiplicity of heterogeneous actors in spite of their differences and under shared and ever-evolving frames. While traditionally studied 'civic networks' are also characterized by powerful integrative dynamics that allow them to 'act on behalf of collective and public interests' (Baldassarri & Diani, 2007, pp. 735–736), the integrative power of online collective action networks is neither purely technological nor purely social. Because it springs from a reciprocal leveraging of social media materiality and social resources, it is a sociotechnical form of power whose forms vary depending on technological developments and also, and perhaps to a larger extent, on how users perceive social media materiality and connect it to their projects. To be sure, different users perceive the same set of features and functions enabled by a certain technology as 'affording distinct possibilities for action' depending on their motivations, goals, expectations, and levels of competence (Leonardi, 2012, p. 37). Thus, different perceptions of affordances, at one point in time or across time, translate into different modes of appropriating and exploiting social media.

However, online networks have been studied so far mainly with reference to pivotal protest and mobilization episodes – such as the massive demonstrations along Tunis streets and in Tahrir square, the Spanish and the American encampments in 2011, and those in Gezi Park in 2013. This focus on pivotal protest events has somewhat bounded our understanding of how online collective action networks exert their integrative power to specific, time-framed episodes of contention. In turn, this affects our capacity to understand the mutable role that social media can play in the long run 'according to the state of the mobilization, the activities sustaining protest as well as the social actors who [are] using them' (Della Porta & Mattoni, 2015, p. 41). In fact, the actual investigation of online collective action networks is often carried out longitudinally (e.g. González-Bailón et al., 2013; Varol et al.,

2014). However, only seldom have researchers considered the different 'temporalities' of movements (Mattoni & Treré, 2014) so to fully grasp the long-term implications of the sociotechnical nature of online networks' integrative power (for an exception focused on users, see Bastos & Mercea, 2016). Furthermore, the overall orientation to the study of social media within 'unusual' patterns of political behavior (Diani, 1992, p. 12) has left behind a systematic reflection on how these tools may become an asset to collective action dynamics above and beyond the adoption of public protests and, more particularly, during institutionalization processes, when movements engage in sustained relationships of 'conflictual cooperation' with institutional actors (Giugni & Passy, 1998, pp. 84–85).

This theoretical blind spot stems, on the one hand, from a general tendency to conceive the recourse to protest repertoires as a defining feature of social movements, although it has long been argued that it is not necessarily the case, especially within movements oriented to personal and cultural change (Diani, 1992, p. 12). On the other hand, this has to do also with the contested status of institutionalization processes in relation to social movement strategies. A first strand of reflection, mainly connected with resource mobilization and political process theories, understands institutionalization as an inevitable step in movements' evolution, necessarily connected with negative transformations of collective action forms and contents (for a review, see Morgan, 2007). The process of institutionalization is thus seen as a co-optation within formal settings and procedures, leading to de-radicalization of claims and routinization of political strategies (Morgan, 2007, p. 281) as well as to an irreparable fracture between 'insiders', adjusting to constraints, and 'outsiders', resisting co-optation and reacting by further radicalizing (Bosi, 2016, p. 342). Equally negatively viewed are processes of professionalization and bureaucratization, as they imply dispersal of the inherent horizontality and participatory features of movements, in favor of a restricted niche of interest groups and protest professionals (Rucht, 1996). Underneath all of these transformations are the challenges that derive from movements' inclusion in institutional arenas: the necessity to adhere and, therefore, adapt to organizational procedures crystallized within the institutions; the urgency of adopting internal labor and roles division to facilitate immediate and efficient responses to political stimuli; and the increased scrutiny from institutional actors to which movements are exposed (Morgan, 2007).

More recently, approaching institutionalization from the point of view of movement outcomes, some observers have depicted institutionalization as resulting from 'joint strategic choices by both the movement and the state' (Suh, 2011, p. 443). Through their inclusion within institutional settings, collective actors are endowed with different possibilities to produce change: from 'incorporating' their claims in the institutional agenda, to 'transforming' the existing social and political system by altering the distribution of power within society, to 'democratizing' society by modifying the 'mutual rights and obligations between the state and their citizens' (Giugni, 1998, p. xii). Such radical transformations of movements' forms and claims may not simply be passively experienced, but intentionally pursued and they can prove highly beneficial. Examples include the electoral success of the Swedish neo-nazi movement (Peterson, 2016) or women's movements organizations in the US, which succeeded in creating 'concrete policy changes' and also 'altered the political opportunity structure' available to the movement itself (Banaszak, 2010, p. 4, see also Ferree & McClurg Mueller, 2004). Albeit connected, this second vision of institutionalization (depending on a more proactive view of movements as 'reflexive actors' that create new opportunities; Jiménez, 2007, p. 149) does not underestimate the challenges that arise from playing in the terrain of formal politics. Whether the effects of voluntary inclusion within official arenas are more or less beneficial depends on both movements and institutions (Suh, 2011, p. 446). In this sense, institutionalization is a nonlinear and multidimensional process (Bosi, 2016), played out within complex and long-term processes of coalition building between collective and institutional actors (Brewster Stearns & Almeida, 2004), and open to a variety of empirical realizations and outcomes (Katzenstein, 1998).

In a context in which observers continue to split over the consequences of movements' inclusion within institutions, and the nexus between social media and collective participation is approached mainly through an event-based and protest-centered perspective, some relevant aspects of the integrative power of online collective action networks remain largely unaddressed. Bringing together these two sets of concerns, the rest of this article addresses the following questions:

- How is the sociotechnical integrative power of online collective action networks played out it in the long run over the dynamic unfolding of movements and their strategies?
- Does the shape of online collective action networks change depending on levels of movements' inclusion within institutional arenas? Do they host different types of communication and participation processes?
- Ultimately, what forms does the integrative power of online collective action networks take when movements institutionalize?

Investigating integrative power

From an empirical perspective, the unique sociotechnical nature of online networks' integrative power requires us to look at systems of digital interactions in a way that allows us to capture simultaneously its material and social aspects.

The material aspects of integrative power concern the unprecedented technology-enabled possibility to construct online networks and, therefore, can be addressed by looking at what types of networks emerge from social media usage. In general, network approaches to movements purport that looking at network structures, in particular focusing on their segmentation and centralization, is crucial to distinguishing between different types of mobilization (Diani, 2003, p. 306). When it comes to online collective action, looking at the structure of networks becomes even more important for two reasons. First, the way in which an online network is structured affects its potential to diffuse claims and individually generated contents (González-Bailón et al., 2013), a key factor to the integration of different actors within collective endeavors. Second, it is crucial to examine whether the inherent networking potential of social media invariably translates into sparse, loose, and centralized structures that simply 'link' individuals and organizations or if, as Bennett and Segerberg suggest comparing different 'power signatures' (2013, 2014), online structures can be molded to promote the integration of different actors depending on the type of mobilization at stake.

To capture instead the social aspects of integrative power, which have to do with how users exploit social media features and affordances, the focus should shift from the structural features of online networks to the type of communication and participation processes they host. One first aspect in this regard is how users choose to exploit social media affordances to engage with others. This element can be addressed by looking specifically at the 'content' of online network ties, which, ultimately, allows us to grasp how online integration practically occurs. On a platform like Twitter, for example, a prominent use of mentions and replies would suggest a greater tendency toward interaction and dialog between users; alternatively, use of tweets containing only hashtags and no handles would point to an informational use of the platform to contribute contents to the discussion; while, finally, a predominance of retweets would suggest a trend toward retransmitting contents produced by others (Barash & Golder, 2011). It is also relevant to investigate with whom users decide to engage, as this element can give us an indication on whether the online integration processes is guided by 'potential leaders' (Diani, 2003, p. 306) as well as on who these leaders may be. Indeed, as shown by Bennett and Segerberg (2013, 2014), it makes a great deal of political difference if online networks are dominated by formal organizations (like Wikipedia and Google during the protest against the intellectual property law in the US Congress) or rather assume the form of 'networks of networks' where no clear leader can be identified (as in the case of Occupy Wall Street).

Looking at network structures at a single point in time may sketch a portrait of collective dynamics that is rather general in comparison to that conveyed by the study 'information cascades', 'diffusion processes' or 'roles evolution' (see e.g. Bastos & Mercea, 2016; González-Bailón et al., 2013; Varol et al., 2014). But by comparing different points in time, this integrative power approach helps us identify broader long-term trends that, in turn, may open the way for more detailed analysis of single temporalities. Moreover, thinking in terms of network structures, ties, and centralities can aid identification of trends both within and beyond public protest dynamics. When it comes to institutionalization processes in particular, looking at if and how online network structures change would help us explore disaggregating effects (e.g. Bosi, 2016). By starting from the macro-structural features of networks, it is possible to explore whether the progressive inclusion of movements within institutional settings generates a 'conversational fracture' within the movement or, conversely, if the integrative power of online collective action networks is used to resist and counteract this trend by keeping 'insiders' and 'outsider' together. Also, examining the ways that relational contents generate online network structures can help us see the extent to which institutionalization processes foster a change of communication strategies adopted by the movement, which may be an online counterpart to the often emphasized change in offline action repertoires (e.g. Morgan, 2007). Finally, reflecting on how actors' centrality in the network may vary provides a starting point to exploring whether offline professionalization is mirrored in the online space (e.g. Rucht, 1996) or if, conversely, online conversations remain multipolar and distributed.

Case study, data, and methods

In the digital age, beside persistent challenges to gender equality, there is also a pressing need to recognize and fight old and new gender-based abuses perpetrated dynamically across the online/offline boundary (UNGA, 2006, p. 155). In response to this situation, the Association for Progressive Communications, with its Women's Right Programme (APC WRP), launched in 2006 the campaign TBTT to reclaim ICTs to end all forms of gender-based violence. TBTT runs officially every year from 25 November to 10 December (the so-called '16 days of activism against gender-based violence' [VAW]). Over these 16 days, TBTT promotes a set of 'daily activities' to foster genuinely gender-aware and gender-empowering uses of ICTs.[1] As part of these activities, the campaign includes (since 2011) a yearly Tweetathon with the hashtag #takebackthetech, which has rapidly become one of its most prominent tools to mobilize support, spread awareness, and publicize its actions.

Outside the '16 days' time frame, the campaign pursues its aims by engaging systematically with other stakeholders in the gender domain. Coalitions and collaborations are built first of all with other civil society organizations all over the globe, like Women's Net in South Africa and the transnational network of JASS – Just Associates (JASS, 2016; Women's Net's, 2016). However, TBTT's representatives are also very active in reaching out to institutional actors by participating in relevant supranational political processes. Examples in this regard are TBTT's involvement in the United Nations Internet Governance Forum (IGF), the main multi-stakeholder venue to discuss how the Internet should be managed and developed, and where the campaign lobbies governments and the private sector to take an active stand in securing a safe and gender-aware online space; also within the Commission on the Status of Women (CSW), the main global intergovernmental body aimed at promoting gender equality and the empowerment of women, where TBTT representatives operate to prioritize the nexus between ICTs and VAW as a critical issue for women's rights.

The regularity with which TBTT is run, together with the centrality occupied by the online space of action within its action repertoire and its effort to engage with both institutional and non-institutional actors, makes this campaign a suitable case study to begin exploring how the integrative power of online collective action networks is exerted over time vis-à-vis the dynamic unfolding of movements' strategies. The TBTT campaign has paralleled its constant use of social media as tools for participation with a fluid interplay with civil society organizations and institutions. This was the case also for the period 2012–2014, during which, for the purposes of this study, three different editions of the TBTT Tweetathon were mapped. In 2012, TBTT's representatives participated in the annual meeting of the IGF. In that same year, the other main commitment of the campaign consisted in realizing a series of workshops and panels during the 12th Association for Women's Rights in Development (AWID) Forum, one of the largest civil society events in the gender domain where women's and feminist movements meet among themselves and with other collective initiatives in the fields of human rights, environment, and social justice (AWID, 2016). In 2013, participation in the IGF was accompanied by a direct involvement of TBTT in the 57th session of the CSW, and in 2014, TBTT remained active both within the IGF and the CSW contexts, lobbying governments to maintain attention on ICTs and on women's access to them.

While the AWID Forum is a very relevant event in the gender domain, it is non-institutional. The IGF is an official venue, but with no mandate to produce binging policy outcomes, with no particular commitment to gender-related issues, and it is characterized by rather loose criteria for participation (IGF, 2016). Conversely, the CSW is a fully intergovernmental body specialized on gender-related issues, with rather restricted access criteria, formalized participation procedures, and producing highly influential outcomes for gender politics. Hence, although in the period 2012–2014, the campaign never operated within a purely informal political terrain, its digital activities over the '16 days of activism', the Tweetathon above all, have been carried out in the context of a progressive institutionalization strategy that unfolded along three main stages: *mild institutionalization*, in 2012, with TBTT working across the boundary between institutional and non-institutional spheres; *inclusion*, in 2013, with TBTT concentrating mainly on institutional venues and, in particular, on CSW; and *consolidation*, in 2014, with TBTT replicating the pattern of the previous year and having to find ways to capitalize the effects of their inclusion by stabilizing their relationship with institutional actors.

Although we identify these three stages as distinct for analytical purposes, TBTT institutionalization path has been neither linear nor incremental. Most notably, even if the campaign did not actively participate in the CSW sessions, it nonetheless took into systematic consideration institutional political dynamics in the gender domain (especially at the supranational level). In the same way, when TBTT oriented its strategy toward a neater engagement within the institutional sphere, it never stopped collaborating with other civil society actors. Moreover, after entering the CSW arena, TBTT faced different working conditions and challenges. In 2013, during the 'inclusion' phase, the campaign worked side by side with governments to address the priority theme 'Elimination and prevention of all forms of violence against women and girls', a core issue for TBTT. Under that banner, a broad coalition between institutions and civil society actors, among which TBTT and its parent organization APC, managed to achieve a final document that also included an explicit reference to the nexus between VAW and ICTs (CSW, 2013, p. 13). The overall working environment of the following CSW session, instead, appeared rather different. As the priority theme shifted to the 'Challenges and achievements in the implementation of the Millennium Development Goals for women and girls', the campaign's claim of the relevance of women's access to ICTs was in fact included into the agreed conclusions. However, negotiations unfolded in a rather conflictual way, splitting governments and civil society sectors among and within themselves over the connection between women's and human rights. In this context, TBTT activists described their participation to the 58th CSW session as an attempt to resist a 'pushback' in the overall discussion, to 'defend' previous achievements, without much progression in the advancement of women's rights (GenderIt, 2014).

Mapping the Take Back the Tech! Tweetathon

For the purposes of this exploratory study, we mapped three different editions of the annual TBTT Tweetathon – a prominent part of the campaign activities during its official period of deployment (25 November–10 December). To trace the three TBTT online networks, we used the NodeXL Network Server, an affiliate software to NodeXL, a free and open network visualization and analysis package for Excel (Smith et al., 2010).[2] The NodeXL Network Server allows scheduling a 'Twitter Search', an automated crawl of tweets containing a specific keyword. For every search it performs, the software gathers tweets and accounts containing the queried keyword and produces a network designed around tweets' authors and users they mention, retweet, or reply to. We programmed the NodeXL Network Server to search for the keyword *takebakthetech* on Twitter every 15 min between 25 November and 10 December every year from 2012 to 2014. By combining subsequent files, we obtained three distinct relational data-sets (one for every Tweetathon edition we monitored) that represent in the form of a network the overall direct communication flow generated around the TBTT campaign.

Thus, online networks traced in this way are structured by different types of ties, depending on the interactions established by users on Twitter by making use of the platform's main options for connecting:

- Mentions: when user A tweets a message that includes the keyword *takebackthetech* and thus explicitly refers to one or more other users, her tweet is translated into a tie going from user A to each and every user she mentions in her message. For example, if @GendetITorg tweets 'Take Back The Tech! Campaign @SayNO_UNiTE – http://t.co/MGyezctg #VAW #16 days #takeback-thetech #fem2 #p2', this mention translates into a tie going from GenderITorg to SayNO_UNiTE;
- Retweets: when user A retransmits a tweet authored by user B and that includes the keyword *takebackthetech*, her tweet translates into a tie going from user A to B. For example, if @ GenderITorg retransmits a tweet originally authored by @takebackthetech with 'RT @takeback-thetech: Wondering how to get the brilliant banners for the #takebackthetech campaign on how violence silences? Right here: htt …', her action translates into a tie going from GenderITorg to takebackthetech;
- Replies to: when user A answers directly to a message sent by user B and thus uses the keyword *take-backthetech*, her tweet translates into a tie going from user A to B. For example, if @GenderITorg replies directly to a tweet sent by @shahanasiddiqui with '@shahanasiddiqui introduces Praggya, the govt portal for violence against women http://t.co/9yZpjUQp #TakeBackTheTech #digital-world12', her reply translates into a tie from GenderITorg to shahanasiddiqui;
- Tweets: when user A tweets some content that includes the keyword *takebackthetech* yet without mentioning explicitly or replying to other users, her tweet translates into a 'self-loop', i.e. a tie going from user A to user A. For example, if @GenderITorg tweets 'Women can defeat VAW by reclaiming technology – so #takebackthetech!', her tweet translates into a tie going from GenderITorg to GenderITorg.

We chose not to trace ties among users based on the following/followed relationship. Indeed, this specific relationship on Twitter represents only a 'potential' communicative interaction as users receive but do not necessarily process the tweets authored by handles they follow. Conversely, mentions, replies, retweets, and tweets point to actual 'communicative acts': the first three correspond to different types of direct interactions between users; the latter to information spreading acts primarily aimed at putting contents in circulation.

Results

Material aspects of integrative power

As we proposed above, the material aspects of the integrative power of online collective action networks can be captured looking at the structure of exchanges that are put in place by users. Two dimensions have been suggested as particularly relevant in this regard: first, network segmentation, which relates to the extent to which communication and exchanges among users flow more or less easily; and, second, network centralization, which points to the extent to which networks tend to revolve around a handful of prominent actors, thus affecting the way in which a movement operates (Diani, 2003, p. 306).

Traditionally, segmentation is addressed starting from nodes reachability, which reflects the distance that separates members of a network (Diani, 2003, p. 306). However, as outlined above, distance between nodes within online networks is typically low as a consequence of the presence of few hyper-connected nodes. For this reason, it is important to look at network segmentation from different angles. In particular, here we look also at the percentage of nodes with no ties to the rest of the network and at what we call 'network inclusivity', which is the percentage of nodes that is included in the network's main component (i.e. the larger subset of nodes that are connected, hence reachable,

Table 1. Overall network features of TBTT online Tweetathon network (2012–2014).

	Year and phase		
	2012	2013	2014
Network feature	Mild institutionalization	Inclusion	Consolidation
N (number of nodes)	858	1175	994
M (number of arcs)	3663	5270	2970
Overall density	0.0022	0.0020	0.0019
Average geodesic distance	300	307	29
Isolates	5.0%	2.4%	4.2%
Inclusivity of the principal component	91.7%	96.9%	93.8%
K (mean degree)	0.40	0.37	0.35
K_{MAX} (max degree)	43.99	41.14	53.17
In-degree centralization	3646%	3305%	4800%

Note: K and K_{MAX} values normalized.

either directly or indirectly, Wasserman & Faust, 1994, p. 109). While the former measure provides an indication on the missed opportunities for integration (an isolated node does not tweet to or provoke the reaction of any other user), the latter points to the extent to which these opportunities are actually seized.

As Table 1 shows, over time, the average distance between nodes remains constant and rather low, as hundreds of participants stay only 'three steps away' one from the other. Furthermore, as shown by density values (i.e. the proportion of ties that are activates on the total number of possible ties), the Tweetathon network is invariantly sparse with minimal, non-significant variations over time. Although sparse, the network seems to be characterized by low levels of segmentation – but this characteristic does not relate clearly to the progressive institutionalization of TBTT in the gender domain. Indeed, already during the phase we labeled 'mild institutionalization' (when TBTT distributes its efforts between the construction of collaborations with other relevant civil society actors during the AWID Forum and its lobbying activity within the IGF), the online network shows only 5% of isolates and around 90% of campaigners linked in the network's main component. As the campaign proceeds toward its 'inclusion' within institutions in the gender domain in 2013, maintaining its effort in the IGF but engaging also in the CSW and thus succeeding to affect its final recommendation, isolates halve and the Tweetathon network becomes even more inclusive, as 97% of campaigners are involved in the principal component. Finally, while TBTT institutionalization 'consolidates' in 2014 and the campaign faces a more difficult phase of negotiation over women's rights, fragmentation slightly rises, although remaining somehow lower than in 2014.

Besides remaining generally 'nonsegmented' (Diani, 2003, p. 310), the Tweetathon network remains also rather centralized. This feature is typically grasped by looking at the disproportion between the highest and the average number of ties in which nodes of the network are involved, which are measured, respectively, through maximum and mean degree (Wasserman & Faust, 1994, p. 173). In fact, the high centralization of the network is not surprising, if we consider that the TBTT Tweetathon is part of a planned campaign effort (see Bennett & Segerberg, 2013, 2014). Thus, across the whole period examined and regardless of the stage along the process of institutionalization, the most prominent position is held by the Twitter official account of the campaign (@takebackthetech), which steadily guides and fuels the process of online integration. Conversely, other campaigners engage on average only in few local interactions. In this sense, they maintain a low, and yet constant, 'level of investment in the building of the network as a whole'[3] (Diani, 2003, p. 310) while renewing their commitment to the collective effort by engaging mainly with the campaign handle.

Nonetheless, a closer look at in-degree centralization indexes suggests that, as the institutionalization process unfolds, the campaign handle is not the sole point of reference that campaigners share. In-degree centralization captures the extent to which network ties tend to flow toward a handful of prominent actors (Wasserman & Faust, 1994, p. 176). As values in Table 1 show, while every edition of the Tweetathon remains highly centralized around the TBTT's handle, after TBTT 'inclusion' in

Table 2. Average daily relevance of tweets, mentions, replies to, and retweets in 2012–2014.

	Average daily relevance 2012	Average daily relevance 2013	Average daily relevance 2014	*t*	*t*	*t*
				2012–2014	2012–2013	2013–2014
Tweet	22.92	17.00	11.94	5.360***	2.779**	2.882**
Mentions	19.27	17.86	14.21	2.493*	0.681	2.341*
Replies to	3.29	3.77	3.29	.005	−.641	.809
Retweet	55.14	61.36	68.47	−4.295***	−2.454*	−2.372*

*$p < .05$.
**$p < .01$.
***$p < .001$.

Table 3. Categories of handles and their aggregate centralities over time.

	2012		2013		2014	
	Mild institutionalization		Inclusion		Consolidation	
Handles' categories	Count	Mean in-degree	Count	Mean in-degree	Count	Mean in-degree
Organization	5	11.76	9	8.53	10	8.02
Activist	5	4.04	7	1.85	–	–
Journalist	3	3.23	5	3.88	1	4.03
Blogger	6	2.72	2	1.45	–	–
Institution	1	4.00	3	6.01	4	8.66
Individual supporter	3	2.25	3	1.59	–	–
New media organization	–	–	1	2.9	–	–
Civil society online platform	–	–	2	2.04	–	–
Researcher	–	–	1	1.618	–	–
Mean in-degre	0.220		0.201		0.188	
S.D.	1.421		1.215		1.721	
Core size	23		33		15	

Note: In-degree values normalized.

the institutional sphere, in-degree centralization diminishes, suggesting that users direct their ties toward a greater variety of actors and, hence, that the campaigning efforts become more horizontal and participatory. Conversely, when TBTT institutionalization consolidates in 2014, the Tweetathon network reaches its centralization peak and the TBTT handle becomes more prominent than ever.[4] Perhaps as a consequence of the difficult phase of negotiation, campaigners seem to reinforce their identification with the campaign, addressing it more systematically, favoring its leadership function, and thus supporting its role of 'insider'.

Social aspects of integrative power

One first dimension of the social aspects of online networks' integrative power, we argued, relates to how users decide to engage with others by choosing between different networking affordances and thus imbuing the network with different relational contents. As a way to explore this dimension, we compare the 'average daily relevance' of the different networking affordances offered by Twitter – i.e. tweets, mentions, replies to, and retweets.[5] Higher daily relevance rates would suggest that some modes of using social media prevail over others and thus a different way to integrate within the online collective effort.

Table 2 illustrates variations of the average daily relevance of tweets, mentions, replies to, and retweets. As the table shows, direct replies to other users always constitute a residual form of interaction, as they account on average only between 3 and 4% of total ties in the network. A more defined pattern seems to emerge from results referred to the other three types of relations. The more the campaign proceeds toward a fuller institutionalization, the less tweets become relevant (their average relevance halves during the observation period) relative to other uses of the platform. In this sense, the strategic contribution and circulation of contents become over time less important than the construction of interactions among users. However, as the process of TBTT institutionalization unfolds, direct interactions among users via mention are substituted by retweets. Thus, increasing levels of institutionalization seem to favor the establishment of instrumental ties that, instead of generating new inputs and contributions, serve the purpose of retransmitting the contents authored by 'insiders' – in particular those of the campaign handle. Particularly in 2014, when TBTT decides to strengthen its engagement within a formal terrain of negotiation, retweets account on average for 68% of overall ties established everyday among campaigners.

Examining who are the actors that campaigners decide to engage with provides a necessary addition to see how modes of pursuing integration vary. Table 3 summarizes the results of the study of nodes' in-degree (i.e. the number of mentions, replies, and tweets they receive), which is a good proxy to determine actors' prominence in relational contexts (Wasserman & Faust, 1994, p. 174). For each Tweetathon edition, we first identified most central nodes and, subsequently, classified them into different groups.[6] Looking at the number of most central nodes and at the average in-degree of each group, we then explored levels of inclusiveness and heterogeneity of this 'network core'.

Our results suggest the presence of significant but nonlinear changes. As TBTT progresses from a 'mild institutionalization' to the stage of 'inclusion', the Tweetathon network core enlarges and ends up including, alongside the official campaign handle, a greater variety of actors. This, in turn, indicates that campaigners distribute their attention more widely, interacting with a greater number of activists, journalists, and also civil society online platforms and new media organizations. Moreover, during the 'inclusion' phase, institutional accounts become more central (in particular, those of UN Women, the United Nations agency for gender issues, and of Say NO UNITE, the UN Secretary-General's promoted campaign against VAW). This element suggests the progressive recognition and, ultimately, acceptance of the relevance of institutional actors for achieving the campaign's goals. Sharply in contrast with this situation, which recalls a 'collective effervescence' moment (Diani, 1992), the consolidation of TBTT institutionalization process leads to a marked resizing and homogenization of the network core, which in 2014 is composed almost exclusively of formal organizations and by the institutional actors that have become its partners in the policy arena.

Discussion and conclusions

Combined together, the longitudinal explorations of the structures as well as of the communication dynamics enclosed in the TBTT Tweetathon networks convey a more nuanced portrait of how social media have been exploited vis-à-vis the different strategies adopted by TBTT in the mutating conditions in which it operated. Over time, social media use during the Tweetathon invariantly results in the creation of non-segmented, centralized networks. Indeed, at every point in time, the online network approaches a 'star' (Diani, 2003), in which integration occurs mainly by engaging with the official account of the initiative. While this pattern distinguishes this type of collective effort from the more horizontal and often disconnected 'networks of networks' that characterizes spontaneous protests like Occupy! (see Bennett & Segerberg, 2013), it is typical of more structured participatory efforts – whether these are pursued online, as in the case of the Robin Hood Tax campaign examined by Bennett and Segerberg, or offline, as Diani (2003) notes with respect to the environmental movement in Italy and the UK and the women's movement in Canada. In this sense, TBTT supporters exploit social media affordances to renew and reinforce their engagement with the campaign, sustaining its efforts outside and inside institutional venues, and creating under all conditions but, in particular when the level of conflict increases, a digital network of support and legitimization.

However, the modes in which this 'structural support' is translated into practice change over time, thus impacting levels of verticality and, most notably, the ways in which integration around the campaign handle occurs. In 2012, when TBTT operates mainly outside the crucial venue of the CSW, social media are used to engage with the campaign and other civil society actors as well as to fuel the discussion with new content through a mixed use of Twitter's networking affordances. As the campaign institutionalization process unfolds, and the collaboration with governments bears some fruit in 2013, the vertical structure of conversation is molded to expand its integrative power. In this phase, campaigners exploit social media to directly interact with and mobilize other users, privileging the construction of interpersonal and inter-organizational alliances via mentions and retweets to consolidate and expand the collective dimension of the campaign. Thus, in this phase, institutional actors become increasingly central and their contribution to the achievement of TBTT's goals is acknowledged and, ultimately, accepted. Finally, over the 'consolidation' phase, while the institutionalization process becomes more challenging and multi-actor collaboration assumes a more conflictual connotation, the online network simplifies. While it remains non-segmented, it becomes even more centralized around a core formed almost exclusively of civil society organizations connected to the campaign and central institutions in the gender domain, and is sustained mainly by actions of content broadcasting. To some extent, this trend seems to reproduce processes of 'de-radicalization' and 'professionalization' feared by negative readings of institutionalization. In fact, the change of communication strategy toward less interactional modes of networking as well as the narrowing and the homogenization of the online network core are not passively suffered but purposely enacted in order to amplify the voice of the campaign and to solicit institutional actors to maintain an active and constructive role in relation to the defense of women's rights.

This article has brought an explicitly sociotechnical perspective to bear on the social media practices of social movements through the concept of 'integrative power'. The empirical study is exploratory and therefore, necessarily somewhat partial. Further research could extend this kind of analysis by looking also at contents that flow along network ties in order to examine how movements' claims modify over time and in particular over institutionalization phases (Morgan, 2007; Peterson, 2016). In the same way, an even more nuanced understanding of the social side of the 'integrative power' can spur from considering how users creatively appropriate social media affordances, for example: adopting a 'via' marker instead of the conventional retweet procedure (Meraz & Papacharissi, 2013). However, taken together and compared across time, network structures, 'conventional' relational contents, and actors' centralities seem to provide a useful entry point to assess more genuinely the meaning of social media participatory practices in conjunction with the different 'temporalities' of movements as well as with the fluid evolution of movement strategic choices, which, within and across single temporalities, entwine with how social media are exploited and can become an asset to collective endeavors.

Ultimately, by delineating and empirically illustrating the integrative power of online collective action networks at work, we have demonstrated the importance of two elements. Firstly, the sociotechnical tradition directs us to consider both material and social aspects of technologically mediated communication practices. While this article is focused on Twitter, any form of networked communication structure may be amenable to this style of analysis. Secondly, we have stressed the way in which integrative power unfolds over time. In this case, it has been possible to connect the ways in which integrative power is practiced to long-observed processes of institutionalization in the domain of global civil society.

Notes

1. An archive on daily actions is available on the campaign website http://www.takebackthetech.net.
2. The software is available in a free version at https://nodexl.codeplex.com/. Recently, the NodeXL Network Server has been substituted by the NodeXL Graph Server importer, see https://graphserverimporter.codeplex.com/.
3. We obtain the same results also by excluding the campaign handle from the network.
4. Over the 'consolidation' stage, the TBTT account reaches a centrality of 479, whereas the mean value is set at 2.
5. We computed this variable as the mean of the daily percentage of ties with a specific content on the total number of ties for every campaign day.
6. Most central nodes are defined as those showing an in-degree score higher than the sum between the mean in-degree score and one standard deviation. Nodes were classified manually starting from information available on their websites or on their Twitter profile.

Acknowledgments

The author would like to thank the editors and anonymous reviewers at Social Movement Studies for their extremely insightful comments on previous drafts of this article. A special thanks goes to Lorenzo Bosi for his precious advices.

Disclosure statement

No potential conflict of interest was reported by the author.

ORCID

Elena Pavan http://orcid.org/0000-0001-8693-5998

References

Association for Women's Rights in Development. (2016). AWID – women's right. Retrieved November 2016, from https://www.awid.org/

Baldassarri, D., & Diani, M. (2007). The integrative power of civic networks. *American Journal of Sociology, 113*, 735–780.

Banaszak, L. A. (2010). *The women's movement inside and outside the state*. New York, NY: Cambridge University Press.

Barash, V., & Golder, S. (2011). Twitter. Conversation, entertainment, and information, all in one network!. In D. L. Hansen, B. Shneiderman, & M. A. Smith (Eds.), *Analyzing social media network with NodeXL* (pp. 143–164). Burlington, MA: Elsevier.

Barassi, V. (2015). Social media, immediacy and the time for democracy: Critical reflections on social media as 'temporalising practices'. In L. Dencik & O. Leistert (Eds.), *Critical perspectives on social media and protest between control and emancipation* (pp. 73–88). Lanham, MD: Rowman and Littlefield.

Bastos, M., & Mercea, D. (2016). Serial activists: Political Twitter beyond influentials and the twittetatiat. *New Media and Society, 18*, 2359–2378.

Bennett, L. W., & Segerberg, A. (2013). *The logic of connective action*. New York, NY: Cambridge University Press.

Bennett, L. W., & Segerberg, A. (2014). Three patterns of power in technology-enabled contention. *Mobilization. An International Quarterly, 19*, 421–439.

Bosi, L. (2016). Incorporation and democratization. The long-term process of institutionalization of the Northern Ireland civil rights movements. In L. Bosi, M. Giugni, & K. Uba (Eds.), *The consequences of social movements* (pp. 338–360). Cambridge: Cambridge University Press.

Brewster Stearns, L., & Almeida, P. D. (2004). The formation of state actor-social movement coalitions and favorable policy outcomes. *Social Problems, 51*, 478–504.

Commission on the Status of Women. (2013). *Agreed conclusions on the elimination and prevention of all forms of violence against women and girls*. Retrieved November 2016, from http://www.un.org/womenwatch/daw/csw/csw57/CSW57_Agreed_Conclusions_(CSW_report_excerpt).pdf

Della Porta, D., & Mattoni, A. (2015). Social networking sites in pro-democracy and anti-austerity protests: Some thoughts from a social movement perspective. In D. Trottier & C. Fuchs (Eds.), *Social media, politics and the state: Protests, revolutions, riots, crime and policing in the age of Facebook, Twitter and YouTube* (pp. 39–65). Routledge: London.

Diani, M. (1992). The concept of social movements. *The Sociological Review, 40*(1), 1–25.

Diani, M. (2003). Networks and social movements: A research programme. In M. Diani & D. McAdam (Eds.), *Social movements and networks: Relational approaches to collective action* (pp. 299–318). Oxford: Oxford University Press.

Diani, M. (2011). Networks and internet into perspective. *Swiss Political Science Review, 17*, 469–474.

Diani, M. (2015). *The cement of civil society. Studying networks in localities*. New York: Cambridge University Press.

Diani, M., & Bison, I. (2004). Organizations, coalitions, and movements. *Theory and Society, 33*, 281–309.

Ferree, M. M., & McClurg Mueller, C. (2004). Feminism and the women's movement: A global perspective. In D. A. Snow, S. A. Soule, & H. Kriesi (Eds.), *The Blackwell companion to social movements* (pp. 576–607). MA: Malden.

GenderIt. (2014). Fighting the backlash: Moving the agenda forward at the CSW. Retrieved November 2016, from http://www.genderit.org/node/3999/

Giugni, M. G. (1998). Introduction: Social movement and change: incorporation, transformation, and democratization. In M. G. Giugni, D. McAdam, & C. Tilly (Eds.), *From contention to democracy* (pp. xi–xxvi). Lanham, MD: Rowman and Littlefield.

Giugni, M. G. & Passy, F. (1998). Contentious politics in complex societies: New social movements between conflict and cooperation. In M. G. Giugni, D. McAdam, & C. Tilly (Eds.), *From contention to democracy* (pp. 81–107). Lanham, MD: Rowman and Littlefield.

González-Bailón, S., Borge-Holthoefer, J., & Moreno, Y. (2013). Broadcasters and hidden influentials in online protest diffusion. *American Behavioral Scientist, 57*, 943–965.

González-Bailón, S., Borge-Holthoefer, J., Rivero, A., & Moreno, Y. (2011). The dynamics of protest recruitment through an online network. *Scientific Reports, 1*(197), 1–7.

Howard, P. N., & Hussain, M. M. (2013). *Democracy's fourth wave*. Oxford: Oxford University Press.

Internet Governance Forum. (2016). All FAQs on the IGF. Retrieved November 2016, from http://www.intgovforum.org/cms/aboutigf/igffaqs

JASS. (2016). *JASS – building women's collective power for justice*. Retrieved November 2016, from http://www.justassociates.org/en/

Jiménez, M. (2007). Consolidation through institutionalization? Dilemmas of the Spanish environmental movement in the 1990s. *Environmental Politics, 8*, 149–171.

Katzenstein, M. F. (1998). Stepsisters. Feminist movement activism in different institutional spaces In D. S. Meyer & S. Tarrow (Eds.), *The social movement society: Contentious politics for a new century* (pp. 195–216). Lanham, MD: Rowman and Littlefield.

Leonardi, P. M. (2012). Materiality, sociomateriality, and socio-technical systems: What do these terms mean? How are they different? Do we need them? In P. M. Leonardi, B. A. Nardi, & J. Kallinikos (Eds.), *Materiality and organizing: Social interaction in a technological world* (pp. 25–48). Oxford: Oxford University Press.

Mattoni, A., & Treré, E. (2014). Media practices, mediation processes, and mediatization in the study of social movements. *Communication Theory, 24*, 252–271.

Melucci, A. (1996). *Challenging codes. Collective action in the information age*. Cambridge: Cambridge University Press.

Meraz, S., & Papacharissi, Z. (2013). Networked gatekeeping and networked framing on #Egypt. *The International Journal of Press/Politics, 18*, 138–166.

Mislove, A., Marcon, M., Gummadi, M. P., Druschel, P., & Bhattacharjee, B. (2007). Measurement and analysis of online social networks. *Proceedings of the 7th ACM SIGCOMM conference on Internet measurement*, 2007, 29–42.

Morgan, R. (2007). On political institutions and social movement dynamics: The case of the united nations and the global indigenous movement. *International Political Science Review, 28*, 273–292.

Morozov, E. (2009, April 24). *Why promoting democracy via the internet is often not a good idea*. Foreign Politics. Retrieved November 2016, from http://foreignpolicy.com/2009/04/24/why-promoting-democracy-via-the-internet-is-often-not-a-good-idea/

Pavan, E. (2014). Embedding digital communications within collective action networks. A multidimensional network perspective. *Mobilization. An international Quarterly, 19*, 441–455.

Peterson, A. (2016). The institutionalization process of a neo-Nazi movement party: Securing social movement outcomes. In L. Bosi, M. Giugni, & K. Uba (Eds.), *The consequences of social movements* (pp. 314–337). Cambridge: Cambridge University Press.

Rainie, L., & Wellman, B. (2012). *Networked. The new social operating system*. Cambridge, MA: The MIT Press.

Rucht, D. (1996). The impact of national contexts on social movement structures: A cross-movement and cross-national perspective. In D. McAdam, J. D. McCarthy, & M. Zald (Eds.), *Comparative perspectives on social movements* (pp. 185–204). Cambridge: Cambridge University Press.

Smith, M., Shneiderman, B., Milic-Frayling, N., Rodrigues, E. M., Leskovec, J., & Dunne, C. (2010). NodeXL: A free and open network overview, discovery and exploration add-in for Excel 2007/2010 (Pro Edition) [Computer software]. California: Social Media Research Foundation.

Suh, D. (2011). Institutionalizing social movements: The dual strategy of the Korean women's movement. *The Sociological Quarterly, 52*, 442–471.

Tilly, C., & Tarrow, S. (2007). *Contentious politics*. Boulder, CO: Paradigm Press.

Tremayne, M. (2014). Anatomy of protest in the digital era: A network analysis of Twitter and occupy wall street. *Social Movements Studies, 13*, 110–126.

United Nations General Assembly. (2006). *In-depth study on all forms of violence against women. Report of the Secretary-General (Document A/61/122/Add.1)*. Retrieved October 2015, from http://www.un.org/womenwatch/daw/vaw/v-sg-study.htm

Varol, O., Ferrara, E., Ogan, C. L., Menczer, F., & Flammini, A. (2014). Evolution of online user behavior during a social upheaval. *Proceedings of the 2014 ACM conference on Web Science*, 2014: 81–90.

Wasserman, S., & Faust, K. (1994). *Social network analysis. Methods and applications*. New York, NY: Cambridge University Press.

Women's Net. (2016). Women's net – strenghtening women's right. Retrieved November 2016, from http://womensnet.org.za/

Tweeting India's Nirbhaya protest: a study of emotional dynamics in an online social movement

Saifuddin Ahmed, Kokil Jaidka and Jaeho Cho

ABSTRACT

Previous research has recognized the role of emotions in protests and social movements in the offline world. Despite the current scenario of ubiquitous social media and 'Twitter revolutions,' our knowledge about the connections between emotions and online protests still remains limited. In this study, we examine whether online protest actions follow the same emotional groundwork for supporting and nurturing a social movement as in the offline world, and how these emotions vary across various stages of the social movement. Through a computer-assisted emotion analysis of 65,613 Twitter posts (tweets), posted during the Nirbhaya social movement (movement against the Delhi gang-rape incident) in India, we identified a strong resemblance between online emotional patterns and offline protest emotions as discussed in literature. Formal statistical testing of a range of emotions (negativity, positivity, anger, sadness, anxiety, certainty, individualism, collectivism, and achievement) demonstrates that they significantly differed across stages of the social movement; as such, they influenced the course of the online protest, resonating parallels with offline events. The findings highlight the importance of anger and anxiety in stirring the collective conscience, and identify that positive emotion was pervasive during the protest event. Implications of these findings are discussed.

New communication technologies have altered how social movements and mass protests are initiated and coordinated. Studies have found that the Internet and social media facilitate and mobilize offline protest efforts (Harlow, 2012), promote participatory behavior (Bennett & Segerberg, 2012; Valenzuela, Arriagada, & Scherman, 2012), instigate public discussion (Eltantawy & Wiest, 2011), disseminate information (Tufekci & Wilson, 2012), and create new connections (Tremayne, 2014). In fact, today, some mass protests are often born online, as a virtual gathering of otherwise isolated actors and organizations, and then move offline (Gonzalez-Bailon, Borge-Holthoefer, & Moreno, 2013; Harlow, 2012). They often have political implications for democracies (Lotan, Graeff, Ananny, Gaffney, & Pearce, 2011). Scholars analyzing collective action have long established the importance of emotions in dynamics of a protest (Jasper, 1998). Although the Internet and social media are open, accessible communication channels used for collective expression and flow of emotions (Martens-Edwards, 2014) yet, scholarly attention to the role of emotions in online protests is marginal. Today, there is a need to go beyond the existing techno-deterministic analyses of the relationship between social media and

Supplemental data for this article can be accessed at http://dx.doi.org/10.1080/14742837.2016.1192457.

protests. This study analyzes this relationship through the lens of emotional expression. It identifies the dominant emotions expressed on Twitter during an online protest, and examines whether they follow the same emotional groundwork for supporting and nurturing a social movement as in the offline world as discussed in literature. Our Twitter analysis focuses on the following key emotions: (a) negative emotions, (b) positive emotions, (c) anger, (d) sadness, (e) anxiety, (f) certainty, (g) individualism, (h) collectivism, and (i) achievement.

A *social movement* is described as 'informal networks, based on shared beliefs and solidarity, which mobilize about conflictual issues through the frequent use of various forms of protests' (Porta & Diani, 2009, p. 16). This implies that a *mass protest*, or *protest action*, is usually a part of a larger, organized social movement (Oliver & Myers, 1998) and comprises a short-term expression of objection by words and actions. Similarly, *online social movements* refer to 'the adoption and use by social movements and community activists of new information and communication technologies (ICTs), such as the Internet and the World Wide Web' (Loader, 2003, p. 1319). Both social movements that use ICTs as well as social movements exclusive to the Internet fall under the online social movement umbrella (Hara & Huang, 2011). The case under study thus qualifies as an online social movement.

In character, an online social movement also displays rudimentary features of offline collective action, such as a crowd sharing its outrage, opinions, and tension around an emotionally charged central event, before consolidating and self-organizing into a social movement with shared objectives and a strategy for action (Dolata & Schrape, 2015). In an online movement, social media users post relevant content as 'online protesters,' who are then considered a part of the collective online–offline social movement.

Posts on social media about mass protests are often posted live, from the ground (Earl, McKee Hurwitz, Mejia Mesinas, Tolan, & Arlotti, 2013; Theocharis, Lowe, Van Deth, & García-Albacete, 2014) and online–offline social movements reflect a paradigm shift and a dual approach of online activism on the Internet and offline activism in a physical location as 'place politics' (Castells, 2012, p. 11). The positive role of the online realm in offline protest action has been exemplified in several recent uprisings such as Arab Spring (Lotan et al., 2011), the 2011 riots in Britain (Vis, 2013), protests in Iran (Burns & Eltham, 2009), and Occupy Wall Street protests (Gaby & Caren, 2012; Theocharis et al., 2014). In most of these uprisings, Twitter was the platform in focus, which was heavily used to facilitate political uprisings (Starbird & Palen, 2012) and civic participation (Burns & Eltham, 2009; Lotan et al., 2011). According to Castells (2012), 'the origins of social movements are to be found in the emotions of individuals and in their networking on the basis of cognitive empathy' (p. 13). Research has long established the importance of emotions in the dynamics of a protest – they glorify ideals that help people to identify with the movement, kindle connections with other members of the movement, and motivate them to participate in protest action (Castells, 2012; Goodwin, Jasper, & Polletta, 2000; Jasper, 1998, 2011). This study has focused on emotional expression in an online social movement – the online, implicit and explicit recognition, declaration and sharing of emotions, moods, thoughts, or experiences relevant to the social movement, by social media users (Derks, Fischer, & Bos, 2008). It aims to address the following questions:

(a) Do the emotional characteristics of online social movements resemble those of offline social movements?
(b) What are the dominant emotions before, during, and after online protest action?
(c) How do these emotions evolve during the course of the online social movement?

This study has drawn on concepts used within the social movement literature to construct a framework of emotional expressions, specifically prevailing *before*, *during*, and *after* mass protests. We focused on a data-set of 65,613 social media posts on Twitter, or 'tweets' pertaining to a social movement in New Delhi, India, with the aim to identify the main emotional experiences, and to relate them to the extant literature on emotions in offline social movements. In this study, the focus is on the Nirbhaya social movement (December 2012), which started as a social media outrage expressing solidarity for a gang-rape victim and horror at the atrocities; it consolidated under the shared cause of 'justice for women' and transcended into a mass offline movement. In this context, we are interested in the online Nirbhaya social movement – the 'waves of emotionally charged outrage on the social web' (Dolata & Schrape, 2015) against the incident. Specifically, we are interested in the period before, during, and after the first major protest held as a part of this movement. Our multi-layered study is the first attempt of its kind: to compare the emotions of an offline and online social movement – their similarities, differences, and key characteristics – and the role of emotions in civic participation. In the rest of this study, we use 'tweets' to refer to the posts by users on Twitter, the social media platform.

ICT in the Indian context

India with a population of 1.2 billion has a mobile penetration rate of 46% and Internet penetration rate of 27%, with an increase of 44% in 2014 itself (IAMAI, 2015a). Nearly half of all the Internet browsing in India currently happens over mobile phones, and this percentage is expected to rise – especially in the rural areas. An average Indian Internet user spends nearly 5 h online every day with approximately 2.5 h spent on social media websites (IAMAI, 2015a). These numbers highlight the growing presence and increasing usage of ICTs in India.

Several technological reforms have been introduced in the past two decades, which have changed the paradigms of local and global communication, and reduced the disparity between digital urban hubs, where 35% of the total population live, and the rural suburbs. An encouraging statistic for technological growth is that the usage of social media in rural areas has grown by an impressive 100% in 2014 as compared to 35% for urban areas (IAMAI, 2015b). India's Internet and social media users mainly comprise the urban population of about 250 million. This socially connected community is influential in most state and civic affairs. Recent events prove that 'India is going through its own version of the Arab Spring. People are demanding more of the system' (Zakaria, 2013) and participating in hundreds and thousands – not as members of a particular party, caste, or religion, but as individuals joining to demand more responsiveness from their government and to talk about changing their culture, attitudes, and schools (Hiatt, 2013). This was visible in 2014 where a pre-election study by the IRIS Knowledge Foundation and the Internet and Mobile Association of India found that social media could influence the electoral outcome in as many as 160 out of 543 constituencies represented in the Lok Sabha, the lower house of the Indian Parliament (IAMAI, 2013). Thus, social media is helping to bolster India's democratic values, by bringing mainstream media and political parties under scrutiny and providing a more people-centric approach to governance and thereby laying the foundation for plurality and transparency in public discourse (South Asia Channel, 2014).

Case study: the Nirbhaya social movement

The events central to this study occurred between 17 December 2012 and 3 January 2013 in New Delhi, India. On the eve of 17 December 2012, five men raped and physically tortured a female student. The news was widely discussed and debated in traditional and social media platforms; the latter became a hotbed of public agitation and indignation, which ultimately went offline, to the streets, as mass demonstrations and protests. It is considered that the main reasons for the protest were their collective frustration at the inability of the justice system to hold the rapists culpable, and of the police to provide basic security and protection to the citizens. Several studies have documented the phenomenal contribution of social media in mass mobilization and protest coordination for the Nirbhaya movement (Ahmed & Jaidka, 2013a, 2013b; Belair-Gagnon, Mishra, & Agur, 2014; Chaudhuri & Fitzgerald, 2015).

'Online spaces' offer a hybrid space to connect online with offline social networks (Castells, 2012, p. 25). In democratic contexts, online spaces are free from the interests of government and media corporations; as such, they afford potential protesters the time and distance to appraise the situation and determine their participation in a safe manner. This is especially crucial in environments where the online movement averts physical curfews and barricades, as was the case of the Nirbhaya movement in New Delhi. Furthermore, online announcements coordinated the offline protest, by announcing the timing, venues, and travel arrangements for the mass protests ahead of time. Online warnings were also issued to alert protesters about impending police barricades and anti-protester charges. The online platform is considered the best way to reach out to the energetic and emotional youth (Castells, 2012) – this was particularly true for India, whose social media users are mostly the young, urban middle class. Nirbhaya movement activists used social media platforms to diffuse critical information among a widespread audience and stir up a nationwide demonstration (Chaudhuri & Fitzgerald, 2015). During the Nirbhaya movement, social media was used to report first-person accounts of the offline happenings at protest venues, discuss the issue being protested, and seek for or provide information (Ahmed & Jaidka, 2013a). The citizens co-constructed a new, unmoderated, online press, thus altering the balance of power in the dependency relationship between the government, media, and citizens and putting forward the real voice of the common person (Ahmed & Jaidka, 2013b).

Social media thus acted as an online information exchanges, creating information flows that thickened the perceived strength of the local Nirbhaya movement, and nurtured the weak ties among strangers connected by the cause. We posit that as online protestors, shared experiences and planned new events, the first bonds of reciprocity, trust, and togetherness for the movement 'were created through the wellspring of online emotional expression' (Castells, 2012, p. 27).

In the following sections, we first motivate our choice of focusing on the emotions inherent in a social movement. Following this, we delve into a discussion of previous findings about the emotions permeating social movements, in order to construct a framework of the key emotions to anticipate in our analysis.

The role of emotions in social movements

Human emotions are moderated by intrinsic factors such as moral values and cultural upbringing, and extrinsic factors which comprise social identity – a set of social expectations recognized as obligations and rights, and an awareness of their place in the social world (Tajfel, 1979). Social identity refers to one's belongingness in a group; strong social identities or 'group identities' can motivate individuals to commit to, and participate in collective action (Tajfel, 1979).

Protests are a form of collective action, and strongly rely on its participants' feeling of belongingness to the identity of the movement (Klandermans, van der Toorn, & Van Stekelenburg, 2008; Tarrow & Tollefson, 1994; Van Stekelenburg, Klandermans, & Van Dijk, 2011) and whether the cause resonates with their political beliefs, cultural ideologies, and emotional instincts (Jasper, 1998; Van Stekelenburg & Klandermans, 2007; Van Stekelenburg et al., 2011). This is why it can be argued that a collective cognitive decision, or group appraisal, is based on the individual emotional reactions of members of a group (Van Troost, Van Stekelenburg, & Klandermans, 2013).

The place of outrage, protest, and emotions in contemporary India can be understood from the several mass agitations routinely held all over the country, to protest the government's apathy toward crime and delayed justice. Beyond the cocoon of the metro cities and its news discourse, which centers on urban problems, there are other protests which do not stay in the public eye for very long – such as the agitations in northeastern India, where women shed their clothes and took to the streets to protest against the sexual crimes committed by Central Reserve Police Force (Singh, 2009, p. 141); there are protests by farmers in the northwest, seeking higher compensation for damaged crops (NDTV, 2015); Irom Sharmila is in her 15th year of a fast-unto-death to protest the Special Forces Act instated to protect the Army in areas of civil strife (Greater Kashmir, 2015) and an upper class caste in western India is demanding privileges in jobs and educational institutions (Indian Express, 2015). The Nirbhaya movement was another example of such a movement – and its coordination by and for the large urban middle-class populace in the national capital could be one of the reasons behind a wide participation and close media attention.

Previous work has explained the triggers of social movements through their emotions (Castells, 2012; Flam & King, 2007; Goodwin et al., 2000). Scholars investigating the success of social movements have relied on the feedback elicited from protest members which comprises a description of their emotional states (Adams, 2003). As Taylor (1989) points out, emotions are an inextricable part of the culture of social movements – they are permeated with emotion in their goals and throughout their timeline; protest action, occurring as a part of a social movement, naturally exhibits all these characteristics as well. This piques our interest in the emotional underpinnings of an online social movement. In the following paragraphs, we have considered the literature on emotions in offline social movements to identify the key emotions of social movements.

A triggering *moral shock* is the first thing to set a social movement in motion; it upsets one's intrinsic emotions toward family, ideology, and culture (Goodwin & Jasper, 2006) leading to feelings of *anxiety, fear, resignation,* or *anger* (Castells, 2012, p. 13). Fear and resignation may prevent individuals from protest action while anger can mobilize them toward collective goals (Marcus, Neuman, & MacKuen, 2000; Rodgers, 2010). Anger, on the other hand, is postulated as the primary activating emotion for collective action (Castells, 2012; Gamson, 1995; Marcus et al., 2000). It is the 'sanctioning emotion' which expresses dissatisfaction toward opponents, and which social movements use to motivate new members to join (Flam & King, 2007, p. 20). Anger is also a prerogative for power, so when social movements are able to re-appropriate the right to feel anger to its members, they also gain a subtle influence over the oppressors.

When protesters and potential protesters appraise the situation – feelings of *anxiety* and *individualism* conflict with *collectivism,* as individuals decide whether or not to participate in protest action. These emotions have been deemed important to build and sustain a social movement (Adams, 2003). Through cognitive appraisal, individuals identify whom to blame – and the more clearly defined the proximate source of the threat is, the more likelihood there is that individuals will feel negative emotions, such as *hatred, suspicion,* and *indignation,* all of which are powerful mobilizers for protest action (Jasper, 1998).

Other than negative emotions, the outcome of a protest is also dependent on positive emotions residing in the collective identity of its participants (Klandermans, 2014; Van Stekelenburg, 2013). The strength of *collectivism* comes from its emotional side, because it represents the shared meanings and reciprocal affective emotion toward other group members, such as *enthusiasm* and *certainty* in the movement's goals. When a movement ends, its outcome is closely related with protesters' emotions – social stigma would lead to feelings of *embarrassment, disappointment*, and *guilt* among protesters; shifting goals and factionalism would cause *frustration.* On the other hand, protesters would feel a sense of *achievement* and be *thrilled, joyful,* and *hopeful* if the protest succeeded in its stated aims (Castells, 2012, p. 244).

Some protesters may feel *cynicism, depression,* or *resignation*, if the result falls short of their expectations. When the structural social network and the ethos of solidarity making up the movement disintegrates, protesters may also may feel *bitter, disconnected* and *disillusioned,* even *impotent,* as they have suddenly lost their sense of purpose (Adams, 2003).

Based on the literature discussed above, we decided to focus on a subset of emotions and cognitive experiences which are representative of social movements. Previous literature affirms that cognitive processes work hand in hand with emotions in social movements – sometimes triggering them, sometimes borne of them – accordingly, we have included four cognitive processes into our emotion analysis – individualism, collectivism, certainty, and achievement. It is our hypothesis that if an online social movement manifests the same emotional characteristics as an offline movement, then we would see the same emotions dominant over the same stages of protest action in our Twitter data-set:

Before protest: negative emotions, anger, anxiety, individualism, and collectivism

During protest: positive emotions, certainty, and collectivism

After protest: positive emotions, achievement, sadness, and anxiety.

We aim to track these all these emotions and cognitive processes, to examine how they evolve through the course of online protest action.

Research objectives

In this study, we analyze the emotions expressed online, in Twitter posts discussing or condemning the Nirbhaya gang rape, in order to:

(1) Identify whether these emotions supported and nurtured the social movement in the same way as they do in the offline world.
(2) Identify the emotions which were dominant at before, during, and after online protest action.
(3) Observe the transition of these emotions through the three stages of the social movement.

Motivating our study with the literature on emotions in offline social movements, we have identified the following emotions to investigate: (a) negative emotions, (b) positive emotions, (c) anger, (d) sadness, (e) anxiety, (f) certainty, (g) individualism, (h) collectivism, and (i) achievement.

Method

In our analysis, we want to identify whether the emotions manifested in the online protest are truly significant as compared to a general conversation on Twitter. In order to test this, we have treated our primary data-set of tweets posted during the online social movement as the experimental condition. To simulate a control group, we adapted the experiment by Pennebaker and Francis (1996) to collect three other user-generated corpora on any other object or event. Next, we measured different corpora on their mean emotional and cognitive dimensions designed to correspond to selected Linguistic Inquiry and Word Count (LIWC: Pennebaker, Booth, & Francis, 2007) dictionary scales. We hypothesize that the findings will reflect a significantly different usage of emotional and cognitive words in our primary data-set, indicating that LIWC successfully measures the emotions and cognitive processes for our purpose.

Data

Primary data

Our primary data-set was collected using Topsy, an archiving service which collects Twitter posts, for a 10-day period from 17 December 2012 to 26 December 2012 – which is the time period covering the build-up, duration, and aftermath of a major nationwide protest against the gang rape. Moreover, the victim's health severely deteriorated post-26 December leading to her demise on 29 December, which led to a mass outpour of sad posts on Twitter. We believe selecting a period post-26 December could have confounded our findings due to this event.

In order to collect the data, we first used Topsy's dashboard to identify the words and topics most frequently appearing in communications about the Nirbhaya social movement within the 10-day period of interest. These words and topics are known as the top trending keywords and the top topic tags (hashtags). We then queried the Topsy archive with the following words and time period information:

DELHI OR gangrape OR rape OR #delhigangrape OR #delhiprotest OR #delhiprotests OR #indiagate OR #stopthsisshame&maxdate = 1,359,743,400 &mindate = 1,365,791,400 &order = date &lang = en

Topsy returned a set of files detailing 72,565 tweets, with the tweets' text, timestamp, username, type of tweet (e.g. tweet, link, image, or video), embedded links, and user mentions. Of these, 65,613 tweets were posted in English and 6952 were posted in other regional languages. Our analysis has focused only on tweets posted in English because LIWC does not support Indian languages.

Secondary data

We have used three categories of secondary data, to identify how far the findings from primary data deviated from the expected results for the given baselines. These data-sets are described in the following paragraphs.

Random tweets

We collected tweets by querying for the hashtags #Newshoursnewsbreak, #1YearOfJaiHo and #FACup, which were the top-three Twitter topics in India during a two-day period in January 2014. Like our Nirbhaya data-set, these were the most talked about topics for the time period we considered. Although they were collected at a different time period, they were collected for the same demographic, so we anticipate that they will reflect the general course, tone, and emotions of topical posts on Twitter in India. Our query returned 10,729 tweets, and we retained the fields corresponding to our primary data-set – the tweets' text, timestamp, username, type of tweet (e.g. tweet, link, image, or video), hits, trackbacks, embedded links, and mentions.

Newspaper articles

We used the LexisNexis search engine to search for newspaper articles containing both words 'Delhi' and 'gang rape' and published by the top three circulating newspapers in India (The Times of India, The Hindu, and The Telegraph India) from 18 December 2012 to 26 December 2012 and identified 487 articles.

Other corpora of user generated content

We have considered a corpus of blog posts and another of transcripts of oral conversations (known as the talking corpora) offered by Tausczik and Pennebaker (2010). The blogs corpora comprises about 150 million words and 714,000 posts from 20,146 authors, collected from LiveJournal.com (written in summer and fall, 2001) and Blogs.com (downloaded in summer, 2004), as a part of two studies. The talking corpora comprises 2014 transcripts collected from 10 studies, with over a million words in total from 850 speakers talking in real-world unstructured settings. Similar to our primary data-set, these corpora also comprise 'user-generated content' written for the purposes of self-expression and discussion.

Analysis

Emotion analysis

In this study, we have analyzed emotions on the basis of the lexical and stylistic features used in social media posts. Computer-assisted emotion analysis was preferred because it enables data processing of large document sets, and helps us understand the qualitative aspects of empirical textual data. A preferred approach for computer-assisted emotion analysis is to apply an existing lexicon, such as SentiWordNet (Esuli & Sebastiani, 2006), EmoLex (Mohammad & Turney, 2010) or LIWC (Pennebaker et al., 2007) to user-generated content, including social media and tweets (Choudhury, Counts, & Horvitz, 2013; Golder & Macy, 2011). In doing so, studies are able to highlight a strong association between certain parts of speech in text and emotional or mental states (Derks et al., 2008) – for instance, positive and negative sentiments were found to relate to health outcomes (Brubaker, Kivran-Swaine, Taber, & Hayes, 2012). Other studies have reported that the use of first-person singular pronouns was elevated for individuals exhibiting signs of depression and suicide ideation (Rude, Gortner, & Pennebaker, 2004). At the community level, the linguistic style of a group of people provides information about the social environment (Eckert, 1996).

We measured the percentage proportion of words related to emotions in protest, identified using the scientifically validated, psycholinguistic lexicon provided by LIWC (Pennebaker et al., 2007; http://www.liwc.net). LIWC is an academic tool that is used to calculate the presence of psycholinguistic categories in a text as a percentage proportion of the total words. The software counts the words in any English text input, against the *dictionary* words that define each of its categories, which are 68 'scales' of emotional, cognitive, content, and linguistic style. It then returns the percentage of each scale found in the input text. For example, it may return a value of 25.5 for 'posemo,' which means that 25.5% of all the words in the input text belonged to the positive emotion category in LIWC. The total number of words defining the LIWC scales is 6400 words and word stems (Pennebaker, Boyd, Jordan, & Blackburn, 2015). LIWC has previously been used to identify social relationships, thinking styles, and other individual differences in text samples (Back, Küfner, & Egloff, 2011; Tausczik & Pennebaker, 2010). It has also been successfully used to measure emotions in social media, such as Twitter (see Bae & Lee, 2012; Choudhury et al., 2013; Golder & Macy, 2011).

We preferred LIWC over other available tools, such as EmoLex and SentiWordNet, because unlike the latter, it also defines words under cognitive processes, some of which are relevant in the group appraisal scenario for protest action. Our confidence in LIWC categories also comes from its extensive use in social science and psychological research, and having been rigorously tested and validated by hundreds of studies in different domains (see Tausczik & Pennebaker, 2010). Details of LIWC's construction and inter-coder reliability are provided in Appendix A (see online supplement).

Key emotion categories in LIWC. Based on previous work in emotional analysis of protests and social movements, we have identified a subset of emotions and cognitive processes to focus on for this study. We then referred to the word lexicon in LIWC, to identify the scales that measure these emotions (see Appendix B; see online supplement).

(1) In prior work, negative emotions – specifically, anger, sadness, and anxiety – have been identified as the main drivers and inhibitors of protest action (Goodwin et al., 2000). Accordingly, we identify LIWC's *Anger* (e.g. cruel, vicious, hellish), *Sadness* (e.g. suffer, crying, ruin), and *Anxiety* (e.g. scary, disturb, horror) categories as relevant to our study, and will be using these for our analysis.

(2) Among positive emotions, previous studies have identified that anticipation is a key driver for protest action, and joy is an indicator of the success, or the end, of a protest. We select LIWC's Positive Emotions category as the over-arching representative of all indicators of joy, anticipation and excitement.

(3) Based on previous work on certainty in social movements (Adams, 2003; Castells, 2012), we select LIWC's *certainty* category (e.g. clear*, definite*, sure*).

(4) Function words have been used in the past as indicators of cognitive and affective processes, especially in the study of mental health (Choudhury et al., 2013) and to indicate feelings of individualism or collectivism (Adams, 2003; Castells, 2012). Based on these previous works, we select LIWC's category of first-person singular pronouns (e.g. I, me, my) and first-person plural pronouns (e.g. we, us, our) to be indicators of *individualism* and *collectivism,* respectively.

(5) In the Current Concerns categories, we identify that the *achievement* category (e.g. honor*, strength*, success*) would be appropriate for our study, based on previous studies of protest which have identified an emphasis on achievement in protest rhetoric (Adams, 2003; Castells, 2012).

Three phases and 4 h time slots

Our literature review identifies that there are three main stages in protest action – before protest, during a protest, and after a protest. For a closer analysis of the emotional transitions during and in-between these stages, we have used the date and time of individual Twitter posts to divide our primary data-set into three subsets:

- Before protest: Tweets posted between 17–21 December 2012
- During protest: Tweets posted on 22–23 December 2012
- After protest: Tweets posted on 24–26 December 2012

We wanted to control for the effects of sudden spikes or slumps in Twitter activity, which were likely to happen if a major offline event happened, or there was a news break, or if there was a lag due to differing time zones. Accordingly, we chose to analyze our tweet data-set using 4-h time slots. This is also in alignment with previous research (Berezin, 2009; Chan, Fung, Xing, & Hagger, 2014), which suggests that moods and emotions may frequently fluctuate over time, sometimes within short spans. Our choice of the length of time slot was also determined by the size and distribution of the primary data, which had high volume during the days when major incidents occurred in connection to the gang-rape incident, and relatively low volume on other days.

We constructed group files of all tweets posted within a 4-h timeslot as a single text file. In this manner, each day was divided into six time slots of 4 h each (Time slots 1–6). These group files were input to LIWC. LIWC is expected to work better on group files as compared to single Twitter posts, which are limited in length to 140 characters (Vargo, 2014). Using group files also allowed our results to be comparable against our baseline corpora, where every text is several hundred words in length.

Results

Twitter activity

Figure 1 shows the trend of Twitter usage across this entire public event lasting 10 days and also identifies the major events which occurred during this period. Tweeting reached its peak on 23 December 2012 which was the second day of major protests at India Gate. On an average, 6561 tweets were posted per day, with a maximum of 15,421 on 23 December 2012, the second day of major protests and a low of 1939 on 17 December 2012, the day when the first story broke out. This finding is in line with previous research where Twitter usage was most common during the days of protest (Earl et al., 2013).

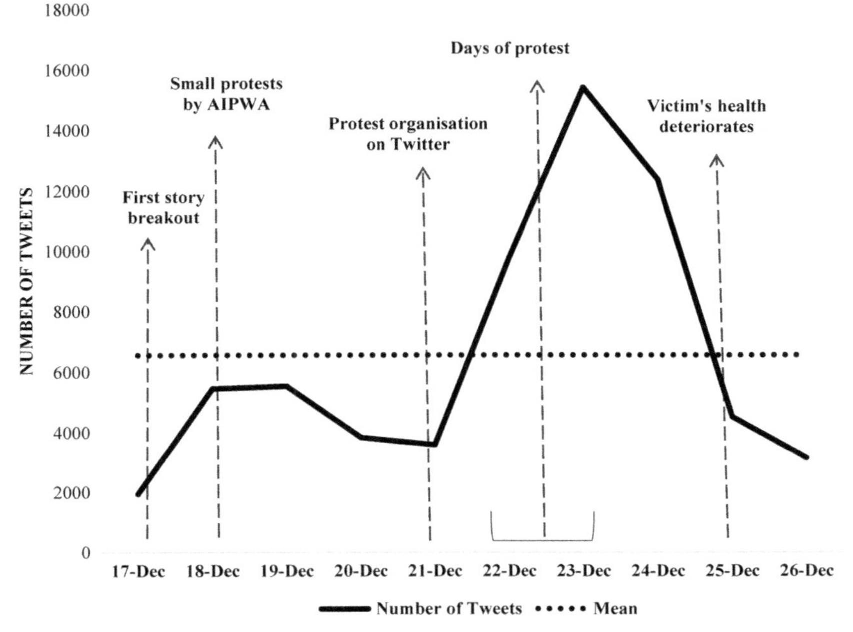

Figure 1. Tweets trend and major incidents from 17 December 2012 to 26 December 2012.

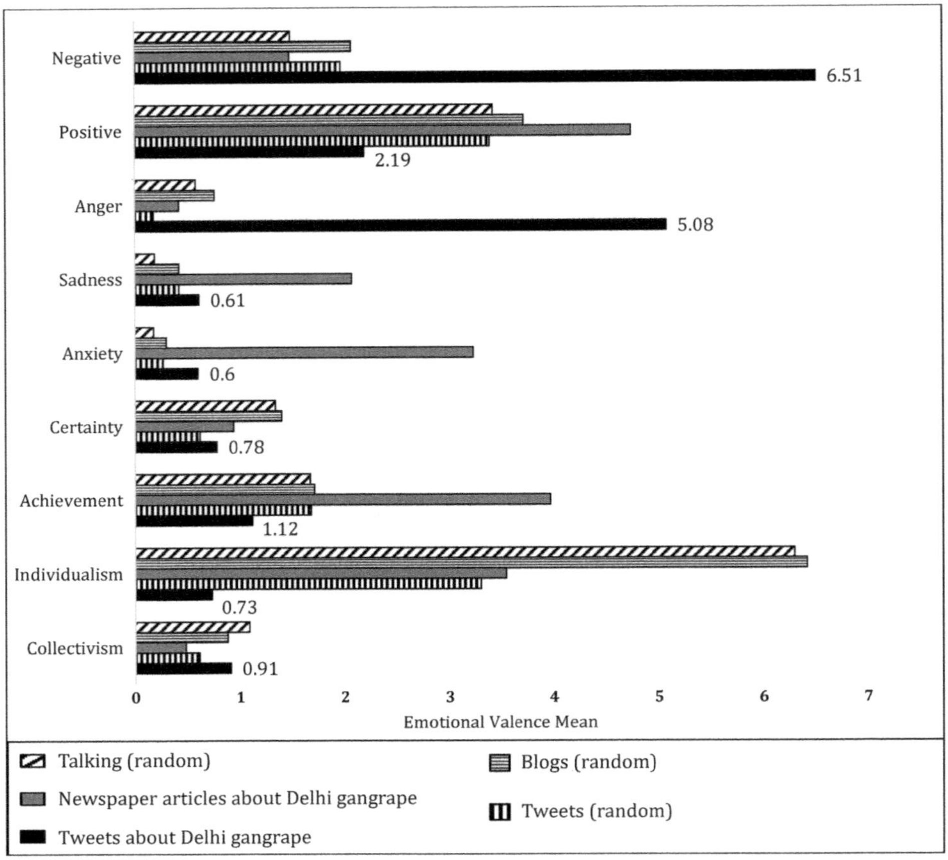

Figure 2. Comparison of means for LIWC categories against means from other corpora.

Descriptive: means

In Figure 2, the clustered columns show a comparison of the emotional valences for our tweet corpus across various categories, against those for random tweets, newspaper articles about the movement against the Delhi gang rape, and the mean percentage proportions for the same categories for our blogs and talking corpora; these were provided by Tausczik and Pennebaker (2010). The corresponding numbers are also provided in Table 1. The figure shows that the negative emotion valence ($M = 6.51$) and anger ($M = 5.08$) for the movement against gang-rape tweets were exceedingly higher than other emotions and also differed from other comparative categories. Anxiety ($M = .60$) was found to be higher than all other categories except newspaper articles ($M = 3.23$). Similar differences were found for individualism and sense of achievement.

Emotion analyses

In the following pairwise emotion analyses, we pair up our emotion categories based on Plutchik's (1980) documentation of bipolar relationships between emotions. Plutchik categorizes and contrasts 'fundamental emotions' based on three main criteria – their subjective quality, reactive nature, and driving behavior (Plutchik, 1980). Several scholars have used Plutchik's dependence of emotional relationships to investigate emotional trends on Twitter (Kim, Bak, & Oh, 2012; Suttles & Ide, 2013). We have followed Plutchik's representation to pair our analyses of negative with positive emotions and

Table 1. Comparison of means for LIWC categories against means from other corpora.

	Tweets about Delhi gang rape	Tweets (random)	Newspaper articles about Delhi gang rape	Blogs (random)	Talking (random)
Negativity	6.51	1.97	1.48	2.07	1.49
Positivity	2.19	3.39	4.74	3.72	3.42
Anger	5.08	0.18	0.42	0.76	0.58
Sadness	0.61	0.42	2.07	0.42	0.19
Anxiety	0.6	0.27	3.23	0.3	0.18
Certainty	0.78	0.62	0.94	1.4	1.34
Individualism	0.73	3.3	3.54	6.42	6.3
Collectivism	0.91	0.61	0.48	0.88	1.09
Achievement	1.12	1.68	3.97	1.71	1.67

anxiety with certainty; individualism and collectivism make a natural pair. We have analyzed anger, sadness, and achievement separately.

Negative and positive emotions

The overall negative emotions ($M = 6.51$, SD = 1.54) clearly outweighed positive emotions ($M = 2.19$, SD = .30, Table 1). As visible in Figure 3(a), we notice a gradual rise in negative emotions till the protests, after which it subsides. The highest negative emotion was on 20 December 2012 – the day the Indian parliament discussed the issue. The lowest negative emotion (4.44) was at the end of our observation period on 26 December 2012, when the victim's medical condition was reported to deteriorate.

Table 2 provides the means of all emotions across the three periods of protest. There was a statistically significant difference in negative emotions across three periods of protest (F (2, 57) = 152.46, $p < .001$). A Tukey *post hoc* test revealed that the negative emotions were highest before the protests ($M = 7.91$, SD = .72) which decreased during the protests ($M = 5.26$, SD = .36) and were lowest after the protests ($M = 5.01$, SD = .56). Positive emotions too significantly varied between the three periods of protest (F (2, 57) = 78.17, $p < .001$) and were found to be highest during the protest ($M = 2.70$, SD = .28), with the highest at 2.99 on 22 December 2012 (the first day of major protest), as compared to before ($M = 2.06$, SD = .13) and after protest ($M = 2.06$, SD = .07).

Anger

Figure 3(b) shows that the high level of anger in the early period dropped as the movement proceeded. One-way ANOVA revealed significant differences for anger (F (2, 57) = 72.64, $p < .001$) across three periods of protests with it being highest before protests ($M = 6.29$, SD = .96) and lowest during protests ($M = 3.82$, SD = .67)

Sadness

There was a spike in sadness a day after the incident on 18 December 2012 which recorded the highest value (0.89), after which there was a large drop during the protest days. Significant differences in sadness were found across three periods of protest (F (2, 57) = 45.92, $p < .001$), highest before ($M = .71$, SD = .06) and lowest after protests ($M = .49$, SD = .11), when the victim was reported to become medically unstable. The trend is visible in Figure 3(c).

Anxiety and certainty

Figure 3(d) shows that the highest value for anxiety (1.10) was recorded on the day before the first day of protest. There was a statistically significant difference in anxiety across three periods of protest (F

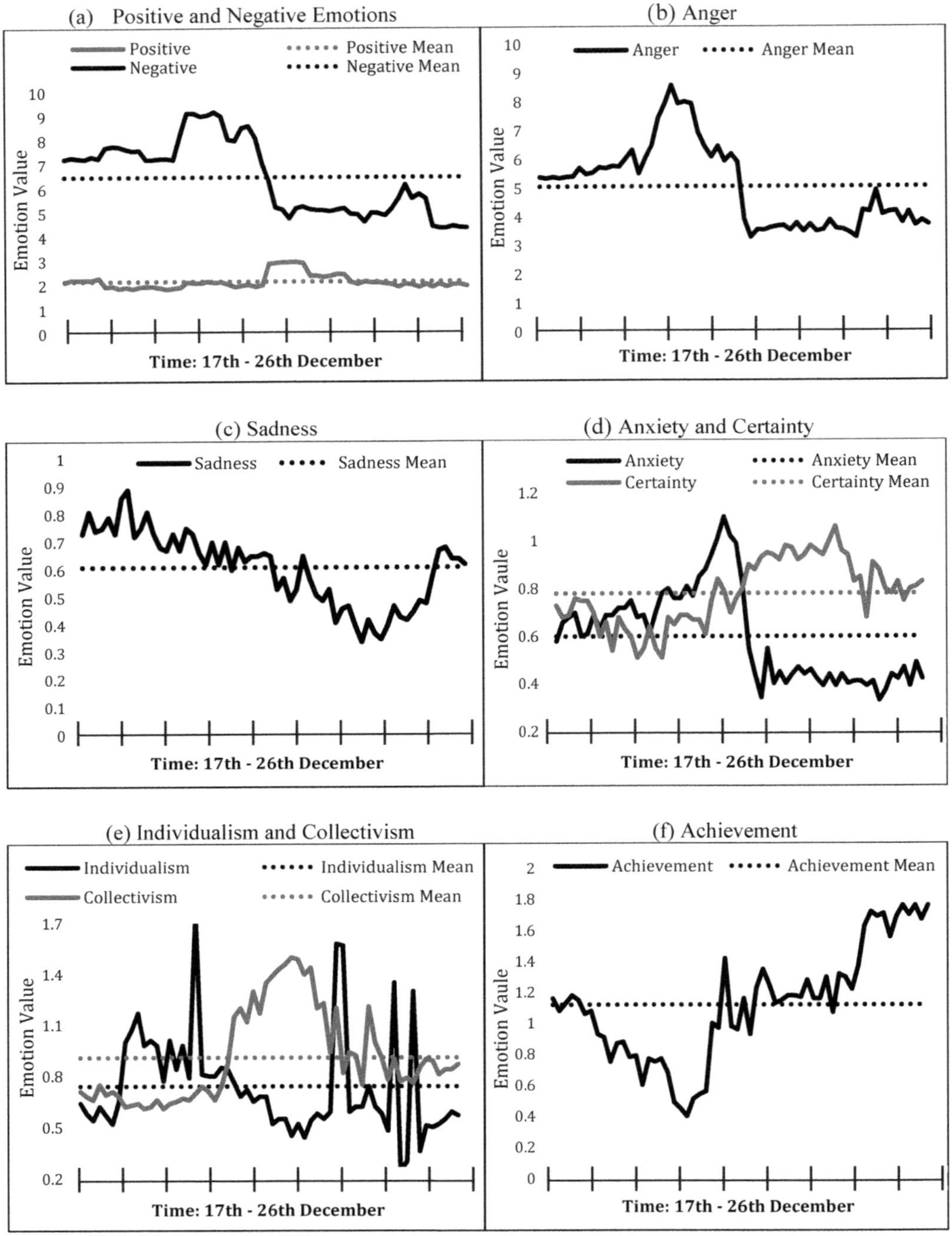

Figure 3(a)–(f). Trends of emotions.

(2, 57) = 63.34, $p < .001$), being highest before the protests ($M = .76$, SD = .14), decreasing during the protests ($M = .48$, SD = .12), and hitting the lowest point after the protests ($M = .41$, SD = .04). For certainty, we notice fluctuating values before the protest – but there was a steady rise during the protest phase, with the highest level (0.98) reported on 24 December 2012, the day following the second day of

Table 2. Means for emotions across three protest periods.

	Before protest		During protest		After protest		Overall
Emotion	*M*	SD	*M*	SD	*M*	SD	*M*
Negativity	7.91	.72	5.26	.36	5.01	.56	6.51
Positivity	2.06	.13	2.70	.28	2.06	.07	2.19
Anger	6.29	.96	3.82	.67	3.90	.39	5.08
Sadness	.71	.07	.51	.06	.49	.11	.61
Anxiety	.76	.14	.48	.12	.41	.04	.6
Certainty	.67	.08	.93	.04	.78	.13	.78
Individualism	.82	.25	.70	.41	.61	.29	.73
Collectivism	.79	.23	1.29	.22	.87	.11	.91
Achievement	.85	.25	1.18	.10	1.52	.24	1.12

protests. Certainty significantly differed across the three stages of protest, (F (2, 57) = 4.66, $p < .001$), being the lowest before (M = .67, SD = .08) and highest during the protests (M = .93, SD = .05).

Individualism and collectivism

Unlike other categories we notice a mixed progression for trend in individualism (M = .74, SD = .31). The scores for the days of protest remained below the overall mean (M = .73). Collectivism was found to be lowest before (M = .79, SD = .23) and highest during protests (M = 1.29, SD = .22). These trends are visible in Figure 3(e). ANOVA did not reveal significant differences in individualism (F (2, 57) = 2.97, $p < .05$) but collectivism was found to be significantly different across the three periods (F (2, 57) = 28.41, $p < .001$).

Achievement

Figure 3(f) shows that starting with the day before the protests, there was a steady rise in the sense of achievement till 26 December 2012. Achievement significantly differed across the three stages of protests (F (2, 57) = 49.68, $p < .01$) with it being lowest before (M = .85, SD = .25) and highest after the protests (M = 1.52, SD = .24).

Discussion

Emotion analysis of social media constitutes the study of unsolicited, self-volunteered feedback in an autonomous environment. Therefore, in order to establish conceptual stability in the age of big data social movement research, it is important to pay attention to the methodological frameworks we utilize. This study followed two methodological decisions which provide a richer understanding of the findings. Most studies in their temporal analysis of digital footprints follow the traditional 24-h day approach. However, when studying the multifarious dimensions of human behavior, like emotions in a protest, in order to get a micro-perspective of temporality, it is important to break down time interval into shortest possible spans as the behavioral dynamics could change within a matter of minutes. Secondly, although analyzing a single platform like Twitter or Facebook does provide us with meaningful insights, a composite picture can be built by analyzing multiple platforms or sources. Our decision to contrast the Nirbhaya movement's online emotions with emotions of news articles, a set of random tweets and other kinds of user-generated corpora helped us to make better interpretations. Our comparison of periodic emotional trends against each other, contributed to an effective story about the evolution of public emotion during the Nirbhaya movement, and corroborated theory about emotions in offline social movements.

Our results show that online emotions transformed when the protest took the form of a physical gathering. Anger, anxiety, and individualism rapidly fell and were transformed into positive emotion and expressions of collectivism. These trends have been observed and predicted in offline protests as well, corroborating the high degree of emotional correlation between online and offline protest activities. However, do the significantly high frequencies suggest that anger 'drove' the online protest? We planned our analysis in such a way as to highlight the significant differences and discard any 'accidental' high frequencies by comparing against four baseline emotional trends. In fact, the dominant emotions we observed in our pre-protest stage have been extensively examined in social movement literature, and identified as triggers for consequent actions and emotions in the later stages of a protest. Thus, our results reflect that the online Nirbhaya movement was able to channel individual expressions of anger into collective action as an offline protest. By corroborating literature on offline social movements, they do establish that anger and anxiety were powerful mobilizers in the online Nirbhaya movement. The following paragraphs theorize how anger, anxiety, and other pre-protest emotions evolved during the other stages of the online protest.

As per the theory of affective intelligence, anxiety reflects an uncertainty about existing norms and mistrust in an existing establishment (Marcus et al., 2000). It paves the way for people to question their loyalties and demand stability, or at least a change for the better, toward stability, by overcoming anxiety through anger, arising from perception of wrongdoing and blame. Anger reflected citizens' outrage at the heinous incident and its perpetrators. When social activists announced a formal social movement with a common cause – 'justice for women' – the pervasive social outrage served to persuade people to participate in the social movement, because they identified with the common cause (Ahmed & Jaidka, 2013a, 2013b). Protesters, now comforted in the collective identity and ideals, were able to shed their inhibitions and individualistic anxieties. This is evident by the dip in anger over the protest days.

For the online Nirbhaya movement, it was to be expected that the fall of negative emotion in tweets would indicate the rise in positive emotion; however, the actual interplay of these emotions is quite complex. There were high levels of positive emotions during the protest – we interpret this to mean that the outrage, directed at the violence of the incident and the perceived inaction of the government, was gradually strengthened into a collective identity as protesters bonded among themselves and expressed solidarity and hope toward each other, effecting a group catharsis. Furthermore, confidence in the strength of the movement gave protesters optimism, and the hope that they could influence a change in the existing status quo. Their desire to build a new, participatory establishment is marked by significant heightening of positive emotion (Jasper, 2011).

In our findings, the transition from high individualism to high collectivism reflects a change in the psyche of the general public. The appraisal processes of social media users are reflected in the high levels of individualism as they coped with the breaking news. The high levels of collectivism reflect that, with time, protestors began to identify themselves as a part of the whole – the bigger Nirbhaya movement. Expressions of achievement steadily rose since the days of the protest. An interim success for the social movement was a large turnout in the offline protest and the support in the online community. Another success could be the government's haste in implementing punitive measures to control those guilty of transgression, and putting in process future steps that could prevent such incidents from happening again. These successes reinforced protesters' faith in the social movement and their strife toward its goals. We infer that this is also why the pre-protest feelings of anxiety gave way to certainty, marking a full circle in the emotional journey of a protester from anxiety to self-actualization.

Emotions of sadness showed a rise during the early outbreak of the news, followed by a dip during protest action; they began to rise again around the time when the health of the victim deteriorated. This corroborates what is known about waning offline social movements (Adams, 2003; Goodwin et al., 2000; Jasper, 2011) – members of a social movement lose interest when they perceive that their actions are not bearing fruit. It is possible that the news of the dying victim made protesters question the impact of the protest.

We can summarize our analysis in the following way:

Online protests reflect the same emotional patterns as offline protests. We have shown that, akin to existing protest literature, online protests are subject to the same tenors and intensity of emotion as their offline counterparts. Anger and anxiety were found to be the main drivers of protest collectivism reached its peak during protest days, and achievement was the primary emotion experienced in the aftermath.

Emotional liberation and cognitive liberation go hand in hand. In our findings, a collective vocabulary and positive emotional words reflect a change in the collective mindset during protest activities.

No proof that positive and negative emotions reinforce each other. We did not identify any significant correlations between overall negative emotions and overall positive emotions, which is not in line with the theory of affective intelligence (Marcus et al., 2000) or Jasper's (1998) claim that positive emotions work with negative emotions to create a 'moral battery' that drives protests.

Emotions in social media reflect contemporary public opinion. Our results have shown a significant correlation between offline and online protests during the Nirbhaya movement. Our findings support the theoretical notes by Kleres (2005), who postulated that the intensity of visceral emotions '[...] depends on the substance of interactions in a changing macro context' (p. 10). In a similar vein, Jasper (2011) adds that, '[emotions] are a part of action and interaction, not simply motivation and outcome' (p. 13).

Online emotions reflect the goals of the offline protest movement. At the end of the period under observation, most online protestors perceived the Nirbhaya movement to be a success. In the scope of this study, it is difficult to attribute the role of the online protest in the success of the movement; however, it can be said that social media created a new-founded recognition and positive perception of the power of social movements among a class of politically apathetic middle-class professionals in India, as well as new meanings and paradigms for future movements to rely on.

Conclusion

The current state of the art in ICT has eased accessibility to the digital footprints of billions, transcending the artificial data ceilings typically encountered in social sciences research. In social movement studies, big data and such digital footprints are an exciting, powerful addition to the existing research toolkit. In order for social science theory advancement within the social movement framework, it is important for future scholars to realize these multi-faceted and complex dynamics of online–offline relationships. In the age of Twitter and Facebook, protest events are going global, beyond place and boundaries, as witnessed in the Arab Spring and the Occupy Movements. Within such an environment, it becomes imperative to follow a multi-dimensional approach. Our study can be taken as a root point, and it would be illuminating to discover whether these findings of online protest emotions are replicated in another environment, dissimilar or similar to the cultural context of India.

Our findings illustrate the close relationship between online and offline protests, where online protests mirror the goals, participation trends, and emotional patterns of offline protests, as seen during the Nirbhaya movement in India. The results validate literature on offline social movements to show that negative emotions were a powerful mobilizer in the online Nirbhaya movement. In the course of the social movement, online protesters underwent a transition in their psyche – from high individualism, to high collectivism, and from anxiety and anger to emotional and cognitive liberation. Furthermore, individual expressions of anger were mobilized into collective action in the offline protest.

Looking ahead, future scholars should focus on multi-method and multi-platform analyses; traditional methods employed in social movement research (ethnography, surveys, etc.) can be complemented using the digital data to attain richer answers. For future studies within this domain, we would like to adopt an 'extended approach' of analyzing big data where, for example, a network of users with similar highs and lows of emotions or the flow of emotions from one platform to other could allow us to strengthen our claims.

To our knowledge, this is the only study about emotions in either the online or offline Nirbhaya movement, so we cannot compare our findings or contextualize them with other known characteristics of this movement. Protestors are using ICT to organize and mobilize movements; other than being an opportunity for protestors and social movements, these communication technologies also provide valuable data for social movement research, which might not be available otherwise. Studies utilizing big data in social movement research are increasing in number. Our primary data-set is modest in comparison – nevertheless, our study reveals the potential of using big data of large volume, variety, and velocity, for social movement research.

Since our analysis was limited to English-language tweets, our results could have been a better representation of the national demographic, if regional language tweets had been included in the analyses. An alternative approach to identify emotions in online protest could have been to conduct *post hoc* surveys with the protestors, investigating their emotions before, during, and after protest – however, this was beyond the scope of the current analysis. Despite these constraints, this study has been able to identify and establish the role of emotions in driving a social media community to online protest participation. Based on the evidence, we recommend future research into the links between cognition, emotion, and vocabulary usage.

Disclosure statement

The authors do not have any financial interest or benefit arising from the direct applications of this study. Kokil Jaidka is affiliated with Adobe Systems Pvt Ltd, but her collaboration in this project was out of her academic interest and skills in the subject. The article was not written for, reviewed or approved by, nor is it necessarily beneficial for Adobe Systems Pvt Ltd, with which she is affiliated.

References

Adams, J. (2003). The bitter end: Emotions at a movement's conclusion. *Sociological Inquiry, 73*, 84–113.
Ahmed, S., & Jaidka, K. (2013a). Protests against# delhigangrape on Twitter: Analyzing India's Arab Spring. *eJournal of eDemocracy and Open Government, 5*, 28–58.
Ahmed, S., & Jaidka, K. (2013b). The common man: An examination of content creation and information dissemination on Twitter during the 2012 New Delhi gang-rape protest. In S. Urs, J. C. Na, & G. Buchanan (Eds.), *Digital libraries: Social media and community networks* (pp. 117–126). Switzerland: Springer International Publishing.
Back, M. D., Küfner, A. C., & Egloff, B. (2011). "Automatic or the people?" Anger on September 11, 2001, and lessons learned for the analysis of large digital data sets. *Psychological Science, 22*, 837–838.
Bae, Y., & Lee, H. (2012). Sentiment analysis of Twitter audiences: Measuring the positive or negative influence of popular twitterers. *Journal of the American Society for Information Science and Technology, 63*, 2521–2535.
Belair-Gagnon, V., Mishra, S., & Agur, C. (2014). Reconstructing the Indian public sphere: Newswork and social media in the Delhi gang rape case. *Journalism, 15*, 1059–1075.
Bennett, W. L., & Segerberg, A. (2012). The logic of connective action: Digital media and the personalization of contentious politics. *Information, Communication & Society, 15*, 739–768.
Berezin, M. (2009). Exploring emotions and the economy: New contributions from sociological theory. *Theory and Society, 38*, 335–346.
Brubaker, J. R., Kivran-Swaine, F., Taber, L., & Hayes, G. R. (2012, June). Grief-stricken in a crowd: The language of bereavement and distress in social media. *Proceedings of the sixth international AAAI conference on Weblogs and Social Media* (pp. 42–49). Palo Alto, CA: AAAI Press.
Burns, A., & Eltham, B. (2009, November 19–20). *Twitter free Iran: An evaluation of Twitter's role in public diplomacy and information operations in Iran's 2009 election crisis.* Record of the Communications Policy & Research Forum 2009, Sydney.
Castells, M. (2012). *Networks of outrage and hope: Social movements in the Internet age*. Cambridge: Polity Press.

Chan, D. K. C., Fung, Y. K., Xing, S., & Hagger, M. S. (2014). Myopia prevention, near work, and visual acuity of college students: Integrating the theory of planned behavior and self-determination theory. *Journal of Behavioral Medicine, 37*, 369–380.

Chaudhuri, S., & Fitzgerald, S. (2015). Rape protests in India and the birth of a new repertoire. *Social Movement Studies, 14*, 622–628. doi:http://dx.doi.org/10.1080/14742837.2015.1037261

Choudhury, M., Counts, S., & Horvitz, E. (2013, April). Predicting postpartum changes in emotion and behavior via social media. *Proceedings of the SIGCHI conference on Human Factors in Computing Systems* (pp. 3267–3276). New York, NY: ACM.

Derks, D., Fischer, A. H., & Bos, A. E. (2008). The role of emotion in computer-mediated communication: A review. *Computers in Human Behavior, 24*, 766–785.

Dolata, U., & Schrape, J. F. (2015). Masses, crowds, communities, movements: Collective action in the Internet age. *Social Movement Studies, 15*, 1–18.

Earl, J., McKee Hurwitz, H., Mejia Mesinas, A., Tolan, M., & Arlotti, A. (2013). This protest will be tweeted: Twitter and protest policing during the Pittsburgh G20. *Information, Communication & Society, 16*, 459–478.

Eckert, P. (1996). Vowels and nail polish: The emergence of linguistic style in the preadolescent heterosexual marketplace. In N. Warner (Ed.), *Gender and belief systems* (pp. 183–190). Berkeley: Berkeley Women and Language Group.

Eltantawy, N., & Wiest, J. B. (2011). The Arab Spring| Social media in the Egyptian revolution: Reconsidering resource mobilization theory. *International Journal of Communication, 5*, 1207–1224.

Esuli, A., & Sebastiani, F. (2006, May). Sentiwordnet: A publicly available lexical resource for opinion mining. *Proceedings of the 5th conference on Language Resources and Evaluation* (pp. 417–422). Genoa: European Language Resources Association (ELRA).

Flam, H., & King, D. (2007). *Emotions and social movements*. London: Routledge.

Gaby, S., & Caren, N. (2012). Occupy online: How cute old men and Malcolm X recruited 400,000 US users to OWS on Facebook. *Social Movement Studies, 11*, 367–374.

Gamson, W. A. (1995). Constructing social protest. *Social Movements and Culture, 4*, 85–106.

Golder, S. A., & Macy, M. W. (2011). Diurnal and seasonal mood vary with work, sleep, and daylength across diverse cultures. *Science, 333*, 1878–1881.

Gonzalez-Bailon, S., Borge-Holthoefer, J., & Moreno, Y. (2013). Broadcasters and hidden influentials in online protest diffusion. *American Behavioral Scientist, 57*, 943–965.

Goodwin, J., & Jasper, J. M. (2006). Emotions and social movements. In J. E. Stets & J. H. Turner (Eds.), *Handbook of the sociology of emotions* (pp. 611–635). New York, NY: Springer.

Goodwin, J., Jasper, J. M., & Polletta, F. (2000). The return of the repressed: The fall and rise of emotions in social movement theory. *Mobilization: An International Quarterly, 5*, 65–83.

Greater Kashmir. (2015). Irom Sharmila completes 15 years of hunger strike. Retrieved November 6, 2015, from http://www.greaterkashmir.com/news/national/irom-sharmila-completes-15-years-of-hunger-strike/200466.html

Hara, N., & Huang, B. Y. (2011). Online social movements. *Annual Review of Information Science and Technology, 45*, 489–522.

Harlow, S. (2012). Social media and social movements: Facebook and an online Guatemalan justice movement that moved offline. *New Media & Society, 14*, 225–243.

Hiatt, F. (2013). India awakens to its grassroots power. Retrieved November 6, 2015, from https://www.washingtonpost.com/opinions/fred-hiatt-india-awakens-to-its-grass-roots-power/2013/01/16/67a291fe-5f8b-11e2-9940-6fc488f3fecd_story.html

IAMAI. (2013). Social media and the Lok Sabha elections. Retrieved November 6, 2015, from http://www.iamai.in/research/reports_details/453

IAMAI. (2015a). India on the go – Mobile Internet vision report 2017. Retrieved November 6, 2015, from http://www.iamai.in/research/reports_details/3647

IAMAI. (2015b). Rural India tops urban India in social media usage with 100% growth. Retrieved November 6, 2015, from http://iamai.in/media/details/3682

Indian Express. (2015). The Patels of Gujarat campaign for downward mobility. Retrieved November 6, 2015, from http://www.telegraph.co.uk/news/worldnews/asia/india/11967837/The-Patels-of-Gujarat-campaign-for-downward-mobility.html

Jasper, J. (1998). The emotions of protest: Affective and reactive emotions in and around social movements. *Sociological Forum, 13*, 397–424.

Jasper, J. (2011). Emotions and social movements: Twenty years of theory and research. *Annual Review of Sociology, 37*, 285–303.

Kim, S., Bak, J., & Oh, A. H. (2012, June). Do you feel what I feel? Social aspects of emotions in Twitter conversations. *Proceedings of the sixth international AAAI conference on Weblogs and Social Media* (pp. 495–498). Palo Alto, CA: AAAI Press.

Klandermans, P. G. (2014). Identity politics and politicized identities: Identity processes and the dynamics of protest. *Political Psychology, 35*, 1–22.

Klandermans, B., van der Toorn, J., & van Stekelenburg, J. (2008). Embeddedness and identity: How immigrants turn grievances into action. *American Sociological Review, 73*, 992–1012.

Kleres, J. (2005). The entanglements of shame: An emotion perspective on social movement demobilization. In H. Flam & D. King (Eds.), *Emotions and social movements* (pp. 170–188). London: Routledge.

Loader, B. D. (2003). Social movements online. In K. Christensen & D. Levinson (Eds.), *Encyclopedia of community: From the village to the virtual world* (pp. 1319–1320). Thousand Oaks, CA: Sage.

Lotan, G., Graeff, E., Ananny, M., Gaffney, D., & Pearce, I. (2011). The Arab Spring| the revolutions were tweeted: Information flows during the 2011 Tunisian and Egyptian revolutions. *International Journal of Communication, 5*, 1375–1405.

Marcus, G. E., Neuman, W. R., & MacKuen, M. (2000). *Affective intelligence and political judgment*. Chicago, IL: University of Chicago Press.

Martens-Edwards, E. (2014). *Social media during the Egyptian revolution: A study of collective identity and organizational function of Facebook & Co*. Hamburg: Anchor Academic Publishing.

Mohammad, S. M., & Turney, P. D. (2010, June). Emotions evoked by common words and phrases: Using Mechanical Turk to create an emotion lexicon. *Proceedings of the NAACL HLT 2010 workshop on Computational Approaches to Analysis and Generation of Emotion in Text* (pp. 26–34). Stroudsburg, PA: Association for Computational Linguistics.

NDTV. (2015). Farmers' protest in Punjab derails train traffic. Retrieved November 6, 2015, from http://www.ndtv.com/india-news/farmers-protest-in-punjab-derails-train-traffic-1230526

Oliver, P. E., & Myers, D. J. (1998). *Diffusion models of cycles of protest as a theory of social movements*. Paper presented at the congress of International Sociological Association, Montreal, Canada.

Pennebaker, J. W., Booth, R. J., & Francis, M. E. (2007). *Linguistic inquiry and word count: LIWC* [Computer Software]. Austin, TX: Liwc.net.

Pennebaker, J., Boyd, R., Jordan, K., & Blackburn, K. (2015). *The development and psychometric properties of LIWC2015*. Austin, TX: The University of Texas at Austin.

Pennebaker, J. W., & Francis, M. E. (1996). Cognitive, emotional, and language processes in disclosure. *Cognition & Emotion, 10*, 601–626.

Plutchik, R. (1980). *Emotion: A psychoevolutionary synthesis*. New York, NY: Harper & Row.

Porta, D., & Diani, M. (2009). *Social movements: An introduction*. Oxford: Blackwell Publishers.

Rodgers, K. (2010). 'Anger is why we're all here': Mobilizing and managing emotions in a professional activist organization. *Social Movement Studies, 9*, 273–291.

Rude, S., Gortner, E. M., & Pennebaker, J. (2004). Language use of depressed and depression – Vulnerable college students. *Cognition & Emotion, 18*, 1121–1133.

Singh, U. K. (Ed.). (2009). *Human rights and peace: Ideas, laws, institutions and movements* (Vol. 4). New Delhi: SAGE Publications Ltd.

South Asia Channel. (2014). How Indian youth are shaking up the 2014 election. *Foreign Policy*. Retrieved October 13, 2014, from http://southasia.foreignpolicy.com/posts/2014/03/20/how_indian_youth_are_shaking_up_the_2014_election

Starbird, K., & Palen, L. (2012). (How) will the revolution be retweeted? Information diffusion and the 2011 Egyptian uprising. *Proceedings of the ACM 2012 conference on computer supported cooperative work* (pp. 7–16). New York, NY: ACM.

Suttles, J., & Ide, N. (2013). Distant supervision for emotion classification with discrete binary values. In A. Gelbukh (Ed.), *Computational linguistics and intelligent text processing* (pp. 121–136). Berlin: Springer, Berlin Heidelberg.

Tajfel, H. (1979). Individuals and groups in social psychology*. *British Journal of Social and Clinical Psychology, 18*, 183–190.

Tarrow, S., & Tollefson, J. (1994). *Power in movement: Social movements, collective action and politics* (pp. 41–61). Cambridge: Cambridge University Press.

Tausczik, Y. R., & Pennebaker, J. W. (2010). The psychological meaning of words: LIWC and computerized text analysis methods. *Journal of Language and Social Psychology, 29*, 24–54.

Taylor, V. (1989). Social movement continuity: The women's movement in abeyance. *American Sociological Review, 54*, 761–775.

Theocharis, Y., Lowe, W., Van Deth, J. W., & García-Albacete, G. (2014). Using Twitter to mobilize protest action: Online mobilization patterns and action repertoires in the Occupy Wall Street, Indignados, and Aganaktismenoi movements. *Information, Communication & Society, 18*, 202–220.

Tremayne, M. (2014). Anatomy of protest in the digital era: A network analysis of Twitter and Occupy Wall Street. *Social Movement Studies, 13*, 110–126.

Tufekci, Z., & Wilson, C. (2012). Social media and the decision to participate in political protest: Observations from Tahrir Square. *Journal of Communication, 62*, 363–379.

Valenzuela, S., Arriagada, A., & Scherman, A. (2012). The social media basis of youth protest behavior: The case of Chile. *Journal of Communication, 62*, 299–314.

Van Stekelenburg, J. (2013). The political psychology of protest. *European Psychologist, 18*, 224–234.

Van Stekelenburg, J., & Klandermans, B. (2007). Individuals in movements: A social psychology of contention. In B. Klandermans & C. Roggeband (Eds.), *The handbook of social movements across disciplines* (pp. 157–204). New York, NY: Kluwer.

Van Stekelenburg, J., Klandermans, B., & Van Dijk, W. (2011). Combining motivations and emotion: The motivational dynamics of protest participation. *Revista de Psicología Social, 26*, 91–104.

Van Troost, D., Van Stekelenburg, J., & Klandermans, B. (2013). Emotions of protest. In N. Demertzis (Ed.), *Emotions in politics: The affect dimension in political tension* (pp. 186–203). New York, NY: Palgrave Macmillan.

Vargo, C. J. (2014). *Brand messages on Twitter: Predicting diffusion with textual characteristics* (Doctoral dissertation). Chapel Hill, NC: The University of North Carolina at Chapel Hill.

Vis, F. (2013). Twitter as a reporting tool for breaking news. *Digital Journalism, 1*, 27–47.

Zakaria, F. (2013). The Indian spring. *The Washington Post*. Retrieved April 21, 2013, from http://articles.washingtonpost.com/2013-01-17/opinions/36410308_1_middle-class-protests-politics

Open networks and secret Facebook groups: exploring cycle effects on activists' social media use in the 2010/11 UK student protests

Alexander Hensby

ABSTRACT
Much has been written in recent years about the growing impact of social media on social movements. While authors have extolled the virtues of Facebook and Twitter as organisational and informational tools for a range of movements from the Arab Spring to Occupy, evidence remains patchy as to under what conditions social media is most effective at engaging and mobilising the wider public. Drawing on the work of Tarrow, this article considers the impact of cycle effects on the effectiveness of social media as a mobilising and organising tool for the 2010/11 U.K. student protests. Although preceding the broader 'movement of the squares' contention cycle, the protests made similar use of social media for generating mass participation. Yet, its mobilising power was dependent on a number of temporal factors, including amplification through mainstream media and the urgency of its initial campaign goal. Moreover, towards the end of the cycle, activists were found to be using social media – via 'secret' Facebook groups – in ways that reinforced emerging group hierarchies, arguably contradicting their initial commitment to open-access networks and participatory democracy.

Since 2011, a great deal of attention has been paid to the 'movement of the squares' contention cycle, incorporating the Arab Spring revolutions, the Indignados movements in Spain and Greece and the global Occupy Movement (Biekart & Fowler, 2013; Gerbaudo, 2013; Kavada, 2015). Although physical encampments were at the core of many of these movements, activists' use of information and communications technology (ICT) and social media networks have arguably gained the most interest from scholars. These networks have quickly become an essential tool for social movement organising, a tool which according to Bennett and Segerberg (2012) facilitates more personalised and interactive forms of communication under an emerging logic of 'connective action'. This creates new opportunities for engaging and mobilising mass audiences, both online and offline. Unlike traditional forms of collective action, the authors claim that this does not rely on organisational resources or binding collective identities as it transmits ideas and messages virally through social media networks such as Facebook and Twitter.

Although recent movements appear to illustrate many of these transformations, Bennett and Segerberg are less clear on the temporal dimensions to connective action. Social movements, Mattoni and Treré (2014) remind us, are 'ongoing and evolving processes', which leads us to question *under what circumstances* social media might be more or less effective for generating protest. Recalling Tarrow's (1998) concept of the protest cycle, one can identify flows and challenges that movements typically face over their lifespan, from the 'flurries of innovation' and 'rapid diffusion' that characterise their inception, to dilemmas over radicalisation or institutionalisation further down the line. These flows and challenges affect how movements – especially at a group level – are organised democratically, and generate forms of collective identity among participants. This article posits that these flows and challenges also affect activists' social media use.

Studies of recent movements have indicated some evidence of cycle effects. Tremayne (2014), for example, claims that the proliferation of social media content created for Occupy Wall Street was a key driver of the movement's upward 'scale shift' to a worldwide phenomenon. In the case of Occupy Boston, Juris (2012) observes how in its initial stages Facebook and Twitter helped quickly mobilise audiences beyond usual activist circles, but that this openness proved difficult to sustain as the physical camp became more organised.

Social media cycle effects are explored further in this article's case study. Although preceding the aforementioned protest cycle as per Gerbaudo (2013) and Kavada's (2015) definition, the UK student protests of 2010 and 2011 shared many of its characteristics, including the use of occupations as radicalising spaces; the advocacy of leaderless self-organisation, and a commitment to spreading informational openness and participatory democracy. Framed by the new Conservative-Liberal Democrat Government's austerity agenda of public sectors cuts, the student protests responded initially to plans to treble the cap on tuition fees for students in England to £9000 per year, as well as cut 95% of universities' teaching budget. Although part of a wider reform programme designed to marketise the entire HE sector (McGettigan, 2013), these proposals were subject to a parliamentary vote only seven weeks after their announcement in October 2010.

To the surprise of many, students quickly responded with a mass campaign, featuring multiple weekly national and regional demonstrations and a reported 51 occupations of campus buildings across the UK (Solomon & Palmieri, 2011, p. 60). With limited involvement from the National Union of Students (NUS), the campaign was mostly driven by a network of occupation spaces (Theocharis, 2012). These drew extensively on social media as 'organising agents' to pressurise parliament – via the mainstream media coverage it generated – into voting down the fees bill. Although the bill was narrowly passed by parliament, the speed and scale through which they mobilised left many activists feeling optimistic about the self-organising potential of social media for building a wider student movement against higher education marketisation. Much of this energy fed into wider anti-austerity protests in the UK throughout 2011 – including the Occupy Movement – but the student movement itself soon stalled, with follow-up mobilisations against the Government's White Paper struggling to engage the wider student body on a scale comparable to the protests the previous autumn.

This article traces the narrative of the 2010/11 student protests through the interview accounts of student activists from four UK universities. Findings show how important social media networks were to the mobilisations of autumn 2010, both in engaging an audience beyond traditional student activism networks, as well as creating an 'informational exuberance' (Chadwick, 2012) which contributed to the campaign's upward scale shift. Analysis then turns to students' use of social media after the fees vote, findings indicating that much of its mass mobilising capacity soon deflated, leaving a nascent movement suddenly short on organisational power. Students' use of social media also began to evolve in unexpected ways, notably contributing to forms of boundary-drawing through its 'secret' Facebook groups. While this reflected the greater costs and risks incurred by core activists, it also reflected emerging collective identity differences.

Social media and social movements

Much of the perceived promise of social media networks stems from fundamental transformations in web technologies over the past 15 years. During this time, we have seen the exponential increase in peer-to-peer ICT usage, from smartphones to Wi-fi networks. According to Hands (2011, p. 79), these technologies have created a platform for the emergence of 'Web 2.0', defined as 'the proliferation of user-created content and websites specifically built as frameworks for the sharing of information and for social networking'. Its fast, memetic distribution is a driver of what Bennett and Segerberg (2012) call the logic of 'connective action'. Within this logic, activists can disseminate first-hand accounts of events via social networking sites – events which previously might have received one-sided coverage in the mainstream media or no coverage at all. Moreover, these sites are extremely popular, enabling activists to connect with like-minded people across the globe, as well as open their campaigns out to wider, less-politicised audiences – particularly younger people (Bennett, 2008).

With these developments forcing traditional political agencies into adopting forms of 'organisational hybridity' (Chadwick, 2007), the range of online tools available – including blogs, discussion forums, crowdfunding pages, media-sharing sites and social networking sites – creates opportunities for more spontaneous, 'entrepreneurial' forms of activism. According to Bennett and Segerberg (2012), this enables large audiences to be engaged and mobilised at short notice and for very little cost. Facebook and Twitter in particular are commonly used for this purpose, functioning as 'stitching technologies' to quickly assemble networks, share information and recruit actors for political participation.

While one can point to numerous examples of mass mobilisations for online protest – such as e-petitions, Facebook page 'likes' and viral videos (Gaby & Caren, 2012; Morozov, 2011) – its mobilising of actors for *offline* protest has drawn more scepticism from scholars. Many subscribe to Diani's (2000) argument that recruitment for higher cost/risk activities such as demonstrations and occupations relies on social ties cultivated through face-to-face interactions. Evidence from recent movements further muddies the waters: Juris (2012), for example, found that social media served as a powerful mobilising tool for Occupy Boston, though its 'smart mobs' of multiple interpersonal networks were found to disaggregate as quickly as they aggregated. Mercea's (2012) study of Climate Camp mobilisations saw potential for more durable engagement, finding that the availability of information, resources and debate online helped 'unaffiliated' actors accrue knowledge independently of activist ties. While this provided a foundation to plan their own participation and 'develop an activist mindset', it did not necessarily extend to feeling an active part of the movement.

Understanding how these affinities are formed brings us to the extensive literature on collective identity formation. Although there has been some debate over the usefulness of the concept when applied to network-based movements (e.g. McDonald, 2002), Melucci's (1996) conceptualisation as a process borne out of 'identization' arguably remains relevant to the sustenance of any movement. Admittedly, these processes are more easily observable at a *group* level, as identization refers to the building of interpersonal trust relations out of day-to-day interactions, as well as protest participation (see Saunders, 2008). However, Flesher Fominaya (2010) argues that these relations can also outlive contention cycles and sustain groups through latency periods while they prepare for new activism opportunities.

Given this emphasis on the day-to-day, one might assume collective identities are more likely to be forged offline than online, but the two can intersect in productive ways. In her study of the Occupy Movement, Kavada (2015) found that collective identity was strengthened through regular communication and codified practices on social media networks, even if this tended to reinforce existing offline ties rather than create new ones. This partly reflected the fact that Occupy was at its core a physical encampment, though the shared rituals, common practices and emotional attachments Melucci considers essential to 'creating the collective' were ultimately a product of sustained activist *conversations*, be they online or offline.

This overlapping of online and offline networks also blurs distinctions of who might be considered 'inside' and 'outside' of the movement, which has consequences for how it practices democracy. In the case of Occupy, Kavada (2015) found that activists' commitment to the principles of autonomism and horizontality resulted in a fluid and open attitude towards rule-making. The practice of group decision-making, however, took place offline via a system of working groups that fed into consensus-based general assemblies. This owed to practical constraints in facilitating multi-participatory discussions online, though it also reflected core activists' tendency to prioritise individual commitment through their physical participation.

As deliberation spaces, online platforms were also found to generate problems of their own. In her study of the Global Justice Network in Madrid, Flesher Fominaya (2016) found that activists' commitment to participatory democracy processes seldom extended to online interactions. Although opening up activist conversations to the public seemingly reflected a commitment to democratic engagement, the nature of these conversations remained implicitly hierarchical. For Flesher Fominaya, this lack of regulation or reflexivity contradicted the movement's commitment to horizontalism as practiced offline, instead conforming to Juris's (2012) pithy depiction of social media as generating 'ego-centred networks'.

Democracy and horizontalism can also be compromised in more structural ways. Despite Occupy's commitment to 'leaderless' practices, Kavada (2015) noted that unintended positions of authority were nevertheless created through camps' Twitter use. Given the increasing importance of social media as the movement's de facto mouthpiece, activists responsible for updating these accounts came to play a more decisive role in shaping the politics and identity of individual camps, leading to frequent struggles over password and administration rights. Kavada (2009) also noted similar unintended hierarchies in an earlier study of email lists in the alter-globalisation movement. In this instance, a 'secret' list was set up to by a sub-group of 'horizontals', as the main list was considered too large and unwieldy to hold more effective discussions or build collective identity relations. In both cases, Kavada noted how these structural machinations appeared to contradict the values of openness and inclusivity seemingly integral to activists' political identity.

In sum, the literature identifies numerous opportunities and challenges for social movements in their use of social media. While its tools and platforms enable fast mobilisation, efficient organisation, and collective identity-building as per Bennett and Segerberg's (2012) 'connective action' logic, recent studies suggest that it can also create more familiar 'collective action' problems, namely divergent identities, accidental hierarchies and barriers to participation for the socially disconnected. Although studies point to the temporality of some of these problems, studying movements' use of social media from a protest cycle perspective may offer a better understanding of when and where these factors come into play.

The case study: research methods

This article makes use of 42 student interviews, ranging from committed activists to non-participants, who were studying in UK universities at the time of the protests. The vast majority were recruited via a survey questionnaire, although certain activist organisers were approached using forms of purposive and snowball sampling. Interviews are taken from four universities – University of Cambridge, University College London, University of Edinburgh and University of Warwick. As large Russell Group universities, the account of the protests presented in this article is not necessarily representative of UK universities overall, but they were selected on the basis that each featured a certain level of high-cost/risk activism throughout the 2010/11 cycle, as well as returning a high number of prospective interviewees.

Interviews were typically conducted on campus, and focused on capturing interviewees' personal experiences of the student protests, depending on their level of involvement. A degree of representativeness was sought in capturing the story of how occupations were organised by ensuring that a minimum of four students were interviewed from each university who took an active role in their initial planning and day-to-day running. Interviews took place in spring/summer 2012, allowing activists to reflect on the 2010/11 cycle in its entirety. Although most remained proud of the protests' achievements, the passing of time enabled activists to be more objective and self-critical with regard to decisions made and how groups and campaigns were organised. This inevitably impacts on how interview data should be interpreted, as discussions at earlier stages in the cycle may have elicited different perspectives.

The material presented in this article additionally draws on informal participant observation in student occupation spaces and on groups' Twitter feeds and Facebook pages between 2010 and 2011. As well as supporting the preparation for student interviews, this 'background ethnography' proved valuable for understanding how students made use of offline and online spaces, including their interactions with the wider student community.

Beginnings and opportunities

In many ways, the university campus is an ideal field for mobilising actors for protest participation. As well as being 'structurally freed up for activism' (Crossley, 2008), the student body represents an interconnected network, with members linked by their collective sharing of courses, accommodation, friendships and the campus itself. Within this broader network, Crossley and Ibrahim (2012) identify a distinct *activism* network, which coalesces around multiple foci such as the student union and political societies. Although tightly knit and sometimes considered cliquey to outsiders, Crossley (2008, p. 18) argues that the interconnectedness of the overall student network creates the potential for activists to generate a 'self-perpetuating dynamic of politicisation', drawing other socially connected students into taking part.

Although Crossley and Ibrahim say little about the role of social media, Loader, Vromen, Xenos, Steel, and Burgum (2015) find that this activism network is replicated online through a virtual architecture of Twitter feeds and Facebook pages. Recalling Bennett and Segerberg's terminology, one of its principal uses is to 'facilitate connective engagement' among the wider student population. This was certainly a key goal in autumn 2010: with the fate of government proposals to effectively treble tuition fees to be decided by parliament in December, students had seven weeks to pressurise MPs into voting down the bill. With the late 2000s representing a relative fallow-period for education-based campaigns, activists' initial efforts to organise were dependent on email lists and Facebook pages from other left-leaning groups, such as Students' Justice for Palestine (SJP) and People & Planet. The organisational flexibility of social media sites therefore enabled activists to quickly and fluidly assemble an anti-fees campaign. Organisers on each of the four campuses recalled initial meetings quickly attracting 80–100 people, including students hitherto unconnected to the activist network.

Invitation processes for student societies and campaign groups drew strongly on Facebook's 'event' function, which enables users to create a specific webpage for an event and invite friends or group members to join. Invitees are encouraged to RSVP by clicking 'join', 'maybe' or 'decline'. For public events, attendees can add others not currently included on the invite list. On university campuses especially, this snowballing effect enables activists to assemble a long list of potential participants very quickly. Echoing the findings of Loader et al. (2015), interviews with students both inside and outside of activism networks noted that Facebook events were the principal means of communication for protest events on campus:

> If you're gonna organise a protest you put it on Facebook – that's how I find out about protests. So I think definitely that's how you spread the word – yeah, it's primarily through Facebook. (Angie[1], Cambridge)

Initially, activist groups and student unions rallied around the NUS demonstration, scheduled for 10 November. This event unexpectedly drew the participation of 50,000 people, generating widespread media coverage. While its turnout owed to a great deal to the organisational power of student unions and the NUS, attention quickly focused on a minority of students who had peeled away from the march to attack Conservative Party headquarters at Millbank. These attacks were quickly condemned by NUS President Aaron Porter, and the organisation's effective withdrawal thereafter created a vacuum for media-savvy alternative voices to define the campaign themselves. For many activists, this had clear advantages as they felt the media coverage caused by 'Millbank' (as the event quickly became known) had given them access to a greater power, namely the ability to shape the mainstream news agenda:

> Millbank gave us coverage in terms of all of a sudden every newspaper in the country would be calling you going 'when is the next big mobilisation?' (Damon, UCL)

In other words, appealing to mass media *directly* was considered more effective for mobilising students and generating publicity than operating via the bureaucratic machinations of the NUS. This fed into the next major event: a 'National Walkout and Day of Action' proposed by emergent campaign network the National Campaign Against Fees and Cuts (NCAFC). Key to the event's power was providing a focal point for student groups to mobilise *simultaneously* across the UK, either by organising new protests or coordinating already-existing plans. Although NCAFC's press release suggested 'university occupations, banner droppings and walkouts' as examples of 'creative forms of political protest and direct action' (NCAFC, 2010), campus organisers were ultimately free to define this in whichever way they saw fit. In this sense, the day of action was a highly effective means of creating a single media-friendly spectacle out of multiple local events, yet one that required relatively little in the way of coordinating resources beyond NCAFC's website and social media pages.

Activists on the four campuses had similar plans in mind for the day of action, namely advertising a march to campus that would finish with the occupation of a university room or building. As well as representing a well-known student protest repertoire, some activists had been involved in a network of occupations across the UK the previous year for the Free Palestine Movement, and saw an opportunity to repeat this on a larger scale. Much of the planning for the day of action took place offline between experienced activists, though advertising of the march again drew strongly on Facebook event pages. This, too, succeeded in mobilising a mass of students which extended beyond the familiar activist core.

Of course, the number of students who attended the march and resultant occupation did not reflect the scale of opposition to the fees increase. Qualitative and quantitative evidence suggests that while Facebook events mobilised students without prior activism experience, they were likely to have had pre-existing social ties to other participants (see Hensby, 2014, 2016). This did not necessarily mean all participants were connected to the event's *organisers*, as the march attracted clusters of 'unaffiliated' friendship groups, but it nevertheless indicates that mobilisation via Facebook events is somewhat dependent on students finding an *offline* social context to their potential participation. This is illustrated clearly in Rick's recollection:

> Most people who were going invited people just through massive Facebook events, and I think for most of those I clicked 'no' or 'maybe' – because 'maybe' is just a polite way of saying 'no' – but I never really had to explain myself for not going [...] because the people who I know who went on those demos are people who I don't tend to interact with too much directly – it's mostly online. (Rick, Edinburgh)

Once in occupation, students quickly established a system of consensus-based general assemblies, and a structure of multiple working groups. This included a media group, which set up Twitter accounts and Facebook pages to share articles, press releases and blogs about higher education funding and the anti-fees campaign. In so doing, members recognised implicitly the importance of generating 'informational exuberance' through its social media output. Although this strategy adhered to the classic counter-hegemonic maxim of 'don't hate the media, become the media', it also, somewhat paradoxically, set out to keep the campaign high up the mainstream news agenda. There were also conscious efforts to mediate the occupation space through posting photos and making videos. The latter, especially had a 'connective action' rationale in seeking to engage wider audiences virally by presenting occupations as fun and creative spaces. This was illustrated most memorably in the UCL vs Oxford occupation 'dance-off', which quickly gained more than 15,000 views on YouTube. To the surprise of more experienced activists, this overall media strategy succeeded in attracting regular mainstream media interest for the occupation spaces, especially at UCL:

> We had journalists coming in all the time – they'd be like, 'do you want to do an interview for Sky News?' 'Do you want to do Radio 5?' The moment where you have any kind of political agency where the media is *coming to you*, that's really rare – most of the time if you're involved in any kind of political activism, you're chasing the most minute bit of coverage. (Brett, UCL)

This informational exuberance was also directed at the student body. Interview accounts indicate that social media enabled students interested in politics, but lacking personal ties to occupiers to develop their own knowledge independently, much like Mercea's (2012) 'unaffiliated' Climate Camp activists:

> I remember reading about [the tuition fees increase] online, probably through Facebook – someone would link a blog and I would read it. I remember reading and just thinking in my head, and speaking to my friends who were more politically engaged than I was at the time. (Danny, Edinburgh)

The occupations' mediation reflected back through the regular stream of supportive wall posts, hashtags and retweets also helped strengthen participants' commitment to the space, as it served to visualise their wider impact and equip occupants with a sense of collective agency:

> I got Twitter that week, and if you're following it online and realising how big it was it was... I'd never been in something that felt that big, this national thing where all these people were feeling similar things and it might've gone somewhere and, you know, achieve something. (Rhiannon, Edinburgh)

In more practical terms, occupation Facebook pages and Twitter accounts were utilised to mobilise for spontaneous marches or flash mobs. These hastily arranged actions had powerful effects, with events quickly attracting crowds far in excess of the occupiers themselves:

> We had two of our own demos whilst we were in occupation. Each time we were getting maybe 400 people or so, not doing any real publicity – just putting it online, tweeting it and saying 'Let's meet here'. (Jeremy, Edinburgh)

> We could get demos weekly by demand – just call a demo, make a Facebook page and a couple of hundred people show up. It was simple. Those were the times we were in. (Eric, Cambridge)

Eric's somewhat elegiac recollection implies a temporality to these mobilisations that will be discussed in the following section, though one can again highlight the ease through which large crowds were mobilised. Indeed, the target for some of these actions reflected a broadening of students' political critique, with protests drawing attention to perceived inconsistencies in the government's austerity agenda, notably its negligence towards corporate tax avoidance:

> We held the first Topshop occupation in the country [...] We showed up and called loads of news cameras – we chose a Monday because we knew it would be a slow news day and we could get it fairly up the agenda. Every time we saw that our space in the media narrative was dropping we would invent something to put us back in. (Gaz, UCL)

Although these actions generated a great deal of media interest – helping promote emerging campaign network UK Uncut in the process – they perhaps also reflected a more general tendency towards the 'mediatization' of activists' repertoire choices (Mattoni & Treré, 2014). Although in many ways justified for the purposes of pressurising MPs into voting against the fees bill, it arguably ran the risk of maintaining a mainstream media profile becoming an end in itself. As Gitlin (1981) recalls from his experiences of student activism in the 1960s, the media can also be a capricious platform on which to base a campaign, especially if it turns on the activists or loses interest in them.

Yet, these issues were not considered problematic by the day of the parliamentary vote in December 2010. November's day of action had established 51 occupation groups across the UK, of which around 30 coalesced into a powerful network of intercommunicative protest hubs for the next fortnight (Theocharis, 2012). This network also helped mobilise for numerous national and regional demonstrations, including one in London on the day of the vote which drew 30,000 people. Moreover, in the effective absence of the NUS, the campaign was mostly run from social media and occupation blog sites, as well as physical occupation spaces. In other words, social media contributed significantly to the campaign's rapid upward 'scale shift', not only through its functionality as an organising agent, but its capacity to quickly gain traction from mainstream media.

After the vote: downward scale shift

With the fees bill narrowly passing in parliament, occupiers recalled feeling physically and mentally exhausted by the time occupations closed down in mid-December. Despite this, many felt that they had undergone a transformative social and political experience over the preceding seven weeks. In collectively bearing the risks of eviction, legal action, not to mention physically sharing the same living space, occupying had generated strong solidarities and friendships among its regular participants. In more practical terms, they felt that these ties, together with the momentum and media traction achieved the previous semester, could and should form the basis of a UK-wide student *movement* against austerity and the marketisation of higher education.

Yet, this momentum and traction proved difficult to sustain. The previous semester's mass mobilisations had at their core a relatively simple issue of grievance, namely the trebling of the fees cap. As Ibrahim (2011) argues, this appealed to students' 'moral economy' and sense of fairness – a position hardened for many by the fact that as junior partners in the Coalition Government, the Liberal Democrats had controversially u-turned on its electoral pledge to oppose any increase to fees. By early 2011, however, the political consensus of the previous semester appeared more vulnerable in the absence of a common grievance and purpose:

> That entire [previous] semester there wasn't much structured political discussion. We had a purpose – we were all there because of the fees thing, and the fact that some people were SJPs and some were anarchists didn't matter – it was kind of like, 'We all agree on this'. That caused problems when the vote happened because it wasn't clear anymore what we were united on. (Peter, Edinburgh)

In addition to joining forces with wider anti-austerity coalitions, student-centric protests resumed in early 2011 in much the same fashion as the previous semester, with Facebook events used to mobilise the wider student population. The difference, however, was that the absence of the fees vote meant that protests focused instead on displaying a more general resistance to the marketisation of higher education, a focus which mobilised far fewer people than the previous semester:

> The first thing we needed to deal with was a lot of people giving up because the bill had gone through, and our numbers shrank because of that. (Andrew, Cambridge)

> We were still very high-profile, we had a lot of support – a lot of *latent* support – but when we didn't have an active issue to grapple around, that became a problem [...] Because we had attached our political actions to the actions of Parliament, we're then subservient to their timescale, and as soon as they stop doing things relevant to us, we cease to be relevant. (Gaz, UCL)

In other words, the fees grievance had given activists an issue that had appealed to the wider student body, but in so doing came to define the protests' perceived purpose and lifespan. While in occupation, students had soon recognised that the fees issue was symptomatic of wider marketisation trends, but as a basis for new protests this did not carry the same sense of urgency as before. This made it harder to mobilise the student body as widely and spontaneously as the previous semester, though as Gaz admitted it also reflected activists' increasing reliance on the attention of mainstream media. The fees issue had made for an appealing narrative for the UK press as it dovetailed with the already-prominent news story of the newly formed coalition government and the Liberal Democrats' policy u-turn. As a result, the events of Millbank and subsequent wave of occupations were given extensive coverage. For activists, this had given greater voice to their arguments while effectively promoting their protest actions through mass media channels. Taken in combination, this served to amplify the protests far in excess of the organisational resources they had at their disposal. As Damon recalls, this amplification had been critical for engaging the wider student body:

> Students believe that a student movement is worth fighting in when they see it reflected by an alternate reality – when the mainstream media is writing the same kind of articles that appear in their student paper, they go 'ah, wait – this one matters then'... [But] there is a limit to how much you can use the Guardian front page as your main communications tool. (Damon, UCL)

It is thus argued that the 'alternate reality' created through mainstream media coverage was an essential component to Facebook event pages' capacity to generate mass mobilisations. For politically engaged individuals who were socially unaffiliated to occupations or activism networks, this coverage provided a context and relevance to Facebook events which transcended the usual hubbub of campaigns on campus, while helping legitimise it as a 'topical' issue. Students receiving these invitations therefore recognised that in attending these protests they were also participating in a significant *national event*.

Yet, recalling Juris's (2012) observation on the 'smart mobs' of Occupy Boston, these were subservient to the campaign's perceived lifespan, meaning that in the absence of strong ties these mobilisations disaggregated as quickly as they aggregated, contributing to an almost-as-rapid *downward* scale shift.

Making a movement

As already noted, much of the power and momentum the protests achieved in autumn 2010 owed to the speed at which they mobilised large numbers. This left many commentators and activists reflecting in the aftermath of the fees vote on the possibilities these new forms of networked mobilising had created. Mason (2011), for example, linked the student protests to unfolding uprisings in North Africa when arguing that 'horizontalism has become endemic because technology… kills vertical hierarchies spontaneously'. Aitchison and Peters (2011) saw its porous network structure as indicative of an 'open sourcing of political activism', but echoed Diani (2000) in noting the importance of affinities forged through autumn's occupations and demonstrations for building a more sustained student movement.

The protests' downward scale shift in early 2011 not only reflected the loss of a uniting cause, but also different levels of collective identification that had formed the previous semester. While core occupiers had forged close ties through the intensity of their involvement, this did not extend as far as members of the Facebook-mobilised 'smart mobs', whose participation soon dropped off after the fees vote. This fed into differing views over how to build a student movement. Recalling the 'institutionalisation or radicalisation' dilemma in the latter stages of Tarrow's (1998) protest cycle, some felt that the drop in mass participation exposed the students' organisational and financial limitations. Consequently, they advocated putting anti-austerity candidates forward for sabbatical positions in forthcoming student union elections to give the movement a stronger organisational base. Others, however, felt that the protests' most powerful legacy was their spontaneous, networked forms of organising. From their perspective, this was what put students on the front pages, and the relationships of trust and solidarity that had formed between participants could be used to mobilise for further empowering actions. These students therefore continued organising impromptu flash mobs and occupations. Such actions illustrated the strength of participants' interpersonal relationships, but they arguably also reflected the extent to which they had become disconnected from the wider student body:

> People became slightly ghettoized, and there were fewer people joining in as the months progressed – it became much more of a group of friends. (Brett, UCL)

These tactics also presented new organisational challenges. The openness through which occupation groups communicated the previous semester – both offline and online – had left them increasingly vulnerable to forms of surveillance: some interviewees reported undercover police officers attending general assemblies, whereas others claimed that their phones had been tapped. Whether these students *were* actually under surveillance is a moot point (for this article at least); what remains significant is that they began to adapt their behaviour because they *felt* that they were being watched. As a result, groups became more selective in the sort of information and language they used to report meetings or planned actions. More problematic, however, was their increasing reliance on invitation-only 'secret Facebook groups':

> With Facebook groups, we have one which is a secret group, which has about 40 people on it, and then there is a broader one that has about 300, so I think that would be the core and periphery balance. We eventually became aware that we were being monitored from the Facebook group by security because they started turning up for our meetings, so we set up this secret group. (Raphael, Warwick)

> We have a [Facebook] page where we broadcast messages, and there's the secret group, which in a way isn't very healthy – it's a terrible way of organising. (Damon, UCL)

When occupations were initially set up, participants had been freely added to this group, but as Raphael suggests, these were later changed to invitation-only. Meanwhile, a separate 'public' page was retained for forms of open discussion and micro-broadcasting. Although partly the outcome of efforts to counter the threat of surveillance, by mid-2011 the invite-only group had effectively become a secret planning and discussion space. Recalling Kavada (2015) and Flesher Fominaya's (2016) cases, this posed obvious problems for occupations' commitment to horizontalism and participatory democracy. As with most protest camps, the student occupations had developed an implicit core-periphery structure among its participants (Hensby, 2014). Yet, in practice these boundaries were arguably more malleable, depending to a large extent on how much time students typically spent at the space. The establishing of public and closed Facebook groups would later replicate this core-periphery balance, but it crucially also gave *structure* to these hitherto-fluid boundaries.

This had consequences for students both inside and outside the 'secret' group. Echoing Flesher Fominaya's (2016) findings, some members admitted that the space had begun to function as an echo-chamber for upholding certain beliefs, with one voicing frustrations at how certain participants could dominate discussions in ways that would not have been tolerated in consensus meetings. For students on the outside, the secret group represented a boundary between themselves and core activists. One such student was Danny, who had political interests but felt insufficiently connected socially to get involved in the 2010 Edinburgh occupation. Over time, he strengthened his social ties to activists, but still had to overcome certain barriers of affinity and trust:

> So there's a secret Facebook page and that's where a lot of organising used to happen. It used to be quite a little hub and I wasn't let on it for several months just to make sure I was all right – if I'm a cop I'm not going to tell you, right? (laughs) [...] If you've got connections then they assume you're good, whereas if they've seen you around campus, they sort of know who you are but they don't really know your politics it takes a while to get their trust, which felt a little bit alie nating to be honest. (Danny, Edinburgh)

While concerns about commitment and trust are typical of most radical movements, it is significant how Facebook – depicted as a driver of networked openness and 'connective action' by many scholars – came to play such a key role in drawing hierarchical boundaries and maintaining network secrecy. Even taken as an unintended consequence of students' concerns over surveillance (as Danny's comment alludes to), the irony that such practices should exist within a year of occupation arguably points to the enduring significance of cycle effects on student activists' social media use. Nor was this irony lost on students when eventually granted access to these groups:

> They made me an admin... I see it as some sort of symbolic thing, like, 'you're in with us now'. No one else was made an admin and I just thought, like, that's not really cool... It's a bit elitist, a bit cliquey. (Bekka, Edinburgh)

Conclusion

In studying activists' social media use across the 2010/11 protests, this article has highlighted the enduring importance of cycle effects in contemporary media-centric movements. Findings have shown that Facebook and Twitter can facilitate connective engagement *and* offline protest mobilisation, enabling grass-roots campaigns to build quickly and effectively. However, the case study has indicated that these powers might be temporal and more susceptible to long-standing collective action trends as the cycle progresses. Moreover, these findings show the malleability of social media as an organising tool, with its capacity to facilitate network secrecy and hierarchy as well as openness and horizontality.

At the beginning of the cycle, students' use of Facebook and Twitter contributed significantly towards the campaign's rapid upward scale shift. The accessibility and adaptability of these tools enabled activists to respond quickly to the fees announcement and build a campaign that communicated directly with students and mainstream media. This was illustrated most powerfully in NCAFC's 'Day of Action', which spawned an interconnected network of occupation spaces. Occupiers took advantage of social media platforms to arrange multiple spontaneous, media-friendly mobilisations, as well as provide a regular supply of tweets, blogs, articles and videos. While their viral distribution through personalised communication networks recalls Bennett and Segerberg's (2012) logic of connective action, generating this 'informational exuberance' was also a deliberate strategy for maintaining the interest of mainstream media.

The emphasis on building and sustaining the campaign's mainstream media presence reflected a need to pressurise MPs into voting down the fees bill. The amplification it created arguably strengthened activists' ability to rally unaffiliated 'smart mobs' in the run-up to the vote, but the media narrative of the fees vote ultimately came to define the students' perceived purpose and lifespan. The resultant downward scale shift echoes Gitlin's (1981) observations on student movements in the 1960s, and the mixed blessings of mainstream media amplification. Moreover, this loss of attention exposed the fragility of students' organisational power, as the lack of strong ties and a uniting cause saw the disaggregation of smart mobs at a time when many core occupiers were trying to build a wider student movement. These occupiers *had* built strong ties, but in their efforts to counter surveillance threats they had become increasingly disconnected from the wider student body. Social media ironically gave structure to this disconnection via 'secret' Facebook groups, arguably contradicting the values of horizontalism and democracy occupation spaces were initially founded upon.

In sum, the case study has identified certain limitations to social media's effectiveness as a mobilising and organising tool, limitations which are perhaps more likely to emerge over the course of a protest cycle. Although it is doubtful whether the accountability structures of the NUS and student unions could have led a campaign as dynamic as activists achieved in autumn 2010, the mobilising power of social media rested on temporalities specific to the cycle's early stages. This is not to say that social media lacks mobilising agency. Rather, it is to point to its constraints for creating mobilisations that extend beyond 'sporadic' episodes (Theocharis, 2012). Nor does this mean that students mobilised initial through Facebook events did not go on to become committed activists after the fees bill passed. The creative means through which occupations formed ensured that they attracted a significant number of participants with little or no prior activism experience. Yet, their development and growing commitment as *activists* arguably owed more to the ties and collective identities formed in the physical space itself.

The organisational expression of these strengthening ties and identities through 'secret' Facebook groups calls into question the perceived affinity between ICT networks and the values of horizontalism as proposed by Mason (2011) and others. Activists' use of Facebook in particular has shown that social media is a malleable organising tool, one that evolves in accordance with activists' changing needs. In this respect, this article echoes Flesher Fominaya's (2016) argument that activists need to be more reflexive in their online organisation in order to sustain their commitments to horizontalism and participatory democracy, particularly in how it responds to authorities' efforts to suppress their connective power.

While findings point to cycle effects in the student case study, it remains to be seen whether cycle effects can be applied to contemporary media-centric movements more broadly. Certainly, studies by Juris (2012) and Tremayne (2014) suggest similar effects in protests' early stages, as do Flesher Fominaya (2016) and Kavada (2015) in their latter stages. It is therefore proposed that future studies of social movements employing elements of a 'connective action' logic take greater consideration of the extent to which these processes evolve, and are shaped by how activists respond to more familiar 'collective action' problems.

Note

1. All interviewee names have been changed in this article.

Disclosure statement

No potential conflict of interest was reported by the author.

References

Aitchison, G., & Peters, A. (2011). The open-sourcing of political activism: How the internet and networks help build resistance. In D. Hancox (Ed.), *Fight back! A reader on the winter of protest* (pp. 44–60). London: Open Democracy.
Bennett, W. L. (2008). Changing citizenship in the digital age. In W. L. Bennett (Ed.), *Civic life online: Learning how digital media can engage youth* (pp. 1–24). Cambridge, MA: The MIT Press.
Bennett, W. L., & Segerberg, A. (2012). The logic of connective action: Digital media and the personalization of contentious politics. *Information, Communication & Society, 15*, 739–768.
Biekart, K., & Fowler, A. (2013). Transforming activisms 2010+: Exploring ways and waves. *Development and Change, 44*, 527–546.
Chadwick, A. (2007). Digital network repertoires and organizational hybridity. *Political Communication, 24*, 283–301.
Chadwick, A. (2012). Web 2.0: New challenges for the study of e-democracy in an era of informational exuberance. In S. Coleman & P. Shane (Eds.), *Connecting democracy: Online consultation and the flow of political communication* (pp. 45–75). Cambridge, MA: MIT Press.
Crossley, N. (2008). Social networks and student activism: On the politicising effect of campus connections. *The Sociological Review, 56*, 19–38.
Crossley, N., & Ibrahim, J. (2012). Critical mass, social networks and collective action: Exploring student political worlds. *Sociology, 46*, 596–612.
Diani, M. (2000). Social movement networks virtual and real. *Information, Communication and Society, 3*, 386–401.
Flesher Fominaya, C. (2010). Collective identity in social movements: Central concepts and debates. *Sociology Compass, 4*, 393–404.
Flesher Fominaya, C. (2016). Unintended consequences: The negative impact of e-mail use on participation and collective identity in two 'Horizontal' social movement groups. *European Political Science Review, 8*, 95–122.
Gaby, S., & Caren, N. (2012). Occupy online: How cute old men and Malcolm X recruited 400,000 US users to OWS on Facebook. *Social Movement Studies, 11*, 367–374.
Gerbaudo, P. (2013). Protest diffusion and cultural resonance in the 2011 protest wave. *The International Spectator, 48*, 86–101.
Gitlin, T. (1981). *The whole world is watching: The mass media in the making and unmaking of the new left*. Berkeley: University of California Press.
Hands, J. (2011). *@ Is for activism*. London: Pluto Press.
Hensby, A. (2014). Networks, counter-networks and political socialisation: Paths and barriers to high-cost/risk activism in the 2010/11 student protests against fees and cuts. *Contemporary Social Science, 9*, 92–105.
Hensby, A. (2016). Campaigning for a movement: Collective identity and student solidarity in the 2010/11 UK protests against fees and cuts. In R. Brooks (Ed.), *Student politics and protest*. London: Routledge.
Ibrahim, J. (2011). The new toll on higher education and the UK student revolts of 2010-2011. *Social Movement Studies, 10*, 415–421.
Juris, J. S. (2012). Reflections on #occupy everywhere: Social media, public space, and emerging logics of aggregation. *American Ethnologist, 39*, 259–279.
Kavada, A. (2009). Email lists and the construction of an open and multifaceted identity. *Information, Communication & Society, 12*, 817–839.
Kavada, A. (2015). Creating the collective: Social media, the occupy movement and its constitution as a collective actor. *Information, Communication & Society, 18*, 872–886.
Loader, B. D., Vromen, A., Xenos, M. A., Steel, H., & Burgum, S. (2015). Campus politics, student societies and social media. *The Sociological Review, 63*, 820–839.
Mason, P. (2011, February 5). Twenty Reasons why it's kicking off everywhere. *BBC Newsnight*. Retrieved October 14, 2013, from http://www.bbc.co.uk/blogs/newsnight/paulmason/2011/02/twenty_reasons_why_its_kicking.html
Mattoni, A., & Treré, E. (2014). Media practices, mediation processes and mediatization in the study of social movements. *Communication Theory, 24*, 252–271.
McDonald, K. (2002). From solidarity to fluidarity: Social movements beyond 'collective identity' – the case of globalization conflicts. *Social Movement Studies, 1*, 109–128.
McGettigan, A. (2013). *The great university gamble*. London: Pluto Press.
Melucci, A. (1996). *Challenging codes*. Cambridge: Cambridge University Press.

Mercea, D. (2012). Digital prefigurative participation: The entwinement of online communication and offline participation in protest events. *New Media & Society, 14*, 153–169.

Morozov, E. (2011). *The net delusion: How not to liberate the world*. London: Allen Lane.

NCAFC. (2010, November 12). *Press release: 24th November national walkout and day of protest against tuition fees*. Retrieved December 19, 2013, from http://anticuts.com/2010/11/12/press-release-24th-november-walkout-and-day-of-action/

Solomon, C., & Palmieri, T. (Eds.). (2011). *Springtime: The new student rebellions*. London: Verso.

Saunders, C. (2008). Double-edged swords? Collective identity and solidarity in the environment movement. *The British Journal of Sociology, 59*, 227–253.

Tarrow, S. (1998). *Power in movement* (2nd ed.). Cambridge: Cambridge University Press.

Theocharis, Y. (2012). Cuts, tweets, solidarity and mobilisation: How the internet shaped the student occupations. *Parliamentary Affairs, 65*, 162–194.

Tremayne, M. (2014). Anatomy of protest in the digital era: A network analysis of twitter and occupy wall street. *Social Movement Studies, 13*, 110–126.

The new information frontier: toward a more nuanced view of social movement communication

Jennifer Earl and R. Kelly Garrett

ABSTRACT
The information environment that social movements face is increasingly complex, making traditional assumptions about media, messaging, and communication used in social movement studies less relevant. Building on work begun within the study of digital protest, we argue that a greater integration of political communication research within social movement studies could offer substantial research contributions. We illustrate this claim by discussing how a greater focus on audiences and message reception, as well as message context, could advance the study of social movements. Specifically, we discuss a range of topics as applied to movement research, including information overload, selective attention, perceptions of bias, the possibilities that entertainment-related communications open up, and priming, among other topics. We suggest the risks of not adapting to this changing information environment, and incorporating insights from political communication, affect both the study of contemporary (including digital) protest, as well as potentially historical protest. The possibilities opened up by this move are immense including entirely new research programs and questions.

The information environment that social movements face is increasingly complex (Gillan, Pickerill, & Webster, 2008). Whether one looks at the fragmentation of media audiences (Webster & Ksiazek, 2012), the rise of social media as an information source (Pew Research Center, 2014), the risks of selective exposure to media (Stroud, 2011), information overload (Graber, 1988), or the ways in which behind-the-scenes algorithms influence what information Web surfers can find online (Pariser, 2011), there is no disputing that important questions about communication practices within social movements have proliferated. Scholars interested in digital protest have been among a vanguard in sociology to examine these issues. However, progress has been incremental and *ad hoc*, and has not diffused to the wider study of social movements despite potentially large payoffs.

The need to make this analytical pivot can be seen as a glass half empty or a glass half full. From the half-empty perspective, social movement studies and sociology more broadly do not have a strong, recent background in theorizing or empirically studying political communication *qua* communication, save research on digital protest. This leaves the field in a lurch: there are increasingly important questions for which we have relatively little experience (Earl & Rohlinger, 2012). From the half-full perspective, though, several allied fields focus precisely on questions about media and communication from which social movement scholars could draw to substantially jump-start our work. Notably, the inter-disciplinary field of political communication – which operates at the intersection of communication and political science and is concerned with how political information is created, distributed, consumed, interpreted, and acted upon – is ripe for this kind of cross-pollination. The central aim of this article is to suggest that by focusing on the audiences for social movement communication, and on how movement messages are received, we could expand and improve social movement scholarship.[1]

Specifically, we discuss two lines of potential research as illustrative examples of what an expanded connection between political communication and social movement studies could bring: (1) social movement scholars could analyze the audiences for social movement communications to understand how they access and process information, instead of more exclusively focusing on the strategic or mediated production of information; and (2) social movement scholars could examine how context affects audience consumption. We close with several important clarifications. First, we see our contribution as inviting further work on this topic, not as an exhaustive review of the ways that political communication research could be usefully appropriated by social movement scholars.[2] Second, we stress that we are not suggesting that social movement scholarship become a subset of political communication, even though some communication scholars have made such an argument (Bennett & Segerberg, 2011, 2013). That would be as problematic as social movement scholars continuing to ignore political communication research.

How has social movement scholarship approached media and communication?

While questions about media and communication were once at the core of sociology, American sociology began to turn away from them in the middle of the twentieth century as high-profile research in the 1940s suggested minimal effects of media coverage on voting preferences (for lengthy discussions on this topic, see: Earl, 2015; Jamieson, in press; Pooley & Katz, 2008). Although the 'minimal-effects paradigm' that this work spawned has been heavily criticized since then, it had an enduring influence on the field of sociology (Jamieson, in press). As American sociology programs were turning away from questions about media, journalism schools in the U.S. were flush with funds and eager to add academic research units, often in the form of communication departments, to drive up their academic prestige (Jamieson, in press). Thus, as sociology pushed away questions about communications and media, independent communication departments were being founded in the U.S. to address precisely these questions.

Social movement studies, as we know it today, was not born until well after the breach between sociology and communication developed. Although the study of collective behavior, which was the progenitor of contemporary social movement studies, emerged during a period when sociologists were more concerned with the media and communication processes, as a subfield collective behavior was often focused on the micro-level (Buechler, 2011; e.g. Kornhauser, 1959; Le Bon 1960 [1895]). Thus, when the study of social movements grew out of the older study of collective behavior (beginning in the late 1960s and early 1970s), there was neither general disciplinary pressure to address media and communication in critical ways nor a legacy of doing so from collective behavior research.

Research on framing, which developed in the 1980s, is a notable exception, but most of this research focused on strategic communication practices and the production, not the reception, of frames. For instance, scholars investigating how movements frame beliefs to motivate participation and support (Snow, 2004; Snow, Rochford, Worden, & Benford, 1986) tended to place more emphasis on how these frames are produced internally than on how they are received (e.g. Gamson & Meyer, 1996; Klandermans, 1996; McCammon, Hewitt, & Smith, 2002). When research did analyze the effects of frames, it tended to be at the macro-level (McAdam & Rucht, 1993; Snow & Benford, 1992), examining questions such as when news outlets would rebroadcast specific frames (Bail, 2012) and whether movements that adjusted their frames improved their futures (McCammon, 2014).

The concept within framing most closely related to audience reception is frame resonance (Snow & Benford, 1988), which speaks to how compelling frames are to audience members. But, in practice, research on resonance often serves as a *post hoc* explanation for the success of particular frames (e.g. frames diffused because they resonated) without enough empirical attention to whether resonance is the best explanation for frame diffusion, how a frame creates resonance, or how frames influence individuals' issue perceptions.[3]

Likewise, a substantial amount of research has gone into understanding what movements can do to gain media coverage of their ideas and actions (Amenta, Caren, Olasky, & Stobaugh, 2009; Earl, Martin, McCarthy, & Soule, 2004; Ferree, Gamson, Gerhards, & Rucht, 2002; Rohlinger, 2002); the role of media such as radio (Roscigno & Danaher, 2001) or books (but see Meyer & Rohlinger, 2012 for a critique of this view) in generating support for movements; and/or the unintended consequences of coverage for social movements (e.g. Gitlin, 1980). Again, the majority of this work either considers the organizer's point of view (e.g. how can movements generate media coverage while avoiding being pushed to more radical ends as they vie for it?) or focuses on aggregate relationships between media availability and movement effects (e.g. proximity to radio stations increased mobilization, see Roscigno & Danaher, 2001).

European scholarship has tended to view meaning and movements as more co-constituted (and less strategic) than Americans, but even here there has not been a large focus on explicitly communicative processes within movements. For instance, while Melucci (1996) and other new social movement theorists are concerned broadly with meaning and collective identity, the focus of this work is on competing meaning systems, which reveal the ways in which the idea of a singular movement is a reification. Likewise, while Eyerman and Jamison (1991) are focused on knowledge interests and cognitive praxis, the focus is largely on knowledge-making within movements, not on communicative processes like the ones we explore below. As is true for American work, research on digital protest tends to be the major exception.

Thus, until the rise of digital protest, few social movement researchers examined how audiences access, consume, or understand these communications (Earl & Rohlinger, 2012; save notable exceptions such as: Gamson, 2004; Gamson, Fireman, & Rytina, 1982; Gamson & Modigliani, 1989; Gamson & Wolfsfeld, 1993), and this research was rare even though these are standard topics of concern in political communication. Earl (2015) argues that digital protest did to social movements research what research on new media was doing to many areas within sociology: it forced a fledgling rapprochement between sociology and communication, and this has been true in both American and European research (Castells, 2012; For a pre-Internet treatment of the information age: Melucci, 1996). As classically trained social movement scholars, largely drawn from sociology but to a lesser extent from political science, began to study online protest, they were publishing alongside communication and political communication scholars interested in digital protest, with each group of scholars bringing very different questions, theories, and approaches to research to bear on the topic. In fact, much of the early work on digital protest was (and continues to be) published in interdisciplinary journals, such as *Information, Communication, & Society*, *Social Science Computer Review*, and *New Media & Society*. The interdisciplinary reviewing pool for these journals forced communication and political communication scholars to become more familiar with and concerned with social movement theory (e.g. work on the free rider dilemma by Bimber, Flanagin, & Stohl, 2005; Flanagin, Stohl, & Bimber, 2006) and social movement scholars to become more familiar with relevant work from communication and political communication (e.g. Earl & Kimport, 2011; Gillan, 2009; Gillan et al., 2008). The result has been the development of an interdisciplinary research area on digital protest which features leading figures associated with political communication and communication more broadly (e.g. Bennett, Bimber, Chadwick, Karpf), and sociology (e.g. Earl, Gillan, Yang).

However, this fledgling rapprochement is limited in two respects. First, even within the study of digital protest, scholars have tended to import singular concepts from communication without building a more systematic connection between the areas. For instance, Earl and Kimport (2011) import a critique of technological determinism from communication and technology studies, as do Gillan et al. (2008). But, Earl and Kimport (2011) don't have much to say about the wider information environment or how participants perceive digital protest. Gillan and collaborators (Gillan, 2009;

Gillan et al., 2008) acknowledge risks identified within political communication, such as information overload and selection effects, and Bennett and Segerberg (2011, 2013) discuss the personalization of politics as part of the rise of 'connected' versus collective action, but we argue that a more systematic integration of social movement studies with political communication is important.

Second, the rapprochement between social movement studies and communication has been limited by its segregation within the study of digital protest. While the rapidly changing information environment affects all forms of protest, including street activism (Gillan et al., 2008), social movement scholarship – as observed in social movement-specific journals, such as *Mobilization* and *Social Movement Studies*, or in social movement-specific imprints, such as the Minnesota series – has not taken up communication-related questions around protest dynamics writ large. Instead, research on more traditional questions (e.g. on framing and media coverage in American research and on collective identity and knowledge work in European research) continues without significant adjustment.

Political communication and new horizons for social movement research

As mentioned earlier, political communication is an interdisciplinary field that primarily draws on the disciplines of communication and political science, though it is also informed by sociology, psychology, and other fields. The fundamental question of the subfield is: How do political messages – whatever their source and mode of delivery – shape audiences' political attitudes and behaviors? This question naturally fits within the wider concerns of communication as a field, which have been famously summarized as describing 'Who/says what/ in which channel/ to whom/ with what effect?' (Lasswell, 1948, p. 37). That is, many of the questions that political communication scholars raise are related to larger questions in communication, but are specifically applied to the communication of political messages. Scholars from political science also contribute to and identify as political communication scholars, meaning that theoretical and methodological influences from political science have informed the development of political communication as well.

Social movement scholars have made headway understanding activists as communicators, beginning to probe the messages they produce, and studying one important medium – large national newspapers. In the rest of this article, we showcase what could be gained by examining a more diverse range of communication questions. In short, we ask what social movement scholars could learn from a fuller investigation of political communication, including studying political communicators, political messages, media that carry political messages, audiences for political messages, and (de)mobilization and other effects of political messages. Given limited space, we focus on two larger issues that we see as uniquely pressing for social movement scholars: (1) problematizing the audience – how do messages reach them, get attended to, get interpreted, and get acted upon; and (2) how does the context in which a message is received shape its reception and its effects?

Table 1 summarizes six key research areas related to these broader concerns. The table identifies a series of problematic assumptions that social movement scholars might implicitly make about political communication, it suggests open-ended research questions that could motivate new lines of social movement inquiry, and it offers examples of specific topics meriting further study. We do not claim that this article, or this table, is an exhaustive accounting of how political communication might enrich social movement research. To the contrary, we acknowledge that our approach to this integration represents one of many possible perspectives, and we invite other political communication and/or social movement scholars to raise alternative pathways to integration.

Problematizing the audience

The *sine qua non* for movement messaging has been media coverage, particularly newspaper coverage. Coverage in the *New York Times*, for instance, has been intensely studied with the presumption that it drives agendas, increases support, and persuades audiences (Amenta et al., 2009; Earl et al., 2004; Ferree et al., 2002).The framing literature reinforces this perspective, assuming that once a movement generates a strategic frame, the hardest moment in the persuasion process is securing distribution of

Table 1. Social movement concerns drawn from political communication research.

	Prompt	Ask	Research questions
1.	Don't assume all media messages are received.	Under what conditions are media messages more likely to reach potential movement audiences?	• Where do members of the public get information about movements in a hyper-competitive media environment? • How do movements' representations vary across diverse media and outlets? What is the audience size and composition associated with those outlets? • What role do entertainment media play in shaping social movement perceptions? • What attributes of message, sender, and receiver shape the 'viral' diffusion of movement messages? • Do theories that help scholars understand reactions to traditional media apply equally to information shared over social media, including 'viral' resharing cascades?
2.	Don't assume that all information crossing the proverbial desk of audience members is consumed.	What conditions increase the likelihood that potential movement audiences will consume the movement messages they encounter?	• How do individuals decide which movement messages to consume, and which to ignore?
3.	Don't assume that media gatekeepers are always most influential.	Under what conditions can more informal and peer-based information exchange be influential in movement processes?	• What are the influences of social recommendations on individuals' response to movement information in both the short and long term? Are socially shared messages more or less persuasive? Under what circumstances, if any, can social recommendations overcome political biases? • How do individuals make sense of viral activist messages absent the larger movement context?
4.	Don't assume that movement messages are received and interpreted as intended.	What factors affect how people interpret and decide whether to trust movement messages that they consume?	• How do individuals' predispositions color their understanding of movement information they encounter? • How do individuals decide what to believe in an information environment offering support for almost any claim? • Are first-hand activist accounts (i.e. user-generated content) uniquely believable or consequential?
5.	Don't assume that the availability of favorable information translates into action.	How and under what conditions do consumed messages affect action by receivers/interpreters?	• Do polarized frames promote a participation gap? That is, do they attract hardened activists while deterring participation among others?
6.	Don't assume that information is context-free.	How does information context matter to message reception, interpretation, and behavior?	• How does the context in which messages are consumed influence actions or judgments based on those messages? • How does priming inform social movement activity? Do messages conveyed by the space in which an action takes place shape individuals' behaviors? • Can activist messaging prime desirable responses among recipients?

that frame. In a fundamental way, both perspectives see information access as key – potential supporters lack access to information about, or compelling frames of, movements, but once they have those, persuasion is straightforward and other structural determinants such as network connections become most consequential. We think that audience attention, reception, and action are far more complex and that in the contemporary saturated media environment – in which it so easy to access an overwhelming amount of information – it is the attention of individuals, not access to information, which is scarce. In other words, the shift to a saturated information environment pushes questions about audience to the foreground. Below we outline several ways in which social movement scholars could attend to audience.

Expanding media environment and dwindling audience

We begin by more carefully considering the transformation of the political information environment, which includes shifts in both traditional media and the emergence of the Internet. There was a time when media coverage was tantamount to reaching a mass audience, but in the contemporary media landscape that is no longer true (Neuman, 1991; Rucht, 2004). In the U.S., for instance, there has been explosive growth in the number and variety of political and movement-relevant information sources (Bimber, 2003), which in turn creates new pressures on these outlets to specialize as they compete for the attention of increasingly selective consumers (Kim, 2009; Tewksbury, 2005).

This has resulted in what political communication scholars refer to as audience fragmentation: the diversity of media sources has fractured audiences such that the vast majority of outlets have audiences that are much smaller than were common just 20 years ago. While this tendency has been somewhat offset by other factors (Webster, 2005) and Americans' more diverse online news diets still often share a handful of common high-profile sources (Hindman, 2009), even major news organizations (which have the widest reach) reach relatively modest audiences today (Pew Research Center, 2015). Although there is less academic research on media audiences in the European context, industry analyses suggest similar declines, at least among newspapers (Bennett, 2014). Furthermore, engagement is often briefer: in 2015, the average time spent with online *New York Times* content was less than five minutes (Pew Research Center, 2015).

In this context, as the first row of Table 1 suggests, while a news story in a paper of record such as the *New York Times* remains important, so too are stories both in competing national media and in partisan online outlets; commentary by influential political bloggers; and social media posts that can include text, images, and video. Given the different goals, news standards, and journalistic practices that undergird these diverse sources of information, it is almost certain that the coverage movements receive in each will differ in important ways. Also, there is evidence of cross-over among these sources: a story might, for instance, migrate from a blog to a paper of record, not just vice versa (Chadwick, 2013). To assert that attracting the media spotlight is a valid measure of movement success is painting with too broad a brush. Instead, it is important to capture empirically the variety of ways in which movements are represented in the media. While there have been limited attempts to do this by comparing newspapers to one another, and movement periodicals to mainstream news sources, we argue that far more work needs to be done in this area so that social movement scholars more actively consider the wide variety of media that might be carrying movement messages. For instance, when judging the uptake of movement messages, or the 'success' of coverage, scholars need to examine audience size and characteristics to fully understand the range of potential impacts.

Entertainment, not news

Some see the dramatic rise in entertainment media consumption as further limiting audiences for political news. For instance, research has shown that less politically-interested individuals have largely abandoned hard news programs (Prior, 2007). However, a range of factors may offset any ill-effects this has for movements. First, a burgeoning literature on political entertainment has demonstrated that entertainment media, from *The Daily Show* to *The Simpsons*, can have important political effects, shaping political knowledge, attitudes, and engagement (Delli Carpini, 2014). Second, persuasion processes function differently in the context of entertainment media (Moyer-Gusé, 2008), suggesting that exposure to movement information through entertainment could be uniquely persuasive. Moreover, repeated exposure to media of any sort shapes users' perceptions of reality (Gerbner & Gross, 1976). The more that entertainment media portray a movement's grievance as a legitimate problem, the more receptive audiences may be to the movement's cause.

Research also questions a bright line distinction between the political world and the rest of the (less obviously political) world. For instance, research shows that online hobby forums and non-political blogs host political discussions that are more deliberative and feature a wider range of views and greater tolerance for disagreement than explicitly political sites (Munson & Resnick, 2011; Wojcieszak & Mutz, 2009). In contrast to discussion spaces organized around controversial topics, where disagreement is often paired with hostility (for example, see Anderson, Brossard, Scheufele, Xenos, & Ladwig, 2014), these less hostile non-political forums could prove essential to the exchange of diverse information and the cross-pollination of ideas. Moreover, given that attitude strength is an important predictor of attitude change (Petty & Krosnick, 1995), sites whose audiences tend to have weaker attitudes may also present a uniquely important opportunity for persuasion.

We argue that social movement scholars should work to understand how entertainment media may be an important driver of opinion change and movement support. Doing so could raise important questions about how activists, grievances, issues, frames, and so on are represented in popular media, including television, film, books, and music, and what the consequences of this coverage are.

Selecting which news to consume

When individuals do choose to pay attention to the news, media exposure is further shaped by their issue positions and attitudes through a process referred to as politically motivated (or partisan) selective exposure (see row 2 of Table 1). Most individuals tend to prefer news content that affirms their prior beliefs over content that challenges them (Stroud, 2011). Although potentially empowering for social movements, which have historically suffered from a lack of media exposure and access to potential supporters, this also poses risk. While fears about online 'echo chambers' (Sunstein, 2001) are unfounded – individuals do not systematically avoid contact with the other side despite being drawn to like-minded content (Garrett, 2009) and news consumers rely on a diverse mix of outlets both online (Gentzkow & Shapiro, 2011) and off (Webster & Ksiazek, 2012) – important selection effects remain. Moreover, as new technologies facilitate repeated exposure to attitude-reinforcing communication, audience members tend to become more polarized: such exposure promotes stronger issue beliefs and political participation, but it can also incite hostility toward individuals holding other viewpoints (Garrett et al., 2014).

Recognizing that media coverage is not tantamount to exposure, and that news consumers play an active role in selecting the content they encounter, is consequential for social movement research. There is no single right way to account for this in empirical work, but attention to media choice is critical. For instance, asking interview informants about their news preferences and media exposure practices may enhance our understanding of their movement perceptions. Models of frame resonance may have more explanatory power when they include indicators of where individuals get their movement information. In some cases, it may be useful to couple measures of where people get their news with an assessment of how movement information is conveyed in the chosen sources. Pairing media exposure with information about the content of that media would offer unique insight into the processes by which attitudes about social movements are formed in today's high-choice media environment.

The rise of social media

It is also increasingly important to understand how messages might be promoted through alternative means, such as online social networks (see row 3 of Table 1). Social networking services are an increasingly important source of news (Pew Research Center, 2014), and scholars argue that the attitudes and information shared across such networks can powerfully influence public opinion (Watts & Dodds, 2007).

As a platform for sharing social movement messages, social media offers opportunities that are profoundly different than traditional news outlets. Although social media users are more likely to share content created by others than to post original content, user-generated content is an important part of the news ecosystem (Pew Research Center, 2014). This presents a unique opportunity for social movements to control their media representation, but it is not without risk. Astroturfing, whereby a small number of individuals use software to create the appearance of a large grassroots social media presence (Ratkiewicz et al., 2010), can mislead the public and undermine trust in more organic online movement activity. Activist reliance on social media as a means of reaching the public also poses risk, as companies that operate social media sites have in some cases shut down activist accounts (Earl, 2012).

The rise of social media might also be important because of the role that peers play in shaping news exposure. The idea that who we know influences what we know about politics is not new – this was the premise of the 'two-step flow,' first introduced in the 1940s (Lazarsfeld, Berelson, & Gaudet, 1944). According to this important model in political communication, media's influence flows through politically attentive opinion leaders who regularly consume news, and who share aspects of what they learn with friends and colleagues, thereby shaping their followers' knowledge and beliefs. The form this influence takes, however, is changing. It is at least plausible that Facebook 'shares' are displacing local opinion leaders' recommendations about what information news consumers should pay attention to (Turcotte, York, Irving, Scholl, & Pingree, 2015). The content featured on social network sites is strongly influenced by other users, especially close ties, and recommendations from these users could have a profound influence on individuals' overall news consumption. Research has already shown that content popular among a peer group is uniquely likely to be viewed, regardless of the individual's political predispositions (Messing & Westwood, 2012): politically motivated selective exposure effectively vanishes in the face of social news recommendations. Indeed, users' consumption of online political news has remained fairly diverse, at least on Facebook (Bakshy, Messing, & Adamic, 2015), and this may be part of the reason.

These considerations put a decidedly different spin on the influence of information sharing by movement supporters. Contrary to the image of 'slacktivists' blithely clicking on links with little real-world effect, these results suggest that online information sharing can have important consequences. Moreover, social recommendations, and the algorithms that online services use to share them (Pariser, 2011), powerfully influence what peers look at, and the resultant shifts in information exposure could shape public opinion. News recommendations, especially those made through one's social network, effectively cut through the noise and complexity of the contemporary media environment, potentially overcoming politically biased exposure decisions along the way.

For social movement scholars, there is also value in understanding virality in the context of activism. What attributes of the message, the sender, and the receiver shape the diffusion of a movement message (e.g. see Aral & Walker, 2012)? And what influence do these messages have? How do audience members, who by virtue of the spread of information across real-world networks may be socially and politically disconnected from the issues represented, make sense of these messages? Can a viral video effectively propagate a movement frame? Can a popular awareness-raising campaign shift or amplify attitudes? Can these messages be mobilizing, and will this mobilization be momentary or sustained? Questions such as these are not new to social movement scholarship, but new technologies and their accompanying social practices demand renewed attention to them.

Resistance to movement messages

We have thus far largely focused on movements' ability to attract an audience, but doing so does not guarantee that a movement's message will have the effect intended by activists or assumed by scholars (see row 4 of Table 1). There are at least three reasons that an individual might respond to new information about a movement in ways that differ from activists' expectations.

First, neutral and factually accurate reporting on an issue may be disbelieved for a variety of reasons. In an effect known as the 'hostile media phenomenon,' individuals are predisposed to see political news coverage as slanted in favor of the opposition even for messages that are relatively balanced (Vallone, Ross, & Lepper, 1985). This means that both sides of an issue may see the same story as favoring their opposition and be disinclined to believe it. The dynamic is evident among more partisan sources, too, although with some differences: individuals on opposing sides of an issue may agree on the direction, but not the extent, of bias, consistently attributing greater bias to the opposition (Gunther, Christen, Liebhart, & Chia, 2001). The tendency to see bias where there is none can also sustain groups premised on false pretenses. Supporters of such groups are likely to dismiss claims that their beliefs are inaccurate or their actions harmful as more evidence of bias on the part of those delivering the message. Witness the persistence of anti-vaccination beliefs in the face of careful fact-based messaging (Nyhan

& Reifler, 2014). Tactics building on these biases have also been effectively used by the climate-change denial movement (Weber & Stern, 2011).

Second, individuals tend to be skeptical of messages that are clearly intended to have a specific effect (Byrne & Hart, 2009). Social movement messages are frequently intended to be both informative and persuasive, and although activists view these messages as pro-social, the broader public (including both those unfamiliar with the movement, and those opposed to it) may view the claims more cynically. Audiences tend to ignore or discount messages that they see as manipulative, and to derogate sources that have a stake in the information provided (Byrne & Hart, 2009). Strategic messages can also inadvertently prime contradictory thoughts, causing the messages to have unintended effects (Cho & Salmon, 2007). For example, an anti-smoking campaign may cause recipients to reflect on the appealing qualities of smoking. In the most extreme cases, strategic communication can have boomerang effects, eliciting changes in attitude or behavior that oppose the desired effect (Byrne & Hart, 2009).

Third, people's prior attitudes influence their information processing, a phenomenon commonly referred to as 'biased assimilation' (Lord, Ross, & Lepper, 1979) or 'motivated reasoning' (Lodge & Taber, 2013). Emotion is commonly cited as a driving force (Lodge & Taber, 2013) of these biases. It is not uncommon for two individuals to reach opposing conclusions in the face of the same evidence, with each finding disproportionate evidence supporting his or her prior beliefs. An implication of this is that although technologies make it easier for movements to share evidence supporting their grievances (e.g. posting confidential documents or activist-recorded videos), this will not necessarily promote agreement about the legitimacy of activist claims. For instance, we would expect radically different reactions to the recent spate of American videos posted on social media showing police shootings and other confrontations with (often African-American) citizens depending on the viewers' prior attitudes: some will see a clear justification for police actions, while others will see blatant use of excessive force.

All of this has implications for activists' ability to communicate strategically. Activists are mobilized, and supporters swayed, by a shared understanding of grievances grounded in an empirical reality, such as working conditions or political injustice. But movements' ability to use communication to promote this shared understanding is threatened by the three types of biases outlined above. Just as it is useful to ask where people get information about movements, rather than assuming that everyone relies on the same sources, it is useful to examine differences in how people perceive the information they encounter. It would be valuable to understand, for example, who trusts first-hand activist accounts (e.g. photos tweeted from a protest) and whether those from-the-street messages do more or less to win over supporters than other types of coverage of the same event. Another important avenue for research concerns how people decide which version of 'the facts' to trust. For instance, claims about vaccine safety are core to the anti-vaccine movement: supporters rally evidence of vaccines' purported dangers while medical experts, public health scholars, government officials, and others work to counteract these activists' claims. The role that media, especially new communication technologies, play in this conflict over meaning is critically important.

The demobilization effect of cross-pressures

Researchers studying deliberation have also confirmed a reaction to discussions and media that are politically contentious that should be troubling to social movement scholars (see row 5 of Table 1). Cross-cutting exposure, including the consumption of counter-attitudinal media and social interactions with those with whom we disagree, does have positive consequences for deliberative democracy, such as increasing awareness of rationales supporting other viewpoints (Price, Cappella, & Nir, 2002) and promoting political tolerance (Mutz, 2002). But it also has more harmful effects: it can increase ambivalence and discourage political involvement (Mutz, 2006). Even more troublingly, there is evidence that these effects are contingent on initial attitude strength: deliberation can make moderates and/or people without strongly held views withdraw from dialogs while polarizing individuals with more radical views and hardened opinions (Wojcieszak, 2012).

These risks should trouble social movement scholars because they suggest that polarized messaging, such as that around pro-choice versus pro-life, may drive bystanders away from movements, even as it reinforces commitment by existing participants. Do movements that use polarized frames draw fewer mainstream supporters, but greater numbers of hardened activists? This also suggests that movements might productively segment their audience into groups based on how they are expected to respond to different messages. For instance, one set of frames or messages may be directed toward the general public, which will include many bystanders and may therefore benefit from less polarizing rhetoric, while other messages might target movement members, who may be bolstered by polarizing rhetoric.

Messages in context

Political communication research suggests that the context in which information is received, or action is to be taken, can affect persuasion (see last row of Table 1). Research on 'priming' has shown that cues embedded in the messaging environment can shape which attributes are most salient when an individual is forming assessments of issues or political actors (Iyengar & Kinder, 1987). For example, media exposure (e.g. watching the news) can influence the weight individuals give to different factors when reporting attitudes about government, political leaders, or issues (Roskos-Ewoldsen, Roskos-Ewoldsen, & Carpentier, 2009). Significant shifts in support can be produced by priming people to think about issues on which the target fairs well or poorly: asking about the economy immediately before asking about favorability toward an elected official might generate different responses than first asking about foreign policy. The attributes activated by a prime may concern specific features of the object being assessed, such as where a candidate stands on a particular issue, or they can derive from more abstract group features, such as stereotypes and prejudice (Valentino & Vandenbroek, 2014). Priming is not focused on simple or direct changes in belief; instead, priming emphasizes how message context shapes its interpretation and how people react behaviorally to that information.

For social movement scholars, deep consideration of potential priming effects could highlight the importance of information and decision-making context to contemporary social justice struggles. For example, a number of scholars have argued that voting might be influenced by the voter's location when casting a ballet (Pryor, Mendez, & Herrick, 2014). This can be quite important to social movements. For instance, it might be possible that the use of churches as polling places might prime negative beliefs about gays and lesbians, effecting support for votes related to gay rights (for research on Proposition 8 in California: Daniels, 2011; Rutchick, 2010). Similarly, voting in schools may influence votes related to education (Berger, Meredith, & Wheeler, 2008). To the extent that primed concerns influence voters' decisions, priming could counteract or reinforce mobilization efforts, although priming effects diminish quickly with time (Roskos-Ewoldsen et al., 2009).

While this suggests important, even potentially decisive, *in situ* effects of priming, research on priming suggests that the information environment is a capacious concept: movement messages may fall flat if consumed in spaces or contexts that prime negative evaluations of the movement or its supporters, or may get a surprising bump if consumed in spaces or alongside other media that prime positive evaluations of the movement or its supporters. When context shapes how messages are attended to, and interpreted, context can have an influence on the developing beliefs different audiences have about movements. Considering such effects could dramatically change social movement scholars' research agenda with respect to media, communication, and even action so that researchers become much more concerned with studying where potential supporters, actual supporters, targets, and opponents gain information about movements and take movement-relevant actions.

Conclusion

Scholars of digital protest have begun to import insights from political communication into social movement studies, raising important questions about information dissemination, consumption, and reception. We hope to extend this to social movement scholarship more generally. While once possible to side-step communication questions, changes in the media landscape and the growth of the Web have made this a dangerous strategy for social movement scholars going forward. Less nuanced understandings of communication processes increasingly imperil social movement scholars' ability to: (1) understand contemporary (and, potentially, even historical) social movement dynamics; and (2) remain the dominant intellectual force in the study of protest-related phenomena (as an increasing volume of research is being published outside of social movement studies outlets). If social movement scholars are to continue to make fundamental strides in understanding protest, we must investigate and learn from research on media and communication processes that has been developed by political communication scholars.

We have attempted to start an explicit and extended dialog between social movement studies and political communication by highlighting some ways in which political communication scholarship can suggest new questions and offer novel perspectives on current social movement research topics. Table 1 summarizes these ideas. We do not claim to have provided an exhaustive review of how these two literatures could be knitted together. We have argued for a focus on audiences and information context, but there are doubtless many other ways to bring these fields into conversation. Instead of being exhaustive, we have tried to provocatively illustrate how this common research territory could benefit from cross-pollination between distinct intellectual traditions. We hope that other scholars will suggest alternative recombinations of these fields, perhaps even from different theoretical traditions including from European scholars since our review has been more American in its focus.

We are not the only ones to note the importance of communication research and concepts to social movement studies. Bennett and Segerberg (2013) have gone so far as to argue that social movements should be recast as fundamentally communicative acts, an argument that implicitly positions communication – and not sociology or political science – as the discipline with the single greatest potential for explaining the inner workings of movements. We think such arguments go too far, ignoring essential structural aspects of social movements and overplaying the role of beliefs in motivating participation (i.e. research has long shown that belief is not enough to compel action and that some people participate who are not believers, but are brought in through social connections). In fact, while not our focus here, there are many things that political communication scholars could learn from social movement studies. We are not arguing for a fundamental rethinking of what social movements are or even a repositioning of beliefs or ideology as causal factors in our models. Instead, we are arguing for a more robust social movement studies that builds on the advances of political communication as it draws on findings and arguments from that literature to advance work on critical social movement topics and open up new research frontiers within it.

Notes

1. We recognize that social movements may actually have multiple audiences, including potential supporters, current and past supporters, opponents, and multiple targets. Differences across these audiences are important, but our goal is to illustrate ways in which attending to message reception is useful more broadly. Fully tracing message effects for every type of recipient is beyond the scope of this article. Likewise, we recognize that movements vary widely across a range of dimensions (e.g. size, coherence, and professionalization), and that this powerfully shapes communication dynamics. Space limitations, however, prevent us from considering how different movements might be differently affected by our arguments.
2. This article largely focuses on research on social movements and political communication from the U.S., although numerous European researchers have studied communication practices related to digital protest (e.g. contributions to the 2015 special issue of *Information, Communication, & Society* on digital protest). Although our focus is weighted toward American theoretical traditions, we view this as not a limit of the approach we recommend but rather of ourselves as authors. We invite European scholars, representing different traditions, to seek different pathways for bringing communication practices into focus within social movement studies.
3. It is also worth noting that resonance-based framing research has been criticized by political communication scholars for being imprecise, and insufficiently distinct from priming (Cacciatore, Scheufele, & Iyengar, 2015).

Acknowledgments

We would like to thank the John D. and Catherine T. MacArthur Foundation for its support of the Youth and Participatory Politics Research Network, which contributed to Jennifer Earl's work on this topic. We would also like to thank the Editor, the anonymous reviewers, and the UA Writing Group, of which Jennifer Earl is a member, for providing helpful comments on an early draft.

Disclosure statement

No potential conflict of interest was reported by the authors.

References

Amenta, E., Caren, N., Olasky, S. J., & Stobaugh, J. E. (2009). All the movements fit to print: Who, what, when, where, and why SMO families appeared in the New York times in the twentieth century. *American Sociological Review, 74*, 636–656.

Anderson, A. A., Brossard, D., Scheufele, D. A., Xenos, M. A., & Ladwig, P. (2014). The "nasty effect:" Online incivility and risk perceptions of emerging technologies. *Journal of Computer-Mediated Communication, 19*, 373–387.

Aral, S., & Walker, D. (2012). Identifying influential and susceptible members of social networks. *Science, 337*, 337–341.

Bail, C. A. (2012). The fringe effect: Civil society organizations and the evolution of media discourse about islam since the september 11th attacks. *American Sociological Review, 77*, 855–879.

Bakshy, E., Messing, S., & Adamic, L. (2015). Exposure to ideologically diverse news and opinion on Facebook. *Science, 348*, 1130–1132.

Bennett, E. (2014). 'European newspaper circulation down another 4% amid calls for more innovation': *World Association of Newspapers and News Publishers (WAN-IFRA)*. Retrieved February 22, 2016, from http://blog.wan-ifra.org/2014/06/05/digital-developments-at-newspapers-must-continue-says-wan-ifra-secretary-general-larry-14.

Bennett, W. L., & Segerberg, A. (2011). Digital media and the personalization of collective action: Social technology and the organization of protests against the global economic crisis. *Information, Communication & Society, 14*, 770–799.

Bennett, W. L., & Segerberg, A. (2013). *The logic of connective action*. Cambridge: Cambridge University Press.

Berger, J., Meredith, M., & Wheeler, S. C. (2008). Contextual priming: Where people vote affects how they vote: Table 1. *Proceedings of the National Academy of Sciences, 105*, 8846–8849.

Bimber, B. (2003). *Information and American democracy*. New York, NY: Cambridge University Press.

Bimber, B., Flanagin, A. J., & Stohl, C. (2005). Reconceptualizing collective action in the contemporary media environment. *Communication Theory, 15*, 365–388.

Buechler, S. M. (2011). *Understanding social movements: Theories from the classical era to the present*. New York, NY: Paradigm Publishers.

Byrne, S., & Hart, P. S. (2009). The 'boomerang' effect: A synthesis of findings and a preliminary theoretical framework. *Communication Yearbook, 33*, 3–37.

Cacciatore, M. A., Scheufele, D. A., & Iyengar, S. (2015). The end of framing as we know it … and the future of media effects." *Mass Communication and Society, 19*, 7–23.

Castells, M. (2012). *Networks of outrage and hope: Social movements in the internet age*. Malden, MA: Polity Press.

Chadwick, A. (2013). *The hybrid media system*. Oxford: Oxford University Press.

Cho, H., & Salmon, C. T. (2007). Unintended effects of health communication campaigns. *Journal of Communication, 57*, 293–317.

Daniels, R. S. (2011). Voting context and vote choice: The impact of voting precinct location on voting for California proposition 8. *Paper presented at the 2011 APSA Annual Meeting*, Seattle, WA. Retrieved from http://papers.ssrn.com/sol3/papers.cfm?abstract_id=1902364l

Delli Carpini, M. X. (2014). The political effects of entertainment media. In K. Kenski & K. H. Jamieson (Eds.), *Oxford Handbook of Political Communication*. Oxford University Press. doi:10.1093/oxfordhb/9780199793471.013.30

Earl, J. (2012). Private protest? Public and private engagement online. *Information, Communication & Society, 15*, 591–608.

Earl, J. (2015). CITASA: Intellectual past and future. *Information, Communication & Society, 18*, 478–491.

Earl, J., & Kimport, K. (2011). *Digitally enabled social change*. Cambridge, MA: MIT Press.

Earl, J., & Rohlinger, D. A. (2012). Introduction: Media, movements, and political change. *Research in Social Movements, Conflicts and Change, 33*, 1–13.

Earl, J., Martin, A., McCarthy, J. D., & Soule, S. A. (2004). The use of newspaper data in the study of collective action. *Annual Review of Sociology, 30*, 65–80.

Eyerman, R., & Jamison, A. (1991). *Social movements: A cognitive approach*. University Park: The Pennsylvania State University Press.

Ferree, M. M., Gamson, W. A., Gerhards, J., & Rucht, D. (2002). *Shaping abortion discourse*. Cambridge: Cambridge University Press.

Flanagin, A. J., Stohl, C., & Bimber, B. (2006). Modeling the structure of collective action. *Communication Monographs, 73*, 29–54.

Gamson, W. A. (2004). Bystanders, public opinion, and the media. In D. A. Snow, S. A. Soule, & H. Kriesi (Eds.), *The Blackwell companion to social movements* (pp. 242–261). Oxford: Blackwell Publishing.

Gamson, W. A., & Meyer, D. S. (1996). Framing political opportunity. In D. McAdam, J. D. McCarthy & M. N. Zald (Eds.), *Comparative perspectives on social movements* (pp. 275–290). Cambridge: Cambrdige University Press.

Gamson, W. A., & Modigliani, A. (1989). Media discourse and public opinion on nuclear power: A constructionist approach. *American Journal of Sociology, 95*, 1–37.

Gamson, W. A., & Wolfsfeld, G. (1993). Movements and media as interacting systems. *The Annals of the American Academy of Political and Social Science, 528*, 114–125.

Gamson, W. A., Fireman, B., & Rytina, S. (1982). *Encounters with unjust authority*. Homewood, IL: Dorsey Press.

Garrett, R. K. (2009). Politically motivated reinforcement seeking: Reframing the selective exposure debate. *Journal of Communication, 59*, 676–699.

Garrett, R. K., Gvirsman, S. D., Johnson, B. K., Tsfati, Y., Neo, R., & Dal, A. (2014). Implications of pro- and counterattitudinal information exposure for affective polarization. *Human Communication Research, 40*, 309–332.

Gentzkow, M., & Shapiro, J. M. (2011). Ideological segregation online and offline. *The Quarterly Journal of Economics, 126*, 1799–1839.

Gerbner, G., & Gross, L. (1976). Living with television: The violence profile. *Journal of Communication, 26*, 172–194.

Gillan, K. (2009). The UK anti-war movement online: Uses and limitations of internet technologies for contemporary activism. *Information, Communication & Society, 12*, 25–43.

Gillan, K., Pickerill, J., & Webster, F. (2008). *Anti-war activism*. New York, NY: Palgrave Macmillan.

Gitlin, T. (1980). *The whole world is watching: Mass media in the making and unmaking of the new left*. Los Angeles, CA: University of California Press.

Graber, D. A. (1988). *Processing the news: How people tame the information tide*. New York, NY: Longman.

Gunther, A. C., Christen, C. T., Liebhart, J. L., & Chia, S. C.-Y. (2001). Congenial public, contrary press, and biased estimates of the climate of opinion. *Public Opinion Quarterly, 65*, 295–320.

Hindman, M. (2009). *The myth of digital democracy*. Princeton: Princeton University Press.

Iyengar, S., & Kinder, D. R. (1987). *News that matters: Television and american opinion*. Chicago, IL: University of Chicago Press.

Jamieson, K. H. (in press). The five decade long evolution of the concept of effects in political communication. In K. Kenski & K. H. Jamieson (Eds.), *Oxford handbook of political communication*. New York, NY: Oxford University Press. doi: 10.1093/oxfordhb/9780199793471.013.27

Kim, Y. M. (2009). Issue publics in the new information environment: Selectivity, domain specificity, and extremity. *Communication Research, 36*, 254–284.

Klandermans, B. (1996). Media discourse, movement publicity, and the generation of collective action frames: Theoretical and emperical exercises in meaning construction. In D. McAdam, J. D. McCarthy, & M. N. Zald (Eds.), *Comparative perspectives on social movements* (pp. 312–337). Cambridge: Cambridge University Press.

Kornhauser, W. (1959). *The politics of mass society*. New York, NY: The Free Press.

Lasswell, H.. (1948). The structure and function of communication in society. In L. Bryson (Ed.), *The Communication of Ideas: A Series of Addresses* (pp. 37–52). New York, NY: Institute for Religious and Social Studies.

Lazarsfeld, P. F., Berelson, B., & Gaudet, H. (1944). *The people's choice*. New York, NY: Duell, Sloan and Pearce.
Le Bon, G. (1960 [1895]). *The crowd: A study of the popular mind*. New York, NY: Viking Press.
Lodge, M., & Taber, C. S. (2013). *The rationalizing voter*. New York, NY: Cambridge University Press.
Lord, C. G., Ross, L., & Lepper, M. R. (1979). Biased assimilation and attitude polarization: The effects of prior theories on subsequently considered evidence. *Journal of Personality and Social Psychology, 37*, 2098–2109.
McAdam, D., & Rucht, D. (1993). The cross-national diffusion of movement ideas. *Annals, 528*, 56–74.
McCammon, H. J. (2014). *The U.S. women's jury movements and strategic adaptation: A more just verdict*. Oxford: Cambridge University Press.
McCammon, H. J., Hewitt, L., & Smith, S. (2002). "No weapon save argument": Strategic frame amplification in the U.S. woman suffrage movements. *The Sociological Quarterly, 45*, 529–556.
Melucci, A. (1996). *Challenging codes*. Cambridge: Cambridge University Press.
Messing, S., & Westwood, S. J. (2012). Selective exposure in the age of social media: Endorsements trump partisan source affiliation when selecting news online. *Communication Research, 41*, 1042–1063.
Meyer, D. S., & Rohlinger, D. A. (2012). Big books and social movements: A myth of ideas and social change. *Social Problems, 59*, 136–153.
Moyer-Gusé, E. (2008). Toward a theory of entertainment persuasion: Explaining the persuasive effects of entertainment-education messages. *Communication Theory, 18*, 407–425.
Munson, S. A., & Resnick, P. (2011). The prevalence of political discourse in non-political blogs. In *Fifth International AAAI Conference on Weblogs and Social Media (ICWSM)* (pp. 233–240). Barcelona: Association for the Advancement of Artificial Intelligence. Retrieved from https://www.aaai.org/ocs/index.php/ICWSM/ICWSM11/paper/download/2871/3268
Mutz, D. C. (2002). Cross-cutting social networks: Testing democratic theory in practice. *American Political Science Review, 96*, 111–126.
Mutz, D. C. (2006). *Hearing the other side*. New York, NY: Cambridge University Press.
Neuman, W. R. (1991). *The future of the mass audience*. New York, NY: Cambridge University Press.
Nyhan, B., & Reifler, J. (2014). The effect of fact-checking on elites: A field experiment on U.S. state legislators. *American Journal of Political Science, 59*, 628–640.
Pariser, E. (2011). *The filter bubble: What the internet is hiding from you*. New York, NY: The Penguin Press.
Petty, R. E., & Krosnick, J. A. (1995). *Attitude strength: Antecedents and consequences*. Mahwah, NJ: Lawrence Erlbaum Associates.
Pew Research Center. (2014). *How social media is reshaping news*. Washington, DC. Retrieved from http://www.pewresearch.org/fact-tank/2014/09/24/how-social-media-is-reshaping-news/
Pew Research Center. (2015). *State of the news media 2015*. Washington, DC. Retrieved from http://www.journalism.org/2015/04/29/state-of-the-news-media-2015/
Pooley, J., & Katz, E. (2008). Further notes on why American sociology abandoned mass communication research. *Journal of Communication, 58*, 767–786.
Price, V., Cappella, J. N., & Nir, L. (2002). Does disagreement contribute to more deliberative opinion? *Political Communication, 19*, 95–112.
Prior, M. (2007). *Post-broadcast democracy*. New York, NY: Cambridge University Press.
Pryor, B., Mendez, J. M., & Herrick, R. (2014). Let's be fair: Do polling locations prime votes? *Journal of Political Sciences & Public Affairs, 2*. Retrieved from http://www.esciencecentral.org/journals/lets-be-fair-do-polling-locations-prime-votes-2332-0761.1000126.php?aid=32194.doi:10.4172/2332-0761.1000126
Ratkiewicz, J., Conover, M., Meiss, M., Gonçalves, B., Patil, S., Flammini, A., & Menczer, F. (2010). Detecting and tracking the spread of astroturf memes in microblog streams. In *20th international conference companion on World wide web* (pp. 249–252). doi:10.1145/1963192.1963301
Rohlinger, D. A. (2002). Framing the abortion debate: Organizational resources, media strategies, and movement-countermovement dynamics. *The Sociological Quarterly, 43*, 479–507.
Roscigno, V. J., & Danaher, W. F. (2001). Media and mobilization: The case of radio and southern textile worker insurgency, 1929 to 1934. *American Sociological Review, 66*, 21–48.
Roskos-Ewoldsen, D. R., Roskos-Ewoldsen, B., & Carpentier, F. D. (2009). Media priming: An updated synthesis. In J. Bryant & M. B. Oliver (Eds.), *Media effects: Advances in theory and research* (pp. 74–93). New York, NY: Routledge.
Rucht, D. (2004). The quadruple 'A': Media strategies of protest movements since the 1960s. In W. van de Donk, B. D. Loader, P. G. Nixon, & D. Rucht (Eds.), *Cyberprotest: New media, citizens, and social movements* (pp. 29–56). New York, NY: Routledge.
Rutchick, A. M. (2010). Deus ex machina: The influence of polling place on voting behavior. *Political Psychology, 31*, 209–225.
Snow, D. A. (2004). Framing processes, ideology, and discursive fields. In D. A. Snow, S. A. Soule, & H. Kriesi (Eds.), *The Blackwell companion to social movements* (pp. 380–412). Oxford: Blackwell Publishing.
Snow, D. A., & Benford, R. D. (1988). Ideology, frame resonance, and participation mobilization. *International Journal of Social Movement Research, 1*, 197–217.

Snow, D. A., & Benford, R. D. (1992). Master frames and cycles of protest. In A. Morris & C. Mueller (Eds.), *Frontiers of social movement theory* (pp. 133–155). New Haven, CT: Yale University Press.

Snow, D. A., Rochford, E., Worden, S. K., & Benford, R. D. (1986). Frame alignment processes, micromobilization, and movement participation. *American Sociological Review, 51*, 464–481.

Stroud, N. J. (2011). *Niche news*. New York, NY: Oxford University Press.

Sunstein, C. R. (2001). *Republic.com*. Princeton, NJ: Princeton University Press.

Tewksbury, D. (2005). The seeds of audience fragmentation: Specialization in the use of online news sites. *Journal of Broadcasting and Electronic Media, 49*, 332–348.

Turcotte, J., York, C., Irving, J., Scholl, R. M., & Pingree, R. J. (2015). News recommendations from social media opinion leaders: Effects on media trust and information seeking. *Journal of Computer-Mediated Communication, 20*, 520–535.

Valentino, N. A., & Vandenbroek, L. M. 2014. Political communication, information processing, and social groups. In K. Kenski & K. H. Jamieson (Eds.), *Oxford handbook of political communication*. Oxford University Press. doi: 10.1093/oxfordhb/9780199793471.013.56

Vallone, R. P., Ross, L., & Lepper, M. R. (1985). The hostile media phenomenon: Biased perception and perception of media bias in coverage of the Beirut massacre. *Journal of Personality and Social Psychology, 49*, 577–585.

Watts, D. J., & Dodds, P. S. (2007). Influentials, networks, and public opinion formation. *Journal of Consumer Research, 34*, 441–458.

Weber, E. U., & Stern, P. C. (2011). Public understanding of climate change in the United States. *American Psychologist, 66*, 315–328.

Webster, J. G. (2005). Beneath the veneer of fragmentation: Television audience polarization in a multichannel world. *Journal of Communication, 55*, 366–382.

Webster, J. G., & Ksiazek, T. B. (2012). The dynamics of audience fragmentation: Public attention in an age of digital media. *Journal of Communication, 62*, 39–56.

Wojcieszak, M. E. (2012). On strong attitudes and group deliberation: Relationships, structure, changes, and effects. *Political Psychology, 33*, 225–242.

Wojcieszak, M. E., & Mutz, D. C. (2009). Online groups and political discourse: Do online discussion spaces facilitate exposure to political disagreement? *Journal of Communication, 59*, 40–56.

A situated understanding of digital technologies in social movements. Media ecology and media practice approaches

Alice Mattoni

ABSTRACT
The article tackles two main aspects related to the interaction between social movements and digital technologies. First, it reflects on the need to include and combine different theoretical approaches in social movement studies so as to construct more meaningful understanding of how social movement actors deals with digital technologies and with what outcomes in societies. In particular, the article argues that media ecology and media practice approaches serve well to reach this objective as: they recognize the complex multi-faceted array of media technologies, professions and contents with which social movement actors interact; they historicize the use of media technologies in social movements; and they highlight the agency of social movement actors in relation to media technologies while avoiding a media-centric approach to the subject matter. Second, this article employs a media practice perspective to explore two interrelated trends in contemporary societies that the articles in this special issue deal with: the personalization and individualization of politics, and the role of the grassroots in political mobilizations.

Introduction

According to *Time* magazine, 2011 was the year of the protester. That year hundreds of thousands mobilized in Tunisia, Egypt, Syria, Yemen, Libya, Barhain, Spain, Greece, Chile, the United States, Russia and other countries across the world. Some of these protests quickly became radical movements, other remained quite reformist in their demands and claims. Some lasted weeks, although rooted in years of minor uprisings, other persisted for months. In the background: one of the major economic crisis of the last decades, which changed the material conditions of millions of people in the Global North and the Global South. In the foreground: the digital native protesters equipped with smart phones and laptops, connected with the world through Twitter and Facebook. As also happened with past upsurges of protest, one of the outcomes of these mobilizations was a renewed interest in social movements and, more specifically, on how the latest digital technologies supported their development. The year 2011, therefore, has also been the year in which scholars, observers and commentators discovered the existence of 'social media revolutions', bringing back interpretations that began to form and spread immediately after the Iranian protests against electoral results in 2009.

Although they concern about other collective actions, which often took shape in more recent years, the articles published in this special issue are rooted in the debate that revamped in 2011 and that brought the relationship between social movements and different types of media technologies to the centre of many academic publications, conferences and seminars. In this article, I will therefore position these articles in the broader context of literature on social movements and media. In doing this, my aim is to contextualize such pieces of research and to discuss further the nexus between social movements and digital technologies both from a theoretical perspective and at the empirical level. Over the years, social movement studies developed a recognized set of concepts, often linked to specific approaches and distinct topics of research (della Porta & Diani, 2015). However, the rich analytical toolbox that social movement scholars employ does not include a systematic theorization of the communicative side of social unrests. Despite increased attention on digital technologies in recent years, this usually lacks a comprehensive theorization of media as a set of social processes that intersect with protest mobilizations. This flaw is widely recognized today (see Cammaerts, Mattoni, & McCurdy, 2013; Earl and Garret, 2017; Mattoni, 2012; Mattoni & Treré, 2014) and there have also been attempts to redefine some of the concepts commonly used in social movement studies through the lenses of media studies (Barassi, 2015; Juris, 2008; Mattoni, 2012), internet studies (Bennett & Segerberg, 2013; Earl & Kimport, 2011) and social technology and society approaches (Milan, 2013). In short, these works ultimately suggest that the understanding of contemporary social movements inevitably passes through the broadening of social movement theories and concepts so as to include their communicative dimensions, also with regard to their use of media technologies. This is even more relevant today, when the academic debate on this issue is shifting away from the role of so-called web 2.0 platforms, devices and technologies to the importance of big data with regard to activism. Although scholars are still discussing to what extent digital technologies transform the very notion of social movements, recent literature on big data assumes a change of paradigm at the epistemological level of knowledge production (Couldry & Hepp, 2017) also within activist communities (Milan & van der Velden, 2016). While this might well be true, once again there is the need to recognize the permeable boundaries between and the coexistence of different media-related interactions within social movements, even within the so-called algorithmic society.

With these issues in mind, and prompted by the articles published in this special issue, in what follows I tackle two main aspects of the interaction between social movements and digital technologies. First, I reflect on the need to include and combine different theoretical approaches in social movement studies so as to construct more meaningful understanding of how social movement actors deal with digital technologies and with what outcomes in societies. In particular, I argue that media ecology and media practice approaches serve well to reach this objective as: they recognize the complex multi-faceted array of media technologies, professions and contents with which social movement actors interact; they historicize the use of media technologies in social movements; and they highlight the agency of social movement actors in relation to media technologies while avoiding a media-centric approach to the subject matter. Second, this article employs a media practice perspective to explore two interrelated trends in contemporary societies that the articles in this special issue deal with: the personalization and individualization of politics, and the role of the grassroots in political mobilizations.

Expanding the study of social movements through media ecology and media practice approaches

Media practice and media ecology approaches are two theoretical perspectives in media studies that an increasingly large number of scholars, mostly but not exclusively based in Europe, engaged with over the past two decades, sometimes combining them to understand the nexus between social movement and media technologies and its recent transformations (media practices: Cammaerts et al., 2013; Couldry, 2004, 2000; Kaun, 2016; Mattoni, 2012; Postill, 2012; media ecologies: Feigenbaum et al. 2013; Mercea, Iannelli, & Loader, 2016; Treré, 2012). While the latter situate specific media technologies in the context of multi-layered media ecologies, the former consider media practices as the heuristic tool through which the communicative dimensions of social movements can be observed and explained from an empirical viewpoint. Such an approach is linked to philosophy of practice theories and it is informed by the so-called turn to practice in the social sciences (Schatzki et al., 2001), according to which social practices can be defined as 'recognised, complex forms of social activity and articulation through which agents set out to maintain or change themselves, others and the world about them under varying conditions' (Hobart, 2009, p. 63). When it comes to social practices that are related to the media, the main empirical question goes beyond the usual dichotomy between media as texts vs. media as institutions, to ask, instead, 'what, quite simply, are people doing in relation to media across a whole range of situations and contexts?' (Couldry, 2004). Definitions of media practice are generally left broad enough to include many types of practices, including the unexpected. However, for a long time the main focus of media practice scholarship remained people's interactions with mainstream media. In connecting that perspective into social movement studies, scholars have begun to develop even broader conceptualizations of practices: while they focus on a specific category of social actors – the political activist and her organizations – they expanded their understanding of media practices to include, among others, alternative media and digital technologies. In this regard, activist media practices can be seen as both routinized and creative arrays of activists' interactions with and understandings of media technologies, professions and roles. One of the main features of this scholarship is an account of the multiple and at times cacophonic constitution of hybrid media ecologies, in which the digital and the non-digital, the online and the offline, the mainstream and the alternative are categories whose boundaries become even more blurred.

Recognition of blurred boundaries is especially important in situating media technologies in their historical context. Each media technology invention has led to interpretations of 'the newest' media technology's ability to create new opportunities for human communication. As adoption becomes more widespread, each new media technology then has some sort of influence on social movement actors as well. An emblematic example is the emergence of national newspapers back in the eighteenth and nineteenth centuries: they contributed to the creation of publics that began to frame protest beyond the local level, shifting the repertoire of contention from a locally based array of contentious performances to modern forms of contention (Tarrow, 2011). In the 1960s and the 1970s, with the diffusion of television, and national television news, battlefield images of the Vietnam War were seen by millions of US citizens including hundred thousands of (potential) activists who were demanding their government stop the war (McAdam, Tarrow, & Tilly, 2001). Due to the centrality of mass media like newspapers, radio and television in the lives of millions of individuals worldwide, it is not surprising that for a long time literature on social movements recognized the importance of the mainstream press for social movements, stressing the fundamental imbalance of power between journalists and activists, news organizations and social movements (Carroll & Ratner, 1999; Gamson & Wolfsfeld, 1993). While mass media are still here today, the fast pace at which digital technologies have developed in past decades changed them deeply and challenged the ways in which social movement scholars look at media technologies, organizations, outlets and professionals. Over the years, the need to enrich social movement studies with new theoretical perspectives, able to acknowledge the communicative and mediatized dimension of grassroots politics, has become ever more established.

In this special issue, Earl and Garrett (2017) discuss a North American political communication literature that rarely paid attention to grassroots politics. According to the authors, political communication studies bring with them the relevant perspective of audience reception of media contents, often neglected when it comes to the interactions between social movements and media. More specifically, scholars could fruitfully analyse how the consumption of information about social movements develops across various media audiences and how the context in which audiences receive such information shapes the processes of consumption. Scholars interested in alternative media already lamented the lack of attention paid to audiences and began to explore the issue (Downing, 2003; Rauch, 2007), but the road that Earl and Garrett point might certainly cast new light on a set of understudied social processes, especially in a time in which the boundaries between media production and media consumption are usually very thin, if not wholly blurred. Earl and Garrett's contribution can be complemented with a discussion on the three ways in which media practices and media ecologies approaches have been able to contribute to social movement studies: (1) to situate the use of digital technologies into the broader palette of activist media practices, hence going beyond the 'segregation within the study of digital protest' that characterize the 'rapprochement between social movement studies and communication' (Earl and Garrett, 2017); (2) to take account of temporal, diachronic dimensions of the relationship between social movements and media technologies, often neglected in studies that focus on the latest digital tools that social movement actors employ today; (3) to develop an in-depth analysis of social movement actors' appropriation of media technologies, hence bringing back activists' agency with regard to media and considering how other, non-media related social practices order activist media practices. In the remaining of this section, I substantiate these the three points.

Multiple media technologies and hybrid media ecologies

Media ecologies and media practices approaches recognize the existence of multiple forms of media technologies, channels and contents with which activists interact in mobilizations settings, hence stressing that the emergence of newer media technologies does not translate into the automatic dismissal of older media technologies. Rather, activists tend to use the two in a cumulative manner, also because emerging technologies are often interpreted through the lenses of older technologies (Dunbar-Hester, 2009) creating multi-modal communication channels resting on mixed technological structures (Gillan, Pickerill, & Webster, 2008). Therefore, activists often combine older and newer media technologies in creative ways: as the repertoire of action in grassroots politics expanded over the past years, so did the 'repertoire of communication' (Mattoni, 2013) that activists might refer to when mobilizing. Since they take into account the broad ecology in which media technologies are situated and focus on how activists employ media in different mobilizations contexts, media ecologies and media practices approaches seem to be particularly well positioned to understand this twofold broadening of possibilities – both at the level of forms of contention and forms of communication – and, in doing this, to deconstruct some of the myths that surround the use of digital technologies in past and more recent movements.

Literature on the topic offers many tales that, read through the lenses of media ecologies and media practices approaches, might take other, less digital-centric, meanings. One emblematic example is the Zapatista movement in the 1990s widely known for the ability of its activists to strategically and tactically use digital technologies hence turning them into a paradigmatic case study of 'information guerrilla' (Castells, 2012) and 'electronic fabric of struggle' (Cleaver, 1998). While it is true that the Zapatistas used online technologies in a conscious and effective way (Olesen, 2004), when considering what they did with media at large, and hence focusing on their media practices, it is clear that their use of internet services did not mean the dismissal of other forms of communication. Local radio and the press also played a pivotal role in strengthening local ties, gaining international attention and activating NGOs (Bob, 2005, Olesen, 2004). At the same time, offline marches and demonstrations performed by EZLN supporters continued to be relevant in the development of Zapatistas mobilizations (Olesen, 2004). Even in some of the most recent uprisings, sometimes enthusiastically labelled as 'revolutions 2.0' (e.g. Bob, 2005), social media like Facebook and Twitter were included into a broader repertoire of communication. Activists therefore frequently used them in combination with other media technologies. Especially in Southern Europe and the Arab countries, where the connective tissue is based on stronger and denser social networks than in North-America, face-to-face interactions were important to spread the news about demonstrations. Activists in Egypt, for instance, also used other forms of communication that those mediated by internet services and platforms to spread information about protests: from emails to flyers; from mobile text messages to pamphlets (Lim, 2012). In a similar vein, for activists in Greece, placards fixed to the walls of specific neighbourhoods, like Exarchia in Athens, continued to be relevant means of communication (Eleftheriadis, 2015).

As these two examples suggest, even in those protests labelled after the activists' use of digital technologies, a broader repertoire of communication was in place. Looking at what activists did with various media technologies within a multi-faceted media ecology might unveil the simplistic nature of dichotomies like the ones that oppose online and offline media, new and old media, or mainstream and alternative media (Treré & Mattoni, 2016).

Media practices and the temporal dimension of social movements

The articles in this special issue show that the temporal dimension is relevant when analysing the relationship between digital technologies and social movements. Digital technologies, indeed, acquire a different meaning and role according to the stage of mobilization in which they are used. Ahmed, Jaidka, and Cho (2017, this issue) illustrate how digital technologies gave room to different expressions of emotions in the Indian uprising against acts of rape. They hence focus on how digital technologies are entrenched with the micro-temporality that characterizes the peak of protest during a specific wave of contention, hence considering 'punctuated events' (McAdam & Sewell, 2001) that have a transformative power in the framework of the same mobilization. There is, then a medium-term temporality often labelled 'cycle of contentions' (Tarrow, 1989, 1994), 'waves of protest' (Koopmans, 2004) or 'tides' (Beissinger, 2002). Despite some conceptual difference, these metaphors convey the idea that social movement activities might cover several years, as it is clear in Uitermark (2017, this issue) investigation of the role of different digital technologies in the Anonymous from a diachronic perspective and in Hensby's (2017, this issue) analysis of how different flows and challenges within a cycle of protest affect the way in which activists use social media. Along these lines, Pavan (2017, this issue) shows how the social media usage also changes over time in the case of the annual 'Take Back The Tech! Tweetathon', in which activists appropriate various Twitter affordances throughout a process of institutionalization of the social movement organization supporting the campaign. Finally, social movement actors do not disappear in between waves of protests: rather, they are in a latent stage and so is their mobilization potential (Melucci, 1989). In relation to this, Liu (2017, this issue) shows how digital technologies are used during latent stages of protest in contemporary China.

Media practices approaches often focus on the micro-level of interactions between activists and the media technologies, professionals and contents that make up the media ecology in which they are embedded. In doing this, they might fruitfully engage with the short-term and medium-term temporality according to which social movements – and their relationship with digital technologies – develop. However, interaction evolves also across more extended times frames: from a long-term perspective, social movements intertwine with 'cultural epochs of contention' in which specific templates of contention are available to protesters (McAdam & Sewell, 2001, p. 112) and their 'repertoires of contention' (Tilly, 1978, 1995) are relatively stable. From this viewpoint, it is possible to see media practices as the building blocks of mediatization processes and the related emergence of different media logics: each "wave of mediatization" (Couldry & Hepp, 2017), for instance, has a temporality which transcends the short-term timescale that characterizes media practices (Mattoni & Treré, 2014). Media ecologies approaches also point to the need to understand transformation in a diachronic perspective (Feigenbaum et al., 2013; Dahlberg-Grundberg, 2016; Rinke and Röder, 2011). Scholars that investigate media practices in social movements show that the exploration of the different media logics emerging in different periods is necessary to understand how such logics are incorporated within activist media practices (Kaun, 2016; Postill, 2012; Scalmer, 2013). In other words, a media practice perspective recognizes that media technologies have evolved over time, but also shows that the focus on the newest technology risks neglecting how social movement actors use older and newer media technologies together. For this reason, the understanding of activists' participation in the creation of political communication flows would also gain from longitudinal comparative research on how activists have changed across time as agents of political communication both within and beyond the social movement milieu. In this respect, a longitudinal study of media practices across several époques of contention seems necessary to grasp how social movement actors incorporated different types of media logics over time, for what reasons and with what consequences (Kaun, 2016).

Activists' appropriation of media technologies

A media practice perspective also illustrates the agency of social movement actors with respect to media. Although much social movement literature on media has focused on the subaltern position of activists with regard to (mainstream) media, an enlarged conception of media practices allows scholars to explore how even social groups that have no voice in the bourgeois public sphere could in any case elaborate their own mediated representation through the appropriation of media technologies. In fact, from a diachronic perspective the history of social movements across different époques of contention is also a history of technology appropriation. In the nineteenth and twentieth centuries, the progressive appropriation of mimeograph machines granted protesters the means to publicize their discourses and demands beyond the dominant national press. Leaflets, posters and underground publications contributed to the creation of counter-publics supporting identification processes of workers, women and other groups of insurgents all over the world (Thompson, 1991). After the invention of phones and their spread across larger portions of the population in the US, activists used them for recruitment and the organization of protest. Telephone trees, for instance, were important to spread information about forthcoming protests from home to home in the U.S. civil rights movement, when activists used them to sustain the massive participation in bus boycotts in Montgomery and other cities (Harding, 1997). After the invention of radio and television, social movement actors across the world also attempted to appropriate these media technologies to support their own activities. During the Algerian liberation uprisings in the 1950s, for instance, revolutionaries struggling against the French colonialist empire employed radio to broadcast news of the revolution through the Voice of Free Algeria, which the central government repeatedly tried to jam without success (Fanon & Gilly, 1994). Late in the 1980s, various social movement actors began to appropriate television: the decreased costs of video-technologies made it easier for activists to produce and then spread their own television content. An emblematic example is Deep Dish TV in the U.S., a public access satellite network established in 1986 that rested on the work of hundreds of volunteers (Stein, 2001). Among other projects, Deep Dish TV aired the work of DIVA TV, a 'video-documenting affinity group' (ACT UP NY, 2003) within the ACT-UP organization, struggling against AIDS related policies: its radical television project 'Be a Diva' asked to activists to tell their stories about protest actions and campaigns representing one of the first examples of media-activism and later developed in the first Indymedia experiments (DIVA TV, 1989).

This brief historical excursus shows that social movement actors appropriated various kinds of media technologies well before the rise of internet tools and web applications. Activists developed specific skills to employ various forms of media technology, hence increasing their overall media literacy while providing a mediated venue in which to express their voices beyond mainstream media. Scholars on alternative media often underline the empowering potential of activist media practices related to the creation of alternative media (Atton, 2001; Rodriguez, 2001). While most recent literature on this topic focused mainly on alternative media produced and diffused through internet technologies (Cammaerts, 2016), according to Rodriguez 'alternative and community media research should re-centre the agency of communicators over technologies and refocus on context, uses and needs.' (Rodriguez, 2016, p. 36). Also in this regard, media ecologies and media practices approaches might orient the analytical viewpoint of researchers towards the actual uses and contexts in which alternative media are created, recognizing the blurring boundaries between these media outlets and other platforms of communication like social networking sites.

Media practices and mundane use of digital technologies

The articles in this special issue employ various theoretical perspectives to delve into the dividing lines between strict definitions of social movements and loose understanding of disruptive political engagement. In particular, the articles by Ahmed et al., Liu and Uitemark question the very definition of social movement actors and the way in which they perform contentious politics. In other words, they point (sometimes implicitly) to two major trends concerning how political participation and mobilization changed in the past decades: personalization and individualization.

On one hand, the political realm became more and more personalized, that is to say constructed around specific personae, including political leaders or grassroots activists, but also ordinary protest participants. Literature highlights the personalization of politics in at least two ways. When looking at more institutional arenas, the personalization of politics mostly refers to the loyalty that the electorate has towards political leaders, and the public characters that they perform, rather than towards the political party and its programmes (Garzia, 2014; McAllister, 2007; Swanson & Mancini, 1996). While that process already began with the rise of the so-called mass media, including radio and television (Mazzoleni, 2000), today social networking sites (and internet technologies more generally) allow political leaders to employ a communication style that is even more direct and personal than in the past, bypassing their political parties to speak with their constituencies beyond any collective intermediaries (Bennett, 2012; Enli & Skogerbø, 2013). Scholars also speak about the personalization of politics in the realm of contentious politics and grassroots participation (Bennett & Segerberg, 2013). However, in this case, the emphasis mainly is on the appropriation of political communication by ordinary protest participants. Thanks to the massive use of ICTs, and especially social media platforms, the meanings and narratives of collective action can be increasingly personalized and hence attached to and frames as the personal experiences of ordinary protest participants, hence going beyond the definitional work of activist groups and movement organizations (Bennett & Segerberg, 2013). On the other hand, today political participation and mobilization revolve more and more around individuals, with collective formations having a secondary role in the organization of political actions. Lay citizens with any specific political affiliations are increasingly important in shaping political participation and mobilization today. In recent decades, new forms of protest spread quickly, which allowed networked individuals to protest, often in a coordinated way, in the online environment that became a new space of struggle (Jordan, 2002; Lievrouw, 2011). But changes went beyond the emergence of distinct forms of protests. Overcoming the traditional and modern repertoires of contention (Tilly, 1978, 1995), the increased use of internet tools and web platforms in contentious politics brought to social movement actors a 'digital repertoire of contention' in which collective actors are less central in initiating protest and being in the same space and time is less important to conduct protests (Earl & Kimport, 2011). As a result, some authors now speak about the rise of a new paradigm of connective action alongside the older processes and mechanisms of collective action (Bennett & Segerberg, 2013).

The literature outlined above claims that personalization and individualization processes bring the individuals' relationship with politics – the way in which we, as individuals, engage with politics at the institutional and grassroots level – to centre stage. Furthermore, the shift from collective to individual is clearly linked to the widespread use of ICTs, and the ways in which they change the temporal and spatial characteristics of political participation and mobilization. Empirically, such literature mostly considers the moments in which political action is already under way, hence focusing on individuals that are already engaging with some form of political action and, at times, considering how collective actors and more experienced activists deal with the presence of individual newcomers in mobilizations. We know a lot less about what happens before lay citizens discover their agency through digital engagement with politics.

The articles in this special issue deal with this last point in reflecting on who is the subject of political agency in today's digitalized mediascapes and according to which forms such political subjects mobilize. They do this by pointing to the ubiquitous presence of digital technologies in the daily lives of people. They show how interactions between people and mundane technologies are relevant to understand, and even to recognize as in the case of Liu's piece of research, the unfolding of political opposition and contention across and beyond national geographies. Other authors have already shown the relevance of email as mundane internet tools for the organization of political participation (Nielsen, 2011), but the literature on this topic lacks depth and for this reason the articles in this special issue are a welcome addition.

In the spirit of media practice theories, I develop a diachronic comparison between media practices related to the digital technologies, on which articles in this special issue focus, and the findings of other scholars, who worked on the use of mobile phones before they became the all-encompassing hub for digital communication that they are today. Previous work done on the role of mobile phones in the massive demonstrations occurring in the Philippines in 2001 (Rafael, 2003) and in Spain in 2004 (Flesher Fominaya, 2011) cast light on how text messages were tactically important in increasing the number of people who participated in large protests that lasted a few days before reaching their explicit objective and then dissolving. From 16th to 20th January 2001, about 1 million people gathered in the streets of Manila, the capital of Philippines, to ask for the resignation of their president, Estrada, impeached for corruption. Mobile phones had an important role in attracting people to the streets to the extent that the People Power II demonstrations, as they are known, became the symbol of the first mobile phone uprising. Four years later, in 2004, the tactical use of mobile phones by a relatively small circle of activists eventually led to a large demonstration that involved about 2 million people in the streets of Madrid, protesting against the misleading governmental framing of the terrorist attacks on March 11. In both countries, existing or emerging communication practices and networks situated outside the realm of politics – like the use of mobile phones to communicate with friends, relatives and colleagues – became almost natural political tools to make individuals' emotions explicit to others and to then mobilize people virally. In this sense, mobile phones acted as tactical socio-technical support for mobilizations in which the act of forwarding text messages, an otherwise common and mundane media practice when performed outside the realm of politics, was central in augmenting protest participation. Contrasted with such use of mobile phones in past uprisings, the use of social media platforms in more recent mobilizations is quite similar in at least two ways. First, as Ahmed et al. in this special issue show, they allow emotions to shift from a highly individualized experience to a high form of collectivism and, parallel to this, from mediatized expressions of discontent to the offline development of mobilizations. Second, as Liu in this special issue argues, similarly to mobile phones also social media platforms are means through which people's mundane activities structure social networks that then become available for contentious activities.

When addressing such mechanisms from a media practice perspective, one relevant question refers to the ability that media practices might have to shape other social practices (Couldry, 2004). Drawing on Swidler (2001), Couldry (2009) refers to the process of 'anchoring' according to which media practices can change the way in which people perform other social practices: like those social practices that sustain even the more ordinary social activities, including having dinner together at home or organizing a trip with friends. Of course, then, it is also possible that this anchoring potential follows a reverse pattern: there might be some social practices that are able to anchor media practices, hence imposing their own logic on the way people interact with the media. That said, and going a step further, we can also expect such anchoring potential at work among different types of media practices. In other words, there are some media practices that might be able to change the very nature of other media practices: the way in which smartphones are embedded into the social practices of ordinary users, for instance, might change the way in which the same ordinary users access political news, express their political opinions, or participate in mobilizations. Starting from these assumptions, then, it is worth asking to what extent social practices that sustain protest activities, like the recruitment of new participants, are able to influence the way in which activists appropriate digital technologies beyond their mundane use. Or, going in the reverse direction, whether mundane media practices, like befriending acquaintances on social networking sites, are then able to shape the way in which activists' media practices unfold in times of mobilizations. Finally, from a more meso-level perspective, it would be also important to understand how the anchoring potential of media practices change according to the types of social movement actors that appropriate media technologies. Although from a different perspective than media practices and media ecologies approaches, articles in this special issue begin to unpack these questions with regard to digital technologies. Again, though, a quick look at the literature on the use of mobile phones, might help us to appreciate a situated and partial answer to the very last question in the list above.

Scholars have illustrated that the ways in which these technologies are appropriated and then integrated into protests can shape the form of protest. From a media practice perspective, this means that media practices might shape other social practices, related to the organization and staging of protest. But they do this differently according to who appropriates the media technology and its affordances. Text messages that virally spread in the Philippines and in Spain through mobile phones informed people about what to do, where and at what time in order to protest. They hence supported a simultaneous coordination amongst (potential) protest participants in a short period of time. But their use, in any case, resulted in rather conventional forms of protest, i.e. large-scale demonstrations (Qiu, 2008). In other cases, though, mobile phones had a more substantial impact on the form of protest itself: mobilizations against the National Democratic Convention and the National Republican Convention in 2004 are an emblematic example with this regard. Through the use of TXTmob, a mobile phone service able to broadcast information to a large number of subscribers, activists were able to spread information during protests (Hirsch & Henry, 2005). Allowing four different model of text message sending, TXTmob supported almost immediate communication within small affinity groups and broad group of protesters adopting the swarming tactic of protest. The implementation and employment of TXTmob broadcasting service rendered mobile phones a tool that had an impact on protest activities in themselves. Although swarming tactics were already known amongst activists, who used them in the Seattle protests against the WTO in November 1999, broadcasting text messages through mobile phones enabled a more fluid coordination of larger numbers of people protesting against the two national conventions.

Conclusions

In this article I have explored the potential of media ecologies and media practices approaches to grasp the role of digital technologies in current social movements. As a preliminary step, I highlighted what these approaches have to offer with regard to three relevant theoretical aspects. First, the contextualization of digital technologies into broader media ecologies, in which older and newer media live side by side, so as to understand how the hybrid nature of current media systems is reflected in the media practices performed in the framework of grassroots politics. Second, the acknowledgement of the temporal dimension of social movements, that leads to the centrality of temporal location in understanding media-related attitudes, knowledge and literacy through the consideration of mediation processes and mediatization logics. Finally, the recognition of the agency that social movement actors have with regard to media, both in past and present times, through a closer look at how activist media practices developed in specific socio-technical contexts of mobilization. In the second part of this article, I then addressed one specific common thread in this special issue: the relationship between the communicative dimension of social movements and the mundane individual use of digital technologies. I diachronically contrasted some of the findings presented by the authors in this special issue, hence comparing the most recent uses of digital technologies with previous research on mobile phones in massive protests. In this regard, I argued that a media practice perspective might enhance our understanding of the relationship between mundane media practices and activist media practices. And, further, I suggested some ways in which media practices might shape other social practices.

This article does not exhaust the many theoretical perspectives and empirical issues that inhabit literature on social movements and digital media today. My contribution to this debate is certainly partial in privileging one specific theoretical perspective and its potentials. Indeed, my aim was to show yet another viewpoint through which we might look at the intricacies that characterize the use of the latest technological devices and platforms in the framework of activism. The media practice and media ecologies perspective is one that might improve our appreciation of the historical, contextual and relational nature of the interactions between activists and a diverse array of media technologies.

Disclosure statement

No potential conflict of interest was reported by the author.

ORCID

Alice Mattoni http://orcid.org/0000-0002-4809-0207

References

ACT UP NY. (2003). *DIVA TV (Damned interfering video activists)*. Retrieved October 19, 2016, from http://www.actupny.org/divatv/

Ahmed, S., Jaidka, K., & Cho, J. (2017). Tweeting India's Nirbhaya protest: A study of emotional dynamics in an online social movement. *Social Movement Studies, 16*(4). doi:10.1080/14742837.2016.1192457

Atton, C. (2001). *Alternative media*. London: Sage.

Barassi, V. (2015). *Activism on the web: Everyday struggles against digital capitalism*. Abingdon: Routledge.

Beissinger, M. R. (2002). *Nationalist mobilization and the collapse of the soviet state*. Cambridge: Cambridge University Press.

Bennett, W. L. (2012). The personalization of politics: Political identity, social media, and changing patterns of participation. *The ANNALS of the American Academy of Political and Social Science, 644*, 20–39.

Bennett, W. L., & Segerberg, A. (2013). *The logic of connective action: Digital media and the personalization of contentious politics*. Cambridge: Cambridge University Press.

Bob, C. (2005). *The marketing of rebellion: Insurgents, media, and international activism*. Cambridge: Cambridge University Press.

Cammaerts, B. (2016). Overcoming net-centricity in the study of alternative and community media. *Journal of Alternative and Community Media, 1*, 1–3.

Cammaerts, B., Mattoni, A., & McCurdy, P. (Eds.). (2013). *Mediation and protest movements*. Bristol: Intellect.

Castells, M. (2012). *Networks of outrage and hope: Social movements in the internet age*. Cambridge: Polity.

Cleaver, H. M. J. (1998). The Zapatista effect: The internet and the rise of an alternative political fabric. *Journal of International Affairs, 51*, 621–640.

Couldry, N. (2000). *The place of media power: Pilgrims and witnesses of the media age*. London: Routledge.

Couldry, N. (2004). Theorising media as practice. *Social Semiotics, 14*, 115–132.

Couldry, N. (2009). Theorising media as practice. In B. Bräuchler & J. Postill (Eds.), *Theorising media and practice* (pp. 35–54). New York, NY: Berghahn Books.

Couldry, N., & Hepp, A. (2017). *The mediated construction of reality*. Cambridge: Polity.

Carroll, W. K., & Ratner, R. S. (1999). Media strategies and political projects: A comparative study of social movements. *Canadian Journal of Sociology / Cahiers canadiens de sociologie* [Cahiers Canadiens de Sociologie], *24*(1), 1–34.

Dahlberg-Grundberg, M. (2016). Technology as movement on hybrid organizational types and the mutual constitution of movement identity and technological infrastructure in digital activism. *Convergence: The International Journal of Research into New Media Technologies, 22*, 524–542.

della Porta, D., & Diani, M. (Eds.). (2015). *The Oxford handbook of social movements*. Oxford: Oxford University Press.

DIVA TV. (1989). *Be a DIVA!* Retrieved from http://archive.org/details/ddtv_34_be_a_diva

Downing, J. D. H. (2003). Audiences and readers of alternative media: The absent lure of the virtually unknown. *Media Culture Society, 25*(5), 625–645. doi:10.1177/01634437030255004

Dunbar-Hester, C. (2009). "Free the spectrum!" Activist encounters with old and new media technology. *New Media & Society, 11*, 221–240.

Earl, J., & Garrett, R. K. (2017). The new information frontier: Toward a more nuanced view of social movement communication. *Social Movement Studies, 16*(4). doi:10.1080/14742837.2016.1192028

Earl, J., & Kimport, K. (2011). *Digitally enabled social change: Activism in the internet age*. Boston: MIT Press.

Eleftheriadis, K. (2015). Queer responses to austerity: Insights from the Greece of crisis. *ACME: An International E-Journal for Critical Geographies, 14*, 1032–1057.

Enli, G. S., & Skogerbø, E. (2013). Personalized campaigns in party-centred politics. *Information, Communication & Society, 16*, 757–774.

Fanon, F., & Gilly, A. (1994). *A dying colonialism*. (H. Chevalier, Trans.). New York, NY: Grove Press.

Feigenbaum, A., Frenzel, F., & McCurdy, P. (2013). *Protest camps*. London: Zed Books.

Flesher Fominaya, C. (2011). The madrid bombings and popular protest: Misinformation, counter-information, mobilisation and elections after '11-M'. *Contemporary Social Science, 6*, 289–307.

Gamson, W. A., & Wolfsfeld, G. (1993). Movements and media as interacting systems. *The ANNALS of the American Academy of Political and Social Science, 528*, 114–125.

Garzia, D. (2014). *Personalization of politics and electoral change*. Basingstoke: Palgrave Macmillan.

Harding, V. (1997). *We changed the world: African Americans 1945–1970*. New York, NY: Oxford University Press.
Hensby, A. (2017). Open networks and secret Facebook groups: Exploring cycle effects on activists' social media use in the 2010/11 UK student protests. *Social Movement Studies, 16*(4). doi:10.1080/14742837.2016.1201421
Hirsch, T., & Henry, J. (2005, April). *TXTmob: Text messaging for protest swarms*. Retrieved from http://web.media.mit.edu/~tad/pub/txtmob_chi05.pdf
Hobart, M. (2009). What do we mean by "media practices"? In B. Bräuchler & J. Postill (Eds.), *Theorising Media and Practice* (pp. 55–76). New York, NY: Berghahn Books.
Jordan, T. (2002). *Activism!: Direct action, hacktivism and the future of society*. London: Reaktion Book.
Juris, J. S. (2008). *Networking futures. The movements against corporate globalization*. Durham, NC: Duke University Press.
Kaun, A. (2016). *Crisis and critique: A brief history of media participation in times of crisis*. London: Zed Books.
Koopmans, R. (2004). Protest in time and space: The evolution of waves of contention. In D. A. Snow, S. A. Soule, & H. Kriesi (Eds.), *The Blackwell companion to social movements* (pp. 19–46). Oxford: Wiley-Blackwell.
Lievrouw, L. (2011). *Alternative and activist new media*. Cambridge: Polity.
Lim, M. (2012). Clicks, cabs, and coffee houses: Social media and oppositional movements in Egypt, 2004–2011. *Journal of Communication, 62*, 231–248.
Liu, J. (2017). From 'moments of madness' to 'the politics of mundanity'—Researching digital media and contentious collective actions in China. *Social Movement Studies, 16*(4). doi:10.1080/14742837.2016.1192027
Mattoni, M. A. (2012). *Media practices and protest politics: How precarious workers mobilise*. Farnham: Ashgate Publishing, Ltd.
Mattoni, A. (2013). Repertoires of communication in social movement processes. In B. Cammaerts, A. Mattoni, & P. McCurdy (Eds.), *Mediation and protest movements* (pp. 39–56). Bristol: Intellect.
Mattoni, A., & Treré, E. (2014). Media practices, mediation processes, and mediatization in the study of social movements. *Communication Theory, 24*, 252–271.
Mazzoleni, G. (2000). A return to civic and political engagement prompted by personalized political leadership? *Political Communication, 17*, 325–328.
McAdam, D., & Sewell, W. H. J. (2001). It's about time: Temporality in the study of contentious politics. In R. Aminzade (Ed.), *Silence and voice in the study of contentious politics* (pp. 89–125). Cambridge: Cambridge University Press.
McAdam, D., Tarrow, S., & Tilly, C. (2001). *Dynamics of contention*. Cambridge: Cambridge University Press.
McAllister, I. (2007). The personalization of politics. In R. Dalton & H. Klingeman (Eds.), *The Oxford handbook of political behavior* (pp. 571–588). Oxford: Oxford University Press.
Melucci, A. (1989). *Nomads of the present: Social movements and individual needs in contemporary society*. Philadelphia, PA: Temple University Press.
Mercea, D., Iannelli, L., & Loader, B. D. (2016). Protest communication ecologies. *Information, Communication & Society, 19*, 279–289. doi:10.1080/1369118X.2015.1109701
Milan, S. (2013). *Social movements and their technologies: Wiring social change*. Basingstoke: Palgrave McMillan.
Milan, S., & van der Velden, L. (2016). The alternative epistemologies of data activism. *Digital Culture and Society*. Retrieved November 16, 2016, from https://papers.ssrn.com/abstract=2850470
Nielsen, R. K. (2011). Mundane internet tools, mobilizing practices, and the coproduction of citizenship in political campaigns. *New Media & Society, 13*, 755–771.
Olesen, T. (2004). *International zapatismo: The construction of solidarity in the age of globalization*. London; New York, NY: Zed Books.
Pavan, E. (2017). The integrative power of online collective action networks beyond protest. Exploring social media use in the process of institutionalization. *Social Movement Studies, 16*(4). doi:10.1080/14742837.2016.1268956
Postill, J. (2012). *New protest movements and viral media*. Retrieved May 27, 2013, from http://johnpostill.com/2012/03/26/new-protest-movements-and-viral-media/
Qiu, J. L. (2008). Mobile civil society in Asia: A comparative study of people power II and the Nosamo movement. *Javnost - The Public, 15*, 39–58.
Rafael, V. L. (2003). The cell phone and the crowd: Messianic politics in the contemporary Philippines. *Public Culture, 15*, 399–425. doi:10.1215/08992363-15-3-399
Rauch, J. (2007). Activists as interpretive communities: Rituals of consumption and interaction in an alternative media audience. *Media Culture & Society, 29*, 994–1013.
Rinke, E. M., & Röder, M. (2011). The Arab Spring media ecologies, communication culture, and temporal–spatial unfolding: Three components in a communication model of the Egyptian regime change. *International Journal of Communication, 5*, 1273–1285.
Rodriguez, C. (2001). *Fissures in the mediascape. An international study of citizens' media*. Creskill, NJ: Hampton Press.
Rodriguez, C. (2016). Human agency and media praxis: Re-centring alternative and community media research. *Journal of Alternative and Community Media, 1*, 36–38.
Scalmer, S. (2013). Mediated nonviolence as a global force: An historical perspective. In B. Cammaerts, A. Mattoni, & P. McCurdy (Eds.), *Mediation and protest movements* (pp. 115–132). Bristol: Intellect.
Schatzki, T. R., Knorr-Cetina, K., & von Savigny, E. (2001). *The practice turn in contemporary theory*. Abingdon: Routledge.

Stein, L. (2001). Access television and grassroots political communication in the United States. In J. D. H. Downing (Ed.), *Radical media: Rebellious communication and social movements* (pp. 299–324). Thousand Oaks, CA: Sage.
Swanson, D. L., & Mancini, P. (1996). *Politics, media, and modern democracy: An international study of innovations in electoral campaigning and their consequences.* Westport: Praeger Publisher.
Swidler, A. (2001). What anchors cultural practices? In T. R. Schatzki, K. K. Cetina, & E. von Savigny (Eds.), *The practice turn in contemporary theory* (pp. 74–92). London: Routledge.
Tarrow, S. (1989). *Democracy and disorder: Social conflict, political protest and democracy in Italy, 1965–1975.* New York, NY: Oxford University Press.
Tarrow, S. (1994). *Power in movement.* Cambridge: Cambridge University Press.
Tarrow, S. G. (2011). *Power in movement: Social movements and contentious politics* (3rd ed.). Cambridge: Cambridge University Press.
Thompson, E. P. (1991). *The making of the english working class.* London: Penguin Books.
Tilly, C. (1978). *From mobilization to revolution.* Reading, MA: Addison-Wesley.
Tilly, C. (1995). Contentious repertoires in Gret Britain, 1758–1834. In M. Traugott (Ed.), *Repertoires & cycles of collective action* (pp. 15–42). Durham, NC: Duke University Press.
Treré, E. (2012). Social movements as information ecologies: Exploring the coevolution of multiple internet technologies for activism. *International Journal of Communication*, 6, 19. Retrieved from http://ijoc.org/index.php/ijoc/article/view/1681
Treré, E., & Mattoni, A. (2016). Media ecologies and protest movements: Main perspectives and key lessons. *Information, Communication & Society, 19*, 290–306.
Uitermark, J. (2017). Complex contention: Analyzing power dynamics within Anonymous. *Social Movement Studies, 16*(4). doi:10.1080/14742837.2016.1184136

Index

Note: Page numbers in **bold** refer to tables
Page numbers in *italics* refer to figures

For Product Safety Concerns and Information please contact our EU representative GPSR@taylorandfrancis.com Taylor & Francis Verlag GmbH, Kaufingerstraße 24, 80331 München, Germany

Batch number: 10726412

Printed by Printforce, the Netherlands